Privacy and Print

Privacy and Print

READING AND WRITING IN SEVENTEENTH-CENTURY ENGLAND

Cecile M. Jagodzinski

UNIVERSITY PRESS OF VIRGINIA
Charlottesville and London

The University Press of Virginia

Printed in the United States of America

First published 1999

∞ The paper used in this publication meets the minimum requirements of the American National Standard for Information Sciences—Permanence of Paper for Printed Library Materials, ANSI Z39.48-1984.

Library of Congress Cataloging-in-Publication Data

Jagodzinski, Cecile M., 1951–
Privacy and print : reading and writing in seventeenth-century England / Cecile M. Jagodzinski.
p. cm.
Revision of the author's thesis (doctoral)—University of Illinois at Urbana-Champaign, 1996.
Includes bibliographical references (p.) and index.
ISBN 0-8139-1839-1 (cloth : alk paper)
1. English literature—Early modern, 1500–1700—History and criticism. 2. Protestantism and literature—History—17th century. 3. Authors and readers—England—History—17th century. 4. Books and reading—England—History—17th century. 5. England—Intellectual life—17th century. 6. Printing—England—History—17th century. 7. Literacy—England—History—17th century. 8. Privacy—England—History—17th century. 9. Authorship—History—17th century. 10. Self in literature. I. Title.
PR431.J34 1999
028′.9′094209032—dc21 98-35586
CIP

For my dearest friend . . .

Contents

Illustrations

Acknowledgments

It is a temptation to regard a book on the private life, one written primarily in solitude, as one's own property, the fruit of individual study and effort. But even as I write these words, I see and hear in my mind's eye the slow procession of teachers, scholars, and authors who have formed my thinking, my beliefs, my self. Their example compels me to abandon the myth of the solitary author in these acknowledgments.

My first thanks go to Achsah Guibbory, Carol Neely, and David Kay, who shepherded this work through its earlier manifestation as a dissertation. I hope that my attempts at improving the original have answered, at least in part, their insightful critiques, questions, and suggestions. Two anonymous readers for the University Press of Virginia challenged my sweeping generalizations about the histories of privacy and of the book; some of my linguistic and logical crudities no doubt remain, but these readers were instrumental in forcing me to rethink, reconsider, and refine my argument.

My friends and colleagues at Milner Library, Illinois State University, deserve special recognition for their support and encouragement throughout the six-year gestation period of this project. Lastly, special thanks go to my mother, who, so long ago, taught me the special pleasures of reading in private.

Privacy and Print

Introduction

It is a commonplace (though a much-disputed one) that the Renaissance was characterized by the emergence of the individual and the awakening of a new subjectivity and a consciousness of the self as a person separate from the community.[1] This tendency has been noted most particularly in seventeenth-century England; indeed, Philippe Ariès, in the introduction to *A History of Private Life,* has called England "the birthplace of privacy."[2]

If we grant the truth of this scholarly commonplace, we might ask how seventeenth-century England, so consumed with revolutions in the public institutions of church and state, could have given rise to the notion of individuality, to self-consciousness? Typically, scholars have linked the rise of the developing private self to the spread of Protestantism, with its Bible reading, its cultivation of a sense of personal sin, its search for a direct relationship with God, and its celebration of the nuclear family.[3] All these conditions set the individual apart from the community, in opposition to the expectations of a more traditional, communitarian, and cohesive society. But how exactly did inhabitants of that century view the idea of privacy? Were our twentieth-century notions of privacy, characterized by personal autonomy and an inner life, greeted with enthusiasm? Which factors contributed to "private life," and, more importantly, what made the notion of privacy acceptable, even desirable, by the beginning of the next century?

I wish to propose that the emergence of the concept of privacy as a personal right, as the very core of individuality, is connected in a complex fashion with the history of reading. My proposal that the reading experience bred a new sense of personal autonomy, a new consciousness of the self, presents a historical problem of sorts; the experience of the great thinkers and writers of the classical era and the Middle Ages hardly reflects an unexamined life or an unsophisticated approach to the individual. One could not argue that the Greek philosophers, the desert Fathers, or the cloistered nuns of medieval monasteries were unacquainted with privacy and the contemplative life. To claim that the seventeenth century was radically different would be to succumb to the charms and simplicity of historical periodization, when, after all, the seventeenth century follows logically and inevitably upon the social and cultural developments of the fourteenth, fifteenth, and sixteenth centuries. Historical change is a gradual process, even when revolutions, wars, and new inventions help it along. However, certain factors do seem to contribute to a changing worldview in seventeenth-century England, the chief of them, I will argue, the widespread availability and accessibility of printed matter.

It was not simply that more people could read (recall the familiar notion that the Protestant reform encouraged literacy as a duty). Rather, the establishment of an English publishing industry, the growth of a merchant class with leisure time, increased opportunities for education for most classes, and the social, religious, and political upheavals of the late sixteenth and seventeenth centuries contributed to a new way of thinking about the individual person. I will suggest that political and religious repression refashioned the ways in which people read and that the chance to get "lost in a book" unsettled long-held notions about the relation of the individual to God, to religious, political, and social structures, and to his or her own interior life and consciousness. The ability to read granted independence from all those communal structures, as the interactions between reader, text, and author moved from the public forums of church and court to the privacy and solitude of the home and even to personalized private spaces within the home. "Equal opportunity" to read coincided with wider participation in the political sphere (for men) and independence in religious choice and practice for both men and women. In short, readers in seventeenth-century England, because they read, began to develop a sense of the private self.

The Notion of Privacy

A reading of the supporting citations in the *Oxford English Dictionary* of the earliest uses of *private* and *privacy* indicate that, for the sixteenth- and seventeenth-century speaker of English, privacy was a concept different from, yet allied to, our modern notions. For the early moderns, privacy carried the suggestion of individual, rather than public, interest, of a person acting in an unofficial, rather than an official, capacity (2.a, 6.a); of privilege or elitism (4.a); of secrecy or concealment (2.b, 3.a); often in an out-of-the-way place (1.a, 2.b). One can infer from the dictionary's illustrative quotations that privacy was a privilege of the elite and upper classes, that secrecy and concealment were suspicious practices, that separating oneself from society was unnatural and irresponsible. Ronald Huebert has classified the developing notion of privacy into four clusters: privacy as absence of status; privacy relating to personal property and ownership; privacy as secrecy (including the use of "private parts" as a euphemism for the sexual organs); and finally, privacy as interiority. Huebert argues, as I will, that written usage indicates a gradual acceptance, even a "cherishing," of privacy, as the concept evolves from More to Marvell.[4]

This valuation of privacy was neither complete nor universal in the seventeenth century. As late as the 1660s there were signs of unease with individual privacy. In a pair of pamphlets published in 1665 and 1667, George Mackenzie and John Evelyn recast the traditional classical debate between action and contemplation in terms of the public and private. The royalist Evelyn took the traditional view that solitude was suspect: political conspiracies, vice, and solipsism are the stepchildren of the private life, he claimed. (Evelyn wrote, perhaps not so coincidentally, in the same decade in which a series of laws forbade private assemblies of worship because they were seen as politically dangerous to the restored monarchy.)[5] Evelyn, interestingly, lays the blame for this chaos on the reading of books; his preference is for a more socially responsible activity, the "reading of men":

> As for *Books,* I acknowledge with the Philosopher [Seneca], *Otium sine literis,* to be the greatest infelicity in the world; but on the other side, not to *read men,* and converse with *living Libraries,* is to deprive our selves of the most useful and profitable of *Studies:* This is that deplorable defect which universally renders our *bookish* men so *pedantically morose* and impolish'd, and in a word, so very *ridiculous:* For, believe it Sir, the *Wisest men* are not made in *Chambers* and *Closets* crowded with shelves, but by *habitudes* and active *Conversations.* (213)[6]

Evelyn deplores bookishness because it seems to capture the essence of the private life, which removes men from their proper place in the society of other like-minded men. The solitude of those "Chambers and Closets," which Evelyn associates with reading and crowded bookshelves, leads to barbarism, not virtue: "The *result* of all is, *Solitude* produces *ignorance,* renders us *barbarous,* feeds *revenge,* disposes to *envy,* creates *Witches,* dispeoples the *World,* renders it a *desart,* and would soon *dissolve* it" (254). Even as he speaks up for the old virtues and the duties of public life, Evelyn represents the clash between old and new values, for Evelyn, as the editor of Evelyn's and Mackenzie's pamphlets points out, had retired to the country and was merely assuming a pose: he had chosen the private life for himself. Though privacy was not yet regarded as a personal right, it was possible, by the 1660s, to withdraw from the ceremonies of public life with impunity.

In time, the persona one assumed in private life came to be seen as the "real" self and public authority was less often equated with personal authenticity. Graham Richards says that the "rise of privacy . . . constitutes the culturally visible beginning of the idea that the individuated ego or personality is the carrier of the authentic self." The traditional view was that one was most "real" when performing in public—in the pulpit, in court or Parliament, or even in the local alehouse.[7] (Note the paucity of places in which women could be "real"—we will return later to the complex relationship between women and privacy.) It would be some time before our late twentieth-century notion of private authenticity swept out those earlier ideas, but the process had certainly begun by the end of the sixteenth century, and privacy became the nurturer of this new "individuated ego." Though "privacy" still often had negative connotations, a cultural transformation was occurring, due, in large part, to new values nourished by private reading.

In the twentieth century, privacy has become a value in and of itself. Sociologists, psychologists, and legal specialists have, for the last one hundred years, been especially concerned with the notion of personal privacy.[8] In the United States, as in many other Western cultures, privacy is seen as a basic legal and human right. Alan Westin claims that individual privacy has four basic functions: "personal autonomy, emotional release, self-evaluation, and limited and protected communication."[9] Westin describes the individual as a series of concentric circles, with the core, or secret self, at the center. The more intimate the relationship, the deeper into a person's psyche may another be admitted. If this is the modern conception of the self (multitudes of concentric circles overlapping with others only in part, Boolean style), we might think of the early modern as a simple circle, the outside supposedly a physical manifestation of the inner person. The early modern preoccupation with proper dress and the passage and enforcement of sumptuary laws signaled the importance of the outer layer: dress was a reflection of one's social station and occupation, of one's proper place in the social hierarchy or the moral sphere. It was commonly assumed that there was a congruence between the inner and the outer man, or between a woman's dress and her chastity and femininity (though this assumption was challenged in stage-plays and in works such as Ben Jonson's epigrams and the protofeminist *Hic Mulier* and *Haec Vir* pamphlets). In printed books, however, characters emerge whose inner and outer lives diverge, whose social persona could hide another sort of person inside.

Today, we assume that "appearances are deceiving," that people may present one face to the world, one to themselves and their intimates. This freedom to reveal all or part of one's inner self to another is basic to privacy; information about the self is regarded as a possession, as tangible psychologically as are material goods. Self-disclosure, then, places the individual in a vulnerable position; hence, the flow of personal information is always opposite to the flow of authority.[10] The transfer of information about the self (whether voluntary or not) always changes the dynamics of personal relationships; the discloser may gain in trust and emotional support what he or she risks by appearing vulnerable; the other person has the options of developing closer human ties with the discloser or of rejecting or exploiting the other. In all cases, the revelation of secrets about the self changes the relationship, makes the relationship "mutually transformative."[11]

Because of the potential volatility of private information, all such revelations must be voluntary if they are to protect the individual's privacy, and the boundaries of disclosure must always be advanced or set back by the person himself.[12] The interactive nature of self-disclosing relationships, the game of moving the boundaries back and forth, is a wonderful paradigm for the negotiations between author and reader, who are engaged in the process of disclosure, of "reading" the other. Authors play a crucial role in this creation of the private self, for they are originators of the text, authoring and authorizing the readers represented within their works. At the same time, they are readers themselves, and so are perhaps the first negotiators of the distance between the public and the private life. Such negotiation is an important component both of setting the bounds of privacy and establishing the relationship between author and reader; the author must find his or her proper audience, decide how distant or how familiar to be in order to capture the reader's fancy or engage the reader's intelligence. The author sends clues with language, message, tone, character—even personal revelation—that the reader may swallow whole, reject, or, even more likely, read to suit him or herself. Authors dissect characters for readers, making them objects of scrutiny, revealing their secrets and silently analyzing their motives. (Sometimes authors dissect their own selves for their reading public, as did John Bunyan figuratively in *Grace Abounding* and John Donne almost literally in *Devotions Upon Emergent Occasions.*) I would like to suggest that, by reading, seventeenth-century readers learned to perform the same sort of analysis: first on characters in books, then on themselves.[13]

Building on these twentieth-century observations on privacy, I intend that the phrase "private self" convey several meanings: the right to personal autonomy, as opposed to the requirement that one submit to authority; a consciousness (and potential manipulation) of the split between the internal self and the public face presented to the rest of the world; and the right to conceal or keep secret the workings of this inner self. I do not want to suggest that this consciousness is complete, sought after, still less approved of during this period. But my examination of actual readers and representations of readers in literary, religious, and historical writings of the late sixteenth and seventeenth centuries will indicate that books awaken readers to new possibilities for the individual, leading to conflict with established social norms and expectations, with filial and religious duty, with political loyalties. The readers in these texts do not so much present a case for personal privacy as demonstrate to other readers that individual private worlds might exist. Even when rebellious readers are presented by authors and narrators as negative examples, the astute reader realizes that there is (despite the potential difficulty) the option of private choice, of withdrawal to the private space of the mind. Reading, I will argue, makes viable the possibility of conversion—a change of mind and heart simultaneously personal, political, religious, psychological, and sociological.

Historical Background: Printing, Publishing, and Authorship

Perhaps it is no coincidence that a technological innovation—the printing press—created a sociological revolution.[14] Reading democratizes; in seventeenth-century England, the publication and reading of pamphlets even helped level a king. Alvin Kernan has discussed the contrast between the hierarchical values of an oral culture and the democratizing power of print, which, ironically, fosters isolation, not community: "Knowledge comes to readers not through the ear but through the eye alone, not from the exchange of views with others *viva voce* but by scanning and interpreting fixed rows of silent signs, not in a noisy community of other persons but in the silence of the library and isolated consciousness."[15] Secrecy and concealment are no longer treasonable but the prerogatives of private life. The mistrust of solitude and aloneness has been transformed into the valuing of private, physical, psychological space.

In an uncanny prefigurement of today's transformation of the world into machine-readability, the technology of printing combined text and image to change the way people thought about and imagined themselves. Today, there is widespread concern about a wholesale withdrawal from public life, as individuals commune with their portable notebook computers, detached from production lines, mainframe computers, their coworkers, and even their families. The results now, as in the seventeenth century, are "individuation and separation."[16] In the early modern era, books were central to this process: reading "liberated the individual from the old mediators, freed him or her from the control of the group, and made it possible to cultivate an inner life."[17]

The first printing press had been introduced into England at Westminster by William Caxton in 1476.[18] But England failed to develop a strong printing industry during the fifteenth century, remaining far behind the leaders in the industry, Italy and Germany, in terms of numbers and geographical dispersion of printshops. (In the incunable period, there were only four in the whole of England: in London, Oxford, and St. Alban's.) Until 1534, when printing was brought under national control, foreign printers carried on their trade in England, and books were imported freely. In addition, the quality of printing, even in comparison to continental work, was "lamentably bad."[19] With government protectionism, local production of books gradually increased, from 54 titles in 1500, to 214 in 1550,[20] 259 in 1600, and 577 in 1640.[21] Edition sizes ranged from about 100 to 1,250 (the upper limit set by the Stationers' Company for most books), although as many as 10,000 copies of grammars, prayer books, and catechisms could be printed.[22] The very existence of the Thomason tracts testifies to the increased productivity of English presses during the Civil War, and the eventual futility of government licensing once the power of print became evident.[23]

Words were everywhere: books were no longer scarce totems but common objects for everyday use.[24] Every parish had its Bible; booksellers posted title pages on walls and the pillars of St. Paul's to advertise their new books;[25] peddlers hawked the wares of illegal presses, both within England and from abroad. The late sixteenth and seventeenth centuries saw the creation of the first parochial and municipal libraries open to their publics.[26] In the period 1560–1635, prices for books ranged from 1d. for one and a half to two sheets (a ballad) to 6d. for Roger Ascham's *The Scholemaster* and 1s. for Spenser's *Shepheardes Calender,* unbound.[27] Whether books were affordable to the average person during this period depends, I suppose, on the value an individual might place on owning a book. In 1520, the 1d. paid for a ballad could have purchased two pounds of cheese or a pound of butter; a pair of shoes cost 6d. In 1595, a sheep cost about 9s., or slightly less than an unbound copy of the Bible.[28] By 1640, book ownership in provincial areas such as Kent rose to over 40 percent, and if only one book was owned, that book was the Bible.[29] However, the interest in more entertaining, if less illuminating, titles has been equally well documented.[30] Even those without personal access to books would have shared in the practice of reading aloud, which had long been regarded as a common courtesy in an era of relatively scarce books.[31] In a newly developing country such as seventeenth-century England, with a rising middle class that had both more education and more leisure time, owning books—owning any personal property—must have been a new experience. Possessions can become an extension and reflection of the self; the totemic book, formerly symbolizing church and state, could now symbolize one's deepest concerns and interests, become an extension of one's personality. The ownership of books can be viewed not only as ownership of property but ownership of knowledge and, most significantly, knowledge and ownership of the self.[32]

Increased literacy and expanded educational opportunities also increased the possibility that individuals were exposed to the printed word.[33] (These opportunities differed in nature as well as in number; during the Middle Ages, reading was distinctly the property of the elite.)[34] From 1500 through 1700, illiteracy declined, with the upper and middle socioeconomic groups enjoying greatest benefits. Occupation had bearing on the ability to read: tradesmen, clergymen, gentlemen, and yeomen exhibited different levels of reading skill, often just enough to carry on their trade.[35] Women always lagged behind men in their ability to read and write and often obtained the first skill without the other. There is evidence, however, that even women who could read and not write served as teachers and were instrumental in teaching their own children to read.[36] In London, people (including women) were more likely to know how to read,[37] but even in the most backward parishes in 1642, one-fifth of the men could sign their names (and evidence suggests that the ability to sign correlated with the ability to read).[38]

Alongside the technological and social changes of the seventeenth century, the idea of common, shared authorship and the virtues of imitation so valued in the medieval era begin to give way to the voice of the individual author. The security and shared friendships of the coterie audience are gradually replaced by the marketplace: publishers, printers, and paying readers are the new coterie. How does the author negotiate with these new audiences? How can he achieve some of the intimacy of the coterie, attain to fame, and not offer himself (and his possibly seditious thoughts) to the power of the anonymous crowd? What happens to readers in this setup? The give-and-take of the coterie disappears as reading moves to private spaces and readings are performed, not by the author, but by readers outside the author's private circles.[39] Even the physical change in the manner of production of a text is significant: writing out or copying a manuscript by hand, in private, is quite different from having to resort to the services of a printer in order to get one's work published. The technological advances of the printshop eliminate, not only the solitary joys and labors of copying, but its drudgery as well. At the same time, the book-buying public eventually does away with the need for wealthy patrons,[40] and the reader becomes more a force to be reckoned with, an unknown quantity who might need to be placated and cajoled. The author's work was out there, on public display, in perhaps five hundred copies, instead of the three or four possible with manuscripts. The prize was fame; the price was criticism, mockery, unwanted self-disclosure.[41] In the new era of print, to read an author's work was to assume a familiarity with him or her. (The intimate relationship between the author and his work has been alluded to by Cathleen Bauschatz, who discusses the "consubstantiality" of Montaigne and his book: to read the *Essais* is to know Montaigne.)[42] The reader was free to participate vicariously in the author's self-display, to replicate the author's experience, even to appropriate (or misunderstand) the text.[43]

It is paradoxical that the rise of authors as highly visible public figures should parallel the development of private life. Should not the claims of publicity and privacy come into conflict? How is it possible that the publication of books could coincide with, even contribute to, a sense of a private self? The two seem at cross-purposes, since publication seems to threaten the privacy both of authors and of the subjects of their books. The answer lies in the role the author chooses to play with regard to his readership. He may simply assume the traditional mantle of authority, setting himself up as the moral and ethical center of the text. John Dagenais comments on the ethical nature of reading in the medieval period: "One of my conclusions about the nature of medieval reading is that it was above all an ethical activity. Where we tend to see our texts as webs of language, medieval readers saw a world of human action for good or ill co-extensive with their own. Texts were acts of demonstrative rhetoric that reached out and grabbed the reader, not so much in the unravelling of meaning as in a series of ethical meditations and of personal ethical choices."[44] Such a statement could just as well apply to the seventeenth century, as we shall see in my discussion of the religious contexts for the act of reading. These texts, reaching and grabbing and calling out to readers, encountered a massive new audience with the advent of the printed book, an audience who would use its newfound privacies to create its own new ethics.

The author, for his part, uses words to ensnare the reader, to demonstrate a rhetorical competence that overwhelms the reader. But this sort of bravura is dangerous; positioning oneself as an authority also sets one up for judgment, or worse, rebellion on the part of the reader. The wiser strategy was for authors to establish a compact with their readers, to identify themselves with their readers. They did this in two ways: by presenting themselves as readers and by creating characters who served as model representations of readers. This practice encouraged intimacy but at the same time deflected possible attention from the author's personal beliefs and feelings. It partnered author and reader in a private experience with the text, made them complicit in the observation of the world the author created. The author invites the reader to share in a kind of surveillance of the readers he or she represents in the text.

Steven L. Nock has examined the role of surveillance in societies such as ours, in which privacy is highly valued. He argues that "the relative absence of privacy in a society is correlated with the relative absence of strangers";[45] that is, there can be no privacy in societies in which everyone's affairs are known to everyone else, as was the case in preindustrial villages and towns. This was surely the situation in most parts of seventeenth-century England, where personal surveillance by one's neighbors was the norm. But where people are strangers to one another, privacy becomes a possibility, and credentials and ordeals or trials, rather than personal observation, must be used to establish reputations and ensure conformity. In the case of our seventeenth-century authors and their anonymous readers, we can observe a situation in which surveillance replaces personal knowledge. The author's credentials (a name on the title page will do) enable him or her to act as agent for the ordeal, for the tests undergone by the subjects of the author's works. The reader, co-opted by the author, can share vicariously in the uncovering of deception, the spying, the establishment of guilt or innocence. In the period of English history with which we are dealing, being subject to surveillance was, at various times, a way of life for persecuted Catholics, Puritans, Jews, and Anglicans. Perhaps Nock's hypothesis should be turned on its head—it may be that surveillance in seventeenth-century

England created a nation of strangers, created the need for privacy. Authors and readers existed in a middle world: not only were they subject to surveillance by religious and political authorities, but they also subversively share in it, writing about, reading about, judging those in power. The essential oppositions between privacy and celebrity, between the desire for a hidden life and the need to know about the lives of others, came together when reader met book.

The need for the reader in early modern England to read between the lines has been well documented by Annabel Patterson.[46] But perhaps a twentieth-century construct can help further explicate the relationship between author and reader during this period. The notion of "private speech," speech directed to the interior self, has been discussed particularly in relation to the psychological growth of children. It has been defined as "a critical intermediate state in the transition from external social communication to internal self-direction . . . the cornerstone of all higher cognitive processes, including selective attention, voluntary memory, planning, concept formation, and self-reflection."[47] Private speech is the language typically used by young children to work out problems by talking to themselves; thus, the conversation is always dialogic: it occurs between the self and the inner self. It is fundamentally social, even though the "I" is the addressee; thus, it is much more than "talking to oneself." In adults, and particularly in creative individuals, private speech is abbreviated, condensed, encoded, cryptic, understandable only to the subject.[48] I would suggest that this habit of using private language recapitulates and symbolizes the experience of readers and writers during the early modern period. The authors of the post-Elizabethan period write in a transitional era: somewhere between the public, social, communal, and oral experience of the text during the manuscript era and the private and individualized reception of the written word today.[49] Authors' literary self-reflections are coded yet are meant to be deciphered by the reader; they are intended to communicate to the reader, but they also promote self-clarification and self-definition for both reader and author. Psychologists and sociologists have argued that personal autonomy can only be attained in relation to the group, to the community. The reading audience is the necessary stimulus, the watcher on the other side of the psychological two-way mirror. Writers allow eavesdropping into their thoughts because it is the only way to maintain the personal contact that once existed between poet and listener or author and reader. As the manuscript era slowly ends, authors only attain the writer's crown by permitting readers to sit in as members of a gigantic coterie.[50] The privacy that appears to have been violated is protected somewhat by the anonymity of the reading audience, who do not know their confrères (or the author), as do coterie groups, and by the shared conspiracy between author and reader. In addition, the public and flamboyant presentation of the author in print is balanced by the reflective nature of reading alone. Not only must the author project a fictive audience because he does not know his readers personally,[51] but the reader is also isolated: "Writing and reading establish a special situation marked by absences, gaps, silences, and opacity. Faced with a text, the reader finds that both the author and original context are absent. The reader himself or herself has to produce the equivalent of both: the equivalent, for he or she can produce neither author nor context in total actuality. The context is no more and the author, often enough, is dead."[52]

It is perhaps incongruous, then, that as readers and authors meet anonymously and in private, the printing press maintains and establishes a "sphere of the public." Like all the mass media, even the handpress was in the "antiprivacy" business.[53] Thus we have the phenomenon of a medium that seeks at the same time to publicize and to privatize. (Jürgen Habermas's seminal *Structural Transformation of the Public Sphere* acknowledges the contribution of reading to the "world of letters," and even England's precociousness in the creation of the notion of "the public," but Habermas's private sphere houses the individual within the family, an economic unit that partakes of the "realm of commodity exchange and labor."[54] My focal point will be the private person as a psychological reality, the individual who acts within, sometimes even in opposition to, the family.)

Private, silent reading encourages the discovery of individuality but also eventually creates a nation of strangers—note that there is no word for the community of readers that parallels the theatrical or musical "audience." And Walter Ong observes that a roomful of people sharing in an oral/aural presentation such as television or radio establishes a community in a way which a roomful of readers does not.[55] As reading became less a communal activity, it also became associated with the private spaces being created in seventeenth-century homes. One aspect of Peter Clark's study of Kentish book owners emphasizes the move from oral, communal reading: in the post-1600 period, books, such as the Bible, migrated from places of honor in public rooms to the closet and bedchamber. This "would suggest the same increasing sense that a book was the private concern of the reader alone"[56] and that more and more family members were capable of reading on their own and without direction—a fact with a great deal of significance for the creation of personal autonomy, as we shall see.

Private Rooms and Personal Space

Essential to the nurturing of privacy is the idea of solitude. (In a study of people's conceptions of privacy, being alone and controlling access to spaces were seen as definitive.)[57] As many social historians have noted, before the sixteenth century, most people did not have the opportunity (or, as far as we know, the desire) to be alone. Life was lived as part of a very public community, and high social status did not guarantee a measure of personal privacy.[58] Even the apparently solitary lives of monastics required conformity to communal regulation; silence and separation from the world did not guarantee privacy. Indeed, Erving Goffman has reminded us that such "total institutions" efface privacy and individuality.[59] Changes in architecture were evident in the great houses first: separate sitting rooms, nonpublic dining rooms for the immediate family, wind porches (internal porches within large, often drafty rooms) provided the propertied classes with quiet spaces for praying, reading, and privacy. The process of royal withdrawal began in England with the reign of Elizabeth I, who frequently dined alone in her privy chamber. Closets for prayer, private chapels for private Masses, cabinets for reading and storing collectibles and oddities all accompanied the increasing compartmentalization of the home. (Bacon's "Of Building" (1625) called for "two Delicate or Rich *Cabinets,* Daintily Paved, Richly Hanged, Glased with *Crystalline Glasse*").[60] By the middle of the seventeenth century, even the laboring classes lived in houses with separate sleeping rooms, which ensured a modicum of aloneness at least part of the day.[61] At century's end, service stairs, closets, and corridors were seen as "part of a defensive strategy against unwelcome and unpredictable territorial encroachments—a defense against potential violation."[62]

Despite the fact that the first private spaces were intellectual and spiritual spaces of repose, they were not gender neutral. Both sexes, to be sure, had their own private rooms, but the aesthetic value of rooms and buildings and the perception of the importance of the activities carried on there were decidedly affected by the gender of the occupant. Leon Battista Alberti was an Italian man of letters and diplomat who had written the first book on architecture since antiquity, *De re aedificatoria.* Published in Florence in 1486, the work, circulated in both manuscript and print, was extremely influential throughout Renaissance Europe (even in England, where it was known only in the original Latin until 1726). Alberti recognized the necessity for private, separate rooms for husband and wife: "The husband and wife must have separate bedrooms, not only to ensure that the husband be not disturbed by his wife, when she is about to give birth or is ill, but also to allow them, even in summer, an uninterrupted night's sleep, whenever they wish. Each room should have its own door, and in addition a common side door, to enable them to seek each other's company unnoticed. Off the wife's bedroom should be a dressing room, and off the husband's, a library."[63]

Female space was regarded, then, as intensely physical: a space in which to be ill, give birth, attend to outward appearance, and (one would presume) make love. The library, on the other hand, served the masculine, intellectual sphere. Private space already had its ambiguities; though it could not be neatly encoded "masculine" or "feminine," its uses could be. Space (like books, as we shall see) could become gendered, and thus valuable and important (a library), or mundane and frivolous (a dressing room).

Sir Henry Wotton, in *The Elements of Architecture* (1624), showed that he had read Alberti and considered him "the first learned Architect, beyond the Alpes."[64] Like Alberti, Wotton wanted to ensure that architectural plans provided for private spaces, and he criticizes the Italians for their lack of such foresight:

> That they must bee forced to make as many common great *Roomes,* as there shalbe seuerall *Stories;* which (besides that they are vsually darke, a point hardly auoided, runing as they doe, through the middle of the whole *House*) doe likewise deuoure so much Place, that thereby they want other *Galleries,* and Roomes of *Retreate,* which I haue often considered among them (I must confesse) with no small wonder; for I obserue no *Nation* in the World, by Nature more *priuate* and *reserued,* then the Italian, and on the other side, in no *Habitations* lesse priuacie; so as there is a kinde of Conflict betweene their *Dwelling* and their *Being.* (sig. K1r–K1v)

Wotton suggests that there should be a congruence between the Italian private (and secret?) nature and their living spaces; he finds the discrepancy unaesthetic. Further, Wotton is making a more general connection between the self and physical space, recognizing that the fulfillment of one's being requires time and place apart. Wotton associates the interiors of buildings, their closed-up spaces with study and recollection: "Let all the principall chambers of *Delight,* All *Studies* and *Libraries,* be towards the *East:* For the Morning is a friend to the Muses" (sig. A4r–A4v). These light-filled "chambers of Delight" encourage the Muses and creativity; rather than seeming claustrophobic, private rooms free the individual for intellectual and spiritual exploration, for the "masculine" activities of writing and study.

Alan Stewart has suggested that private rooms and closeted spaces were associated not just with individual withdrawal but with sex, surveillance, and secret, nonpublic transactions between men.[65] Wotton himself is intensely concerned with making a house too open, with too many windows, "all *Eyes,* like *Argus.*" It is ingenuous of Wotton to claim, as he does, that these concerns are related to protection from extreme heat and cold. Certainly Wotton was aware of the means and methods by which the Elizabethan state carried out its work. Earlier in his treatise, he cautions against building too near powerful neighbors, lest one lose one's place in the sun, so to speak. That would place one in the same situation as Mercury, "euer in combustion, or obscuritie, vnder brighter beams then his owne" (sig. A3r). Distance from political powerhouses ensures an independent stance, individuality, a certain autonomy, even princely power: "Every Mans proper *Mansion* House and *Home,* being the *Theater* of his *Hospitality,* the *Seate* of *Selfe-fruition,* the *Comfortablest* part of his owne *Life,* the *Noblest* of his Sonnes *Inheritance,* a kinde of priuate *Princedome*" (sig. L1v).

Wotton is the diplomat and public servant carefully balancing the personal and the public in this passage. He assumes the wise man will fulfill the social responsibilities of hospitality and the legal obligation of father to son, but he extends the notion of property to include the home as a place for the independent, autonomous pursuit of literary and spiritual self-communication and, most importantly, personal sovereignty.[66] The ability to remove oneself from the demands of court or one's neighbors, even the use of doors (Wotton devotes a whole section to this) for shutting out unwarranted intrusions, enables the individual to create a space for self-transformation and self-determination.[67]

It is difficult to tell whether the creation of separate living areas was a response to, or the genesis of, a need for privacy. The inviolable rooms of a man's home were mirrored by a growing sense that "the closet of the heart" deserved its own kind of sanctum, free from the intrusion of any other persons, but especially from structures of authority.[68] Certainly, authority figures soon discovered problems with this trend: cabinets became not only "refuges of intimacy" but also repositories of secrets.[69] And books joined personal souvenirs, erotica, and forbidden religious objects in these secret cabinets.[70]

Sixteenth- and seventeenth-century readers and publishers were quite aware that the publication of books was a means to discovery, to laying out truths and making revelations. Consider, for example, the revelations implied in titles such as *The Discouerie of Witchcraft* (1584); *New Englands Prospect. A True, Lively, and Experimentall Description of That Part of America, Commonly Called New England . . . Laying Downe That Which May Both Enrich the Knowledge of the Mind-travelling Reader, or Benefit the Future Voyager* (1635); *The Plot Discovered and Counterplotted Commended in a Letter to a Private Friend* (1641); *Naaman the Syrian His Disease and Cure. Discovering Lively to the Reader the Spirituall Leprosie of Sinne and Self-love* (1642); or, *Virginia Impartially Examined and Left to Public View* (1649). Books could provide intellectual breadth, sustain spirituality, or reveal political secrets. It was easy to make the link between the "discovery" power of print and the private rooms or storage places known as cabinets.[71] The metaphor was a simple one: either could contain treasure (words or jewels) or hide secret corruption.

The first such bookish "cabinets" contained spiritual and literary jewels, collections of quotations or prayers. Their titles bear witness to their contents: *Psalmes of Confession Found in the Cabinet of the Most Excellent King of Portingal, Don Antonio* (1596); *The Golden Cabinet of True Treasure Containing the Summe of Morall Philosophie* (1612); *The Audi Filia, or, A Rich Cabinet Full of Spirituall Jewells* (1620); *A Cabinet of Spirituall Jewells* (1657); *A Cabinet of Choice Jewels or, A Box of Precious Ointment Being a Plain Discovery of, or, What Men Are Worth for Eternity, and How 'tis Like to Go with Them in Another World* (1669). These follow in the tradition of the medieval florilegia and commonplace book, with sermons, aphorisms, prayers, and meditations.

If books could preserve and provide moral and religious guidance, they could also be dangerous and thus had to be limited to a few initiates. In *Curiosities: or The Cabinet of Nature* (1637), R. Basset, in catechism-like question-and-answer style, offers revelations of the curiosities of Nature, who is depicted on the engraved title page:

> The Goddesse (like her selfe so plac't on high,
> So open breasted, freely doth descry
> Her love, which heretofore shee long conceal'd
> Wisely, to make thee love what's here reveal'd,
> She opens her closet, richly set
> With high prize'd gemmes, her richest Cabinet.[72]

Basset emphasizes that Nature's mysteries are not freely available to all, despite her "open-breasted" demeanor. His dedication reminds the reader that "the ever-verdant and private walkes of *Naturall Philosophie,* (which are not accessible to all, nor every one admitted, but onely Students, by their prerogative and Priviledge) where (having an eye not incurious) it being lawfull to enter the very bowels (as I may say) of her secresies, not without infinite pleasure I penetrated her *Arcana,* and opening her *Cabinet,* finding her full of *Curiosities,* and having free licence to take what I thought fit" (sig. A5r–A6r). Becoming a student, having access to the cabinet, is still a "Priviledge," and literacy itself is not the entrance key. Basset's gendering of Nature and Natural Philosophy as feminine poses some interesting questions about the nature of discovery and of reading. If Nature is female, are the only appropriate "readers" male? Who is more powerful: Nature/author, who can conceal or reveal, or the student/reader, who may "penetrate" and invade her "private walks"?

The genre, if you will, of cabinet-literature compensated for the paradoxical partnership of secrecy and publication by developing into two strains: the public, dealing with the observable in science, medicine, and the physical world, and the private, dealing with private life and lives and political and religious intrigue. The first group corresponds to the scientific revolution of the seventeenth century; books become museums between covers. The second type of cabinet-book, however, cultivates an air of secrecy, voyeurism, even prurience, in its revelations of "truth." The titles are indication enough: *The Wandring-Whores Complaint for Want of Trading Wherein the Cabinet of Her Iniquity Is Unlockt and All Her Secrets Laid Open* (1663); Richard Head's *The Canting Academy, or, The Devil's Cabinet Opened* (1673); *Holborn-drollery, or, The Beautiful Chloret Surprized in the Sheets . . . to Which Is Annexed, Flora's Cabinet Unlocked* (1673); *The Cabinet Open'd, or, The Secret History of the Amours of Madam de Maintenon* (1690). Books, like cabinets, could contain learned philosophies or titillating gossip, the new science, or old stories of sin, sex, and amorous play. Each attended to different facets of our modern preoccupation with secrecy, privacy, and the private self.

Privacy and the History of Books and Reading

This discussion of the creation of private space, the gendering of that space, and the association of books with those closed spaces is presented as preliminary to my main concern: exploring the connection between the rise of the "private self" and the publication and reading of books in seventeenth-century England. Seventeenth-century England was a society in flux, even apart from the political uncertainties that often seem peripheral to the average person's life. Alongside the quite visible changes in modes of building, both churchmen and lay people were striving to complete (or stave off) the Protestant Reformation; the ready availability of books then, like computer technology today, must have been seen as the sign or symptom of the disappearance of old ways of thinking. In what way did the conditions of that culture militate against or encourage the acceptance of privacy? Can we show, by examining how and what people read at the time, that reading precipitated what we would call a psychological revolution in thinking about private life (in tandem with the era's political, religious, and technological revolutions)? Or does the evidence only indicate the beginnings of such a transformation, or none at all? Secondarily, what can we discover about the traditional association of authorship with the public, male, active domain and reading with the private, female and passive? Can reading be a transgressive activity? If so, how does the female reader participate? How do the roles of author and reader overlap and challenge each other?

As a way of answering these questions about what seems to be a crucial period in the recognition of the private self, I will attempt to recover the experience of readers and reader-authors of the past. Methods for doing so have been suggested by Roger Chartier, Robert Darnton, and David Hall in their essays on the history of reading.[73] By referring to the concerns invoked by those definitions from the *OED,* I will focus throughout this study on several issues that arise in the history and sociology of reading: physical space (where to read); the distinction between the elite and the common reader (who should read);[74] and authorized as opposed to personal readings (how one should read). The function of secrecy and concealment and the complementary roles of author and reader will be a particular concern, as will the role of female readers. Women, constrained by limited educations and generally deprived of public status and personal autonomy by parents, husband, and custom, make especially apt models for all early modern readers. The private person par excellence, the woman reader exemplifies the possibilities for the realization of the private self in the seemingly powerless, supposedly sexually and textually vulnerable newly literate reader.[75]

I will examine, first of all, literary and thematic representations of reading and readers' accounts of their experiences in personal narratives, autobiography, and letters, as well as fictional and dramatic depictions of readers. Secondly, I will take into account reading manuals and guidance given by religious and educational authorities on methods for reading. Thirdly, since the material aspects of books provide clues to their use—that is, how earlier readers approached the reading process—I will scrutinize the presentation of the text itself. Iconography and illustrations make the reading experience easier and more pleasurable and must have held a great deal of significance for readers whose roots lay in the Catholic pictorial tradition. Prefaces and dedications may have offered a substitute for the background provided by oral performers of texts or for authors and printers prevented by law or distance from interacting with their readers.

My organization will be generic, for several reasons. Alastair Fowler has called genre "a communication system, for the use of writers in writing, and readers and critics in reading and interpreting."[76] In an age in which oral presentation was beginning to be supplanted by print, genre provided useful clues on how to read particular texts. At the same time, the Renaissance was a period of innovation for genre; though the historical context was important, the author's challenge, as Rosalie Colie says, was both to imitate and outdo.[77] The generic instability of the period also neatly mirrors the parallel uncertainties about the nature of the self.[78] And if, as Mary Gerhart claims, "genre testing . . . and the issue of genric competence is a correlate of the ability to read at all,"[79] then genre offered new groups of readers the opportunity to test their interpretive skills as well as their basic reading ability. The contract genre establishes between author and reader guarantees the author will follow some conventions and still be permitted to introduce new ones.[80] The very notion of contract implies an agreement between equals and individuals; thus it seems appropriate to my investigation of the fashioning of the private, autonomous self for both readers and authors.

The five chapters in this study explore five instances of readers and authors negotiating their experiences of privacy and print with one another, with religious and political authorities, with their families and lovers, with society, even with God. Many of them challenge their traditional roles in the public and private spheres, not just as economic or spiritual or sexual beings, but as individual, autonomous persons.

Chapter 1 examines the way in which the religious differences that sparked the English Protestant Reformation also played a role in the creation of a reading public, regardless of sectarian affiliation. Questions about religious ceremony and spontaneity in prayer, the locus of authority (whether the individual or an organized church or the crown), and the need for human priestly intermediaries evolved into questions about, and methods for, personal spiritual reading. Religious suppression demanded that believers make radical choices about their faith, and this frequently came to mean that individuals often expressed their beliefs, not when they attended Sunday services, but when they sat down with a book. At various times between the 1590s and the Civil War, all Christian denominations—Catholic, Puritan, and Anglican—came to rely on the book as a mode of religious expression. For Catholics, spiritual reading was a substitute for their outlawed traditions and ceremonies and fugitive priests; the possibility of legal reprisal meant that recusants not only had to develop a religious imagination fostered only by books but also had to develop a secret religious self, one at odds with official doctrine. Radical Protestants read as a matter of principle, for they regarded the book as the true manifestation of God's word. Though the Protestants of the middle way resisted extemporaneous prayer and individualized interpretations of texts, they too came to see books as vehicles for dissent during the 1640s. As members of the major religious denominations came to reading as a substitute for, and central expression of, religious practice, it became apparent that this private reading had larger implications: private reading freed one from the community, from established religious authority—perhaps even from all authority. Religious leaders come to realize that reading moved the locus of control from popes, bishops, official churches, and even holy books to the individual.

In chapter 2, my interpretation of four seventeenth-century conversion narratives points to the beginnings of the split between canonical and popular literature. Parental and religious authorities face off against readers who wish to control not only their approach to the text but their personal lives. While biographical and autobiographical conversion narratives continued the earlier tendency of religious literature to sermonize, to have the author's work act as a "domme preacher" that would convert the reader, later, more sensational narratives displaced the author in favor of the emoting, feminine, and self-authorizing reader. In these cases, the private experience of reading is explicitly associated with women and with the appurtenances of the novel. If my reading of these early modern conversion stories is accurate, it may be correct to conclude that canonical literature becomes canonical because it assumes the public, discursive, authoritative mantle of religious literature, while the more seductive and entertaining strain of the conversion narrative helps explain the centuries-long suspicion of fiction, with its emphasis on women, social convention, and the private life of the mind and the emotions.

Chapter 3 explores the effects of the revelations of publication on individuals and illustrates the powerful implications of the new medium of print for the invasion of personal life. The publication of the letters of Charles I not only raised questions about "the king's two bodies," disturbing the carefully created aura of divinity surrounding anointed rulers, but created an environment for speculation on the place the physical body plays in the establishment of psychological boundaries between people and the possibility that two "bodies," or two personalities, might coexist within one person. Like Charles I, the poet John Donne shared a penchant for secrecy, for cloaking his writing in actual or metaphorical codes; both men attempted to shield their writings from the eyes of unauthorized readers and represented their letters as the embodiment of their true, undisguised selves. What is significant is that their efforts at control are erased, or at least weakened, by readers of their texts; the posthumous publication of Donne's letters by his son and the unauthorized publication of the king's letters demonstrate the growing power of the reader to arrange and interpret the work of the author without authorial intervention. More importantly, the publication of these two sets of letters offered individual readers the opportunity to consider secrecy and disclosure, the body and the self, in personal terms, and not simply as oblique and distant political and literary questions.

Margaret Cavendish, royalist, exile, and ambitious author, felt the need to erase suspicions about privacy and about female authorship by situating her work in the context of the virtuous life. As a woman of her time, she concurred with the popular notion that female virtue consisted in chastity and in womanly silence. In order to reconcile this belief with her equally strong desire for fame and for public recognition of her talents, she rewrote contemporary attitudes about publishing by depicting female authors, orators, and generals in her plays. She demonstrated that the actions of these women—public women all—were rooted, not only in solitude and the contemplative, hidden life, but in a physical and spiritual integrity that guaranteed their chastity. This chastity, not incidentally, gave her characters an actual and psychological independence from men that freed them for personal autonomy without the loss of their reputations. And the private life of women became, for Cavendish, not a state of exclusion, of nonparticipation in the life of the state, but a school of virtue, the preparation for sharing (or surpassing) government by men. In Cavendish's female characters, reading, study, and contemplation burst forth, manifested themselves in authorship and publication.

Aphra Behn's *Love-Letters Between a Nobleman and His Sister* puts a different twist on Cavendish's thinking about the uses of privacy. She depicts what Cavendish had feared: that privacy might be used, not for the good of the Commonwealth, but for personal gain and self-interest. Behn's female protagonist is the embodiment of the Protestant private spirit;[81] she comes to regard personal desire as her sole authority. Behn's central character, Silvia, takes up the "masculine pen" and is able to manipulate both her acquaintances and the book's readers with her skillful concealments and discoveries. In escaping the traditional female role of fallen woman, in her calculated self-authorization, Silvia demonstrates the power and the indecipherability of the private self.

Behn's depiction of Silvia illustrates the ambivalence of the seventeenth-century mind toward personal privacy. There was a recognition that individuality and personal autonomy could exist and that it could be nourished by private reading. It was also accepted that the author's role was pivotal: his or her authority resided in books, which had the ability to guide (or misguide) the reader. Over the course of the century, the "author" was created, religious wrangling led people of good faith to question the lawfulness of authority, and a king was imprisoned and executed. It is perhaps significant that the information explosion of the seventeenth century, due to the ready availability of printed books, had a hand in each of those public events. Because books were available and because more and more people could read them, social and political events were no longer public matters of interest only to the governing elite. When books came into the home, public events became private concerns as well; they could change the *mentalité,* the way of observing the self and the world, of the early modern English citizen. Private life and personal autonomy may not yet have been considered an individual "right," but the evidence of reading and writing habits in seventeenth-century England at least marked out a space for consideration of that possibility.

I

Reading and the Creation of the (Protestant) Private Spirit

"And what haue kings, that Priuates haue not too,
Saue Ceremonie, saue generall Ceremonie?"
—Shakespeare

"I was no private but a person rais'd
With command from Heav'n to free my Countrey"
—Milton

THE QUOTATIONS that serve as epigraphs to this chapter pinpoint a central concern of the seventeenth century: the relationship between the private person and authority. Traditionally and etymologically, the "private" person was one who held no public office or official position,[1] one who was disempowered because he (and certainly she) could not speak with authority for the community. Here, ironically, it is Milton the revolutionary who hints at the potential religious and political powerlessness of the individual. In contrast, Shakespeare's Henry V ascribes equality to private persons and kings, an equality that is obscured only by the outward trappings of "generall Ceremonie"; Shakespeare (or his character) seems to undermine the authority of that most public of persons, the king. Separated by two generations, these quotations exhibit no progress toward a definition of privacy; rather, they indicate the unsettled attitude of the seventeenth-century mind toward the concept of "privacy." If privacy as we think of it existed at all, it was regarded as a negative—as the absence of station, of authority, of the divinely bestowed right or ability to lead a nation. Being a public person, on the other hand, seemed automatically to confer these qualities on individual persons, whether priests, kings, or prelates. The disengagement of this notion of authority from public persons, and the beginnings of its attachment to private individuals, is the subject of this chapter. I shall attempt to locate the roots of this gradual congruence of authority with the private person in devotional reading, with its particular emphasis on the notion of the solitary reader, alone with God and his or her book.

The tensions between public and private in the early modern period arose first in the religious sphere, where they were embedded in the oppositions between official church teachings and the call for individual interpretations of the word of God. Proponents of traditional church authority and hierarchy, sacramentalism, and ceremony were forced into extreme conservative and legalistic positions, in (apparent) opposition to the authority of the individual believer. The catholic, universal church faced off against the enthusiasts of the English reform, whose claim to authority lay in the private reading of Scripture by individuals. I will argue that an evolving notion of privacy may be situated in the religious struggles of post-Reformation England; further, that these religious controversies eventually ratified the right to individual autonomy in all things (including religion); and that the catalyst for these changes lay in the practice of private spiritual reading, regardless of religious persuasion or doctrinal belief. One could say that attitudes toward the private self during the seventeenth century were evolving, but that gives the impression of some progressive, forward movement. Privacy encompassed both individualism and a dangerous anarchy, both subversion of religious and political authority and spontaneity (not so positive a quality for the early moderns as it is for many of us). Secrecy and privacy were almost synonymous, were regarded as suspect and possibly even immoral; the private self was certainly subject to surveillance by both religious and political authorities. Only gradually did the meaning of privacy become more neutral, even positive and humanizing.

In the contemporary pamphlet literature, there were three principal foci for the conflict between received public religious authority and private (individual) interpretation: private prayer, private (or lay) preaching, and Bible reading. Reading lay at the heart of all three of these issues; from prayer books to sermons to the Bible, the individual person reading became the site of the conflict. The central arguments on both sides of these questions almost always revolved around the right of the individual to bypass public ceremony, to read and pray outside the community of believers, to become, as it were, simultaneously author, reader, and editor of one's own religious texts. I will trace these arguments through an examination of the practices associated with spiritual reading in the Catholic, Anglican, and Puritan traditions. While it is tempting to stereotype and make radical distinctions between religious bodies (e.g., the Catholic as conservative, reactionary, and authoritarian, the Puritan as radical, individualistic, and repudiating earthly authority, and the Anglican as happily midway between the other two), individual spokespersons for each discipline muddle the distinctions between churches. And laypeople sometimes were oblivious to doctrinal distinctions, often sharing the same reading materials, no matter the doctrinal source.[2] The extremely popular medieval genre of the book of hours, for instance, was equally beloved in its Protestant manifestion as a primer; the revised primers of Queen Mary's reign exhibited an amazing mix of Catholic and Protestant spirituality and theology.[3] In a devotional work on the Eucharist, Thomas Wright, a Jesuit missionary, does not restrict his addresses to Catholic readers, but rather seems to take into account the widest possible audience.[4] The three prefaces (one for Catholics, one for Protestants, and one for "Catholike-lyke Protestantes") to his *The Disposition or Garnishmente of the Sovle to Receiue Worthily the Blessed Sacrament* (1596) illustrate the variety of possibilities for believers (and for readers) at the time: "I preconceiued, that these my sclender Meditations, shoulde come to the vew and censure of three sortes of persons; Catholicks, protestantes, & demi-catholickes, or catholique-like protestantes, or externall protestantes, & internall catholikes: some call them Churche-papistes, others Scismatiques."[5] Wright's complicated naming of the various sectarian possibilities indicates the variety of religious choices open to individuals. And it is significant that such options appear in the preface to a book printed secretly in England: the Antwerp imprint is false. Concealment and choice converge in Wright's text. It is the practice of private spiritual reading that becomes instrumental, not only in encouraging personal choice in religious matters, but in linking the idea of privacy and autonomy.

The Tradition of Devotional Reading

The rise of silent reading was a radical development in the history not only of reading and literacy but of privacy. It encouraged a new level of literacy: that of silent comprehension of the text. The eyes became the channels through which impressions reached the heart and worked their effects. This made possible private devotion and private scholarship unmediated by an official church.[6] Silent spiritual reading was not, of course, an invention of the age of print and reform. The *lectio divina* was part of a long monastic tradition,[7] and the *Devotio Moderna,* a lay movement of the late fourteenth century, encouraged solitary contact with the text. Albert Hyma has claimed an influence for the *Devotio* on such disparate religious personalities as Calvin, Luther, and Ignatius of Loyola.[8] Gerard Zerbolt (1367–98), an early leader in this movement, encouraged lay reading of the Bible in the vernacular and stressed the need for a personal, living faith. His directives for the spiritual life emphasized the role of reading:

> Take up some reading apt to spiritual progress, one that admonishes toward constant ascent and exhorts to progress. What you choose to read should speed your ascent toward purity and charity, show you the way through holy exercises and works, warm your affections for the ascent, instill fear, or raise hope. Therefore, as someone said, reading should be a form of admonishment for a Christian philosopher and not just busywork. This will easily happen if, following the teaching of Augustine, you begin your reading in the fear of the Lord, and it regulates your intention and affections so you seek nothing but spiritual advance toward purity of heart.[9]

The goal of such reading is self-admonishment and the regulation of the affections; reading is almost a passive activity, which the reader initiates, but which God directs. The end result is a conversion, a turning away from things below, and especially a turning away from the self to the things of heaven. (*The Imitation of Christ,* a byproduct of the *Devotio Moderna,* is the premier example of this model of self-abnegation, and continued to be popular for devotional reading into the post-Reformation period by Catholics and Protestants alike).[10] Members of the monastic orders and the adherents of the *Devotio Moderna* were an elite group: they were among the few who could read in the pre-Reformation era. By the end of the sixteenth century, however, literacy had increased and spiritual reading among laypersons assumed a much more important role.

Reading and the Catholic Imagination

Historians have long connected reading and literacy with the Protestant reform: Protestantism being the religion of the book and of individual spirituality, Catholicism supposedly the religion of outdated ceremony and rigid hierarchies. But the peculiar condition of Catholics in post-Reformation England separated English Catholics from their confrères on the Continent and made them more likely to assume the religious practices of their English Protestant neighbors. Moreover, I would like to suggest that the repression of Catholics during this period became a spark that fired a particularly English notion of privacy; later arguments over the validity of private belief and interpretation arose precisely because the early Catholic controversy had foregrounded questions about civil disobedience, public presentations of the self, and private choice in matters religious. The "Protestant" private spirit, then, was not peculiarly Protestant; during what Keith Thomas has called the "Age of Conscience," cases of conscience concerned every believer and theologians representing every religious stripe.[11]

In 1559, the celebration of the Mass was made illegal in England, and the parliament of 1562–63 extended the Oath of Supremacy as a test of loyalty to a wide range of laymen and clerics. In 1571 it became treasonous to import or publish any writings emanating from Rome; in 1581, treasonous to become reconciled with the Catholic Church. The same year, the fine for recusancy was raised to twenty pounds for each four-week period, a fine only the most wealthy could afford. It became a capital offense to aid a Catholic priest at all in 1585, and it was treasonous for a priest to set foot on English soil.[12] The English college at Douai was established in 1568 in order to educate missionary priests to return and serve in England.[13] These conditions of life in late sixteenth-century England may have, as John Bossy says, led to the "death of a church," but the repression of Catholic practices also fostered something new: a private spirituality for Catholics and the growing experience that their personal religious practices need not be affected by outward adherence to official doctrine and attendance at Church of England services. Outward conformity permitted interior religious freedom.[14] The Catholic mission created a self-conscious body that relied on Catholic lay individuals more than it did priests. Because illegal, Catholicism became an underground movement, and as with all underground movements, an underground mentality prevailed.[15] The prospect of principled civil disobedience first arose for Catholics during the last half of the sixteenth century, in the aftermath of antipapist legislation, in a way it did not for the Puritans until the beginning of the next century.[16] With their loyalty to civil authority constantly in question, Catholics experienced a split between public and private presentations of themselves. The specialized doctrine of equivocation permitted mental reservations that protected "the secrecy of man"[17] (and, not incidentally, provoked the scorn of Protestants whose lives were not imperilled by possible charges of treason). Catholics could choose to attend Church of England services, becoming "Church papists" (and so apparently deny their beliefs through their actions), or they could choose recusancy, an open refusal to conform. In either case, an individual choice was imperative, and mistrust, suspicion of others, and reliance on one's own resources were a given. Among these personal resources was the practice of devotion. English Catholics borrowed devotional techniques from the Continent; with the suppression of Catholic writing and the liturgy in England, translations of prayer manuals and other devotional works abounded.[18] Devotional reading became a substitute for forbidden ceremonies and for increasingly unsuccessful polemical works. The secret presses of Jesuit Robert Parsons and others produced titles for the laity that aimed not only to educate but to create a spirituality suited to the secular person.[19] Though based in Scripture, Catholic reading relied, not directly on the Bible, but on an imaginative encounter with scriptural persons and events. Meditation and private prayers such as the rosary led to an intimacy with the self and the development of a personal spirituality, often held to be the fruit of the work of the Protestant reformers alone. Indeed, the Catholic Church experienced an early corruption of this type of spirituality, in the extreme privatism and distorted mysticism of Illuminism in sixteenth-century Spain and quietism in Catholic Europe during the late seventeenth century.[20]

The necessity of books became clear to the minority Catholics.[21] *A Memoriall of a Christian Life* (1586) is a translation by Richard Hopkins of Luis de Granada's *Memorial de la vida Christiana.* In "The Prologve to the Christian Reader," Hopkins, interestingly, assigns books, and not sacrament or ceremony, the power of creating "a perfecte Christian": "Nowe this is the thinge (good Christian reader) which I haue so manie yeares desired: to wit, to see some booke that should treate particulerlie howe to forme a perfit Christian, and that might conteine a briefe somme of all such thinges as do appertaine vnto the professio[n] of this heauenlie life."[22]

Hopkins acknowledges that priests (it is noteworthy that he calls them preachers) have the obligation to assist Catholics in their pursuit of the devout life, but he recognizes that books offer a substitute that may be safer, and even preferable, because instruction can be controlled by the individual:

> And although it be the office of Catholique preacher to cure this blindnes with the light of godes worde: yet notwithstandinge theise be not euerie where to be founde, neither do all preachers treat of theise so necessarie matters, nor yet can they well (speakinge generallie) desce[n]de to such particularities, as this moral doctrine re-

> quireth. . . . And for all theise causes the readinge of deuout Catholique bookes is verie profitable: for somuch as they be vnto vs as it were domme preachers which are neither tedious for lengthe, (because we may leaue them of when we list,) neither do they leaue vs with a greedie appetite by reaso[n] of their briefnes, for that it is in our owne power to continewe the reedinge of them so longe as we mynde to take profit thereby. (sig. A6v)

Hopkins makes several points here: priests are scarce, and so books offer a substitute spiritual guide; books can address individual moral concerns, something impossible for a preacher speaking before a congregation; and finally, books are "domme preachers," always available at the convenience of the reader. Not only can a book preach eloquently without fear of the law's retribution (save perhaps the danger of its being burned); books can be tailored to individual needs. One may pick up or leave off a book whenever one likes; books are neither so boring nor so inadequate as human preachers can be. Personal preferences can be satisfied with books and are even a necessary adjunct to Mass and the sacraments:

> For in olde time in the primitiue churche the priestes and Curattes were so feruent and carefull in preachinge of the worde of God, that that might suffice to preserue and increase the faithfull people in vertue without any other readinge: but nowe alas, the priestes, and euen suche as haue cure of soules, do beleue that they are bounde to nothinge els, but onlie to minister the sacramentes, and to saie a *masse* at their times appointed, and herewith they content themselues for the moste parte in villages, and townes, yea and in some populous cities also. Wherefore the greater the wante is that we haue at this daie in this behalfe, the greater neede we haue to supplie the wante of good Catholike pastors, and Curattes, with good and deuout bookes. (sig. B1v–B2r)

Someone supplies a marginal note at this point: "Both townes and citties haue in this corrupt age to manie lewde bablinge hereticall preachers: but the Awthor compleyneth of the great want of good Catholike preachers." Even as Hopkins laments the lack of good Catholic priests (and the laxity of those who restrict their service to routine administration of the sacraments despite the many heretical preachers about), he emphasizes personal responsibility for reading: the burden for spiritual growth falls squarely upon the individual reader.

The attention paid to the reading of lay Catholics in the Counter-Reformation literature is significant. Catholics are not expected to spend their lives as hermits or solitaries, yet silence, private prayer, and reading play a substantial role in a good Catholic's life. Robert Southwell, the Jesuit priest and poet who was tried and executed for treason in 1595, wrote one such layperson's guide to the spiritual life, probably for the use of the countess of Arundel.[23] In chapter 6 of *Short Rules of a Good Life,* Southwell advises on "An Order How to Spend Every Day." Prayer and meditation are to begin the day: "After I am up, for a good pretty space it is good not to talk, but at the least for half a quarter of an hour to busy my mind in prayer and meditation, and then to talk if need be."[24] After this morning period of recollection, Southwell advises that the reader think about how best to conduct the "necessary business" of the day. Then, on to formal prayers. The method of prayer first requires a recollection of the presence of God; vocal prayers are acceptable, but better still to occupy one's prayer time with meditation on the Passion or one's own sins. All of these instructions presuppose silence, reflection, inwardness. Though God is the center and end of these practices, there is a good deal of concentration on the self—from one's routine activities to the state of one's soul. There is also a sense in these rules of an essential loneliness, a sense that strength is to be derived from private spirituality, not the communal life. (This stands in strong contrast to the monastic tradition of communal recitation of the Divine Office, or even lay participation in liturgical services.) There are chapters on duties toward neighbors, children, and superiors, but the text, significantly, is written in the first person, and the focus on the interior life predominates. Two practices support and furnish this interiority: reading and the imaginative life arising from prayer.

The *Rules* allow for the reading of "a good book" each day before supper. Southwell emphasizes that the reader continue in one book before beginning another; he somehow regards floating from book to book as incompatible with the examined life. Here is a variation on the "intensive" reading of the centuries before books became commonly available: reading few books over and over again, rather than reading many books "extensively." Roger Chartier associates intensive reading with the reverence due to scarce objects; extensive reading is nonchalant, an act of pleasure, and becomes the rule when reading becomes individualized and the book is desacralized.[25] Because the habits of the spiritual life necessitate such intense absorption with the self, Southwell seems to be using the manner of reading as a sort of discipline: to control spiritual pride and self-interest, to steel the soul for possible future contests. Books, though tools of the moral life, may perhaps also be dangerously attractive. Restricting oneself to one book at a time may be a small exercise in self-denial.

The time after supper might be spent in talking, walking, or in reading "some pleasant yet profitable book, as Catholic histories or the like" (44). On holy days, reading may occupy some of the time ordinarily spent at work: "Instead of my work I must bestow those days in reading good books, hearing sermons, and suchlike godly exercises, not lightly running over them thinking it enough to have read or heard good things, but pausing upon such things as move my affection and printing them well in my mind and memory" (45). And because one is apt to be "troubled with company" on holy days, Southwell advises prudent and charitable conversation in place of the usual quiet and intimacy with God. Southwell's insistence on creating a private space for one's spiritual life is especially important for the Catholics he is addressing, challenged, as he will be in his own life, with the possibility of torture and martyrdom.

This private space is to be peopled by the imagination. Louis Martz has written of the influence of Jesuit meditative tradition on Southwell and the poets who followed him: Donne, Herbert, Vaughan, and Crashaw.[26] The new interiority attributed to these poets (particularly to Donne) is perhaps linked to the Catholic imaginative tradition fired by various methods of meditation and private devotions such as the rosary.[27] Books were the starting points for prayer, but scenes from the life of Christ and the Virgin Mary became the substance of devotion and the measure against which to judge oneself. The examination of conscience was to be a daily task, not just an occasional one preceding confession: "Towards the hour of going to bed . . . I must examine my conscience touching the thoughts, words, and deeds of that day, and especially concerning the purposes that I have made in the morning, and how I have observed these rules, and what faults I have committed of any moment. After I have abstained from talk that night (unless some just occasion require the contrary) that my mind may be free from idle thoughts when I go to sleep" (44). The repeated injunctions to avoid unnecessary talk exist for a particular reason, and not only the traditional ones of containment of the affections and the senses.[28] Silence encouraged the believer's cohabitation with Christ and his saints: "Also, when I lie down, I may imagine to lie by the pillar, Cross, manger, or some such place where Christ was present, that when I wake in the morning he may be the first that shall come into my mind" (44–45).

And, as another actual "exercise of devotion," Southwell suggests the following: "I must in every room of the house where I dwell imagine in some decent place thereof a throne or chair of estate and dedicate the same and the whole room to God himself, that whensoever I enter into it I enter as it were into a chapel or church that is devoted to him and therefore in mind do that reverence that is due unto him. And thus will that place be to me in manner a paradise" (68). For the closed churches of England, Southwell substitutes a chapel of the mind. The private person, rather than a public building, becomes the seat of God's presence. As an aid to this creative process, Southwell relies on the iconographic tradition of the Catholic Church:

> But to help my memory and to avoid confusion, it is good to appoint in every room some certain and determinate pictures to be patterns and examples unto me in that action for which that room principally serveth: as in the dining chamber or parlor, saints of spare and regular diet, of sober and virtuous conversation; in the bedchamber, saints given to short sleep and watchfulness. . . .
>
> . . . likewise, instead of these saints, I may place some lamentable history of the Old or New Testament, or some representation of death, hell, or judgment. Likewise, in other rooms, to place some glorious, fair, and comfortable saints, histories, or figures, withal suitable to joy, that may serve me in time of my heaviness to allay my sorrows; and the like in fear, hope, presumption, despair, and such other passions, but especially in those which I find myself most inclined unto. (68–69)

Visual images, books, and the imagination become linked in the prayer life of the Catholic. The routine association of the Protestant religion with the book, Catholicism with ceremony and imagery, fails to take into account the fact that both books and images are, first of all, visual.[29] The Puritan hatred of images that accompanied the emphasis on literacy and the ability to read Scripture may have encouraged individualism, but this does not mean that the same development did not occur among Catholics, particularly in England. Imbued with a sacramental and iconographical mindset that looked for meaning in images and forced into disguise and equivocation by constant political threats, Catholics took to the interpretive exercise of reading to sustain their ancient liturgical and paraliturgical traditions. Even the rosary, a late medieval devotion much attacked by the Protestant reformers, took its part in the new print culture. An oral prayer, the rosary was defended vehemently by Catholic apologists. Supporters of the practice couched this remnant of the old faith in terms of a book culture, a culture that promoted the private encounter of the soul with God. Oral prayers were to be accompanied by meditation on the mysteries of Christ's and the Virgin's lives, not unlike the Ignatian *Spiritual Exercises.* Henry Garnet, the Jesuit who was executed in the aftermath of the Gunpowder Plot, wrote one such apologia for devotion to Mary, *The Societie of the Rosary* (1596–97). Garnet likens the rosary to reading: "Euery deuout Catholicke, dailye when he saieth his beades, doth as it were in a booke read and reuerently laith before his eies, Christ our Sauiour incarnat in his Mother, sanctifying Iohn Baptist his holy Precursor, lying in a manger, offered vp to his Father in the Temple, teaching the Doctors, praying in the Garden, cruelly whipped with thornes, carrying his Crosse and exalted theron for our redemption, rising againe, ascending into heauen."[30] Garnet goes on to "page through" all fifteen events meant to be recollected by the mysteries of the rosary. Though the imagery is visual, the activity of prayer is internal and private, not oral and communal.

I shall close this section by making a connection between the devotional practices described above and the social and political conditions of Catholics in the late Elizabethan and Jacobean period. The cultivation of the imagination and the consciousness of the individual self that derived from prayer, silence, and devotional reading were closely linked with the suppression of Catholics. As would become the case with the Anglican/royalist party during the Civil War, the proscription of public worship and the danger of imprisonment forced a retreat into the private conscience. (The two groups, Catholic priests and cavaliers, even shared some of the same "priest-holes," or hiding places, in the great houses of England.)[31] As Josephine Evetts Secker has shown, Boethian freedom of mind was invoked by recusant consolatory literature and was particularly associated with prison literature.[32]

The Rosarie of Our Ladie, Otherwise Called Our Ladies Psalter (1600), a set of meditations on the rosary, is presented as the work of an imprisoned priest, Thomas Worthington. "Depriued, both of bookes and Beades" and thrown back on the resources of his own imagination, he had written the book as a "priuat Exercise"; the prison work has now, however, been released in print: "This priuat Exercise, albeit very vnperfect (as not purposed for the print, but rudely writte[n], and geue[n] to a priuat freind) yet did so content and please some wel disposed persons, that presently, without knowledge of the author, they caused it to be printed, and so made common to manie."[33] The trope of unauthorized publication can be attributed to more than authorial modesty in this case: the author notes that possession of a rosary was "inhibited" (sig. *3v); publication and importation of Catholic works was illegal. The book not only makes private meditation public; its very publication valorizes the imprisonment and presents the imaginative fruit of that solitary experience. The priest, "prisoner for the Catholike religion," makes his private thoughts "common to manie" in order to sustain his fellows in their own "priuat" spiritual lives.

Along with "necessary points of Christian doctrine," Worthington's publisher includes woodcut images to aid in meditation: "For as meditation without knowledge is erroneous: so knowledge without meditation is drie and fruitlesse." Reading as an intellectual exercise will simply not suffice; images engage the imagination and the emotions as a text alone cannot: "Likewise out of this varietie, and copie of diuine Mysteries and benefites, the wel disposed may at al times and occasions, choose sufficient and fit pointes to meditate vpon, in al their prayers vocal or mental. And finally, by diligent viewing and beholding the pictures here placed, euerie one may better conceiue and consider the Mysteries by them represented, and be perhaps more moued to deuotion by sight thereof, then by only reading" (sig. *8r–*8v).

In one of his final meditations, based upon apocryphal events not recorded in Scripture (and not even part of traditional Catholic legend), Worthington links together the themes of privacy, imprisonment, reading, and the imagination. The meditation, entitled "The actes of our Ladie from Christs Resurrection to her owne death and Assumption," depicts the Virgin Mary after the events of the Passion:

> Wherupon she retyring to her chamber, after that she hath awhile meditated vpon the sacred woundes of her deare sonne and Lord, and other torments by him suffered, she turneth her cogitatio[n]s from that tragical act, to thinke what he now doth where he is. And so as wel in the sepulchre she adoreth him as God, knowing that his humaine flesh, albeit without soul, yet is continually vnited to his Godhead, by which it was assumpted: as also in Limbo, where his soule by his excellent brightnes driuing away the wonted darknes, triumpheth ouer death, loseth the captiuitie of the old fathers, and by his most glorious presence maketh that place, which hitherto was a prison, to be to them as heauen or paradise. (sig. D12r)

On the page facing this text is an illustration of the Virgin seated at prayer, opposite a resurrected Christ (fig. 1). The picture is a Dutch interior, a

1. *The Rosarie of Our Ladie* (by permission of the Folger Shakespeare Library)

resetting of an Annunciation scene, down to the traditional and anachronistic book before her. The caption above the picture, "Conseruat omnia verba haec conferens in corde suo," quotes Luke 2:19, and recalls the new mother Mary pondering in her heart the mystery of the incarnation. In this private chamber, the Virgin meets in prayer a God who released souls from the imprisonment of Limbo. Her meditation is the promise to Worthington and his readers that their imprisonment is temporary, that his presence can turn what looks like a prison into a paradise.

Solitude, reading, and privacy, then, were not foreign to the Catholic experience of the late sixteenth and early seventeenth century. However, the move toward private life, for a Catholic, was not solely a rational enterprise; thought had always to be leavened by the devotional imagination. The Catholic tradition of spiritual reading harked back to the medieval sacramental notion of the book. In a sense more modern than the iconoclasts, Catholics expected *both* words and images, both reason and feeling. The interior imaginative sphere had to become real enough to inhabit in case of capture and imprisonment. As Elizabeth Hanson has noted, the lies elicited under torture defined for Catholics a new inner realm of experience, "interior, private, and subjective *as though* it were external reality."[34] The imaginative constructs of prayer, fed by visual images, differed from, and therefore seemed at odds with, the Protestant approach to the word. Only later, in the emblematic and intensely private religious poetry of the seventeenth century are word and image conjoined in a suitably Protestant way. Poetic collections (such as Herbert's and Vaughan's) substituted verbal imagery for the visual in the printed books that valorized and highlighted the achievement of the individual author.

The Protestant Controversy over Private Prayer

If Catholics identified privacy with self-examination, surveillance, and the exercise of the imagination, Anglicans (a term I shall use to represent supporters of the official Church of England) associated it with the dangers of spontaneity in private prayer, with departures from the official prayers and pronouncements of the church. Reading became associated with private prayer, which held a great range of meaning for seventeenth-century believers. The debate about the propriety of private prayers arose from a fear that the official English church stood too close to the hated ceremonies and set prayers of the papists. The Church of England's claim that it was a return to the pure and primitive devotion of the church fathers was disputed by the more radical Protestant groups, which preferred a complete break with outward ceremony and an emphasis on spontaneous, inner communion with God.[35]

Several challenges presented themselves to Protestants on both sides of the private prayer question: how to maintain a proper respect for the majesty of God; how to reconcile the multiple voices of separate individuals all clamoring for God's ear; how (and whether) to incorporate the Bible and set prayer into one's own spiritual devotions. The possibilities for prayer were multiple: the ceremonial ritual of the Catholics, the private, set prayers of both the Catholics and the Anglicans, and the extemporaneous prayer (either in public or private) recommended by the Puritans.[36] Writers of every religious persuasion seem, eventually, to fall back on method (whether free or structured) to provide form for the believer. Even the most Puritan of writers gives readers specific directives for the conduct of their spiritual lives, and all polemicists face the crucial question of the proper role of spiritual books (including the Bible) and of the reader's relationship to sacred texts. Many of the arguments revolved around the right relationship between reading and prayer. The differences cannot be neatly aligned with a religious sect (i.e., Catholics and Anglicans opposing private prayer, Puritans espousing it). Though Protestantism saw the Bible as central to belief and practice, the most radical Puritan sometimes saw even books as symbols of authority, and therefore inimical to the freedom of the children of God. Books could alternately be vehicles for personal autonomy or instruments of religious authority or oppression. The gradual acceptance of private devotion seems to have occurred through a series of increasing accommodations between the religious left and the Anglicans and royalists who represented the old forms of political and religious authority.

Puritan John Robinson, in *Of Religious Commvnion Private, & Publique* (1614), argued that spiritual communion exists outside the bounds of formal church structures, that each person stands individually before God. Gathering to pray in an assembly puts one in danger of becoming one body with Satan; the true temple is made of the lively stones of individual persons. Reading prescribed texts, the service book so revered by the Anglicans, is nothing less than idol-worship. Robinson finds reading as a substitute for prayer totally repugnant:

> And we do therefore repute the *service book* an *Idoll,* because it is, & is apoynted to be read by the Minister, for his, & the Churches prayers. . . . we doubt not but it is lawfull to read privately the

> prayers, or sermons of any godly men that come to our hands for instruction & provocation in & vnto any good duty, & to have the heart therewith affected acccordeingly: but to conclude, that therefore it is lawfull to bring the some into the Ch: & to read them publiquely for that end, & (which is more) that the so reading of them as the preaching, & praying which the Ministers of Christ are to *give themselves* vnto . . . is to make ropes of sand. . . .
>
> They further call this *the reading of Decluses prayer:* & therein confess theyr Ch: praying to be reading. And is reading praying? or are not these two distinct exercises, & for divers ends? Do men read to God, (which if to read be to pray) they must do? In praying, we powr matter out of the heart: but in reading we receav matter in, as common reason teacheth. How ignorant then or obstinate soever men are in theyr customes & traditions receaved from theyr auncestours, theyr set service read for prayer is but an humayn devise for Gods worship (& that vnreasonable also:) & so an Idoll & agaynst the 2[d] Commaundment; with which no fellowship is to be had.[37]

Robinson reaffirms the duty of Christians to read and pray privately, but he cannot tolerate what he sees as an abuse of God's word. Reading by itself—the way the Anglicans read—is seen by this Puritan as a passive activity, inseparable from the mindless oral prayers of Catholics. The reader at an Anglican service is swallowed up in ceremony, is merely an observer of a group ritual; Anglicans are consumers, not authors of prayer. True private prayer is an autonomous, creative act, in which "we powr matter out of the heart." It is significant that, from a Puritan point of view, reading in and of itself cannot be connected with the trend toward interiority in religious practice. Habits of reading that parallel the older oral traditions and ceremonies of Catholicism, in which the listener simply imbibed the spoken text, do not lend themselves to the creation of a private self. Passive religiosity breeds subjection, not an interior subjectivity.

The Anglican response to the Puritan accusation that rote prayers were by definition mindless is represented in works such as Robert Hill's *The Pathway to Prayer and Pietie* (1613). Hill's book was issued in several editions; it is only in this, the fifth, that the author must have felt a need to respond to Puritan attacks on private prayer, for the publisher announces on the title page the inclusion of an "Apologie for publicke, and priuate set Prayer." Hill, an Anglican minister, presents his arguments in the form of a dialogue between Euchedidascalus, a teacher of prayer, and Phileuches, a lover of prayer.[38] Euchedidascalus is the Socratic questioner, posing theological test questions to Phileuches. The first issue to be dispensed with is the lawfulness of set prayer. Phileuches cites God's ordinance, the "iniunction of Godly Kings and Magistrates," tradition, and lastly, "the inconueniences which will follow upon the disallowance of a set and stinted Prayer."[39] He expands upon this last reason: "In this age so farre inferiour to that of the Apostles, without set praier, there would be such distraction and diuersity not onely in the matter, but also in the forme of prayer, and such deformity and discordance in Leiturgie, leauing it to the discretion of every priuate Minister, that whereas God is the God of order and consent: 1.Cor.14.33. we should be like the people of confusion" (sig. L1r). Private prayer, untrammeled enthusiasm, and individual approaches to God breed disunity and an unseemly dissonance among churchgoers. (In his preface, Hill had counseled readers, in public prayer to "conforme your selfe to the laudable custome of that Church in which you are.")

Noting that churches separated from the Anglican communion argue against prayers drawn from books, Euchedidascalus asks whether set and written prayers do not simply illustrate the faculty of memory and the ability to read, and not the spirit of God. (Note the increasing problematic of reading: for the Puritans, reading Scripture, a set text, is acceptable, but reading set prayer, and most especially, substituting it for the true devotion expressed by ex tempore prayer, is not.) Phileuches' response argues for the sacredness of reading; in fact, he sees it as a repetition of the work of the Holy Spirit, the reader, as it were, sharing in the divine authorship: "And like as the Scripture did not only manifest the spirit when it was first endited, but doth also when it is read: so praier which manifested the spirit when it was first endited, serues also to manifest the spirit, when it is repeated or read" (sig. L3r). Despite Hill's apparent approval of spiritual reading, he agrees that there may be excesses, that public religious order may be threatened by private worship. Staying home and reading "a good Sermon priuately" (sig. T5r) is not preferable to attendance at church services, for "Experience teacheth, that the liuely voice is more effectual, then ocular reading" (sig. T5v). The word of God is meant to be heard, dispensed by a preacher who leads a unified public assembly, not a diverse collection of individual penitents.

In *Abba Father: or, A Plaine and Short Direction Concerning Priuate Prayer* (1618), Elnathan Parr finds that praying from a book is more expedient in congregations, but agrees with the Puritan stance that, ideally, each

Christian should be able to formulate his or her own prayers.[40] Parr offers his book for those who lack the memory and understanding to formulate their own. However, he expresses some discomfort with a total reliance on book-prayers:

> The reason why I haue vndertaken this businesse, considering there are so many good Prayer-bookes in euery mans hand, is, first, because, though it bee comendable to vse a booke, yet it is more comfortable to pray of our selues, whose wants may be such, as that we shall hardly finde them sufficiently expressed in any booke: for euery man is best acquainted with his owne heart.
>
> Secondly, a man may be cast into prison, and his booke taken from him: how vncomfortably must he needs passe his time, if he cannot pray without his booke. The booke cannot be vsed in the darke, when we may haue iust occasion to pray. The booke may be forgotten, or lost: but if thou attainest this gift, thou canst neuer loose it, unless thou loosest thy selfe.[41]

Parr wants it both ways: he would like people to buy his book and find its set prayers useful, but he must side with the Puritans in the superiority of private extemporaneous prayer. The "selfe" is more authentic and more revealing than any book, and the possibility of the ultimate privacies, prison and death, require an independence from the authority and physicality of the book. Parr goes on, nevertheless, to present some guidelines for praying well. His first directive is to find a fit place: "But priuacy is to be chosen, that being sequestered from company, we may the more fully descend into our owne hearts" (sig. A10r–A10v). Cultivating a spirit of repentance, finding a fit time, and freeing oneself from thoughts of the world follow. Lastly, he recommends reading a chapter of the Bible or a Psalm as a preparation to prayer, "both for the increase of knowledge, and for the better calling home of the mind to the businesse in hand" (sig. A11v–A12r). The creation of a spiritual self comes to be linked to a separation from others: alone, the Christian may penetrate the recesses of his heart, enter more easily into the interior castle.

For Parr, reading becomes a means to prayer, but it also requires that the reader/believer move from passive recipient to active respondent. In order to pray well, the reader should create a spiritual commonplace book, so that the multiple activities of praying, reading, and writing become intertwined:

> If he can write, let him make a book of clean paper, and in sundry leaues, write in the top the particular parts of prayer, with their seuerall branches, allowing a whole leafe to each part & branch; and then whatsoeuer excellent and speciall phrase or sentence hee readeth or heareth of any of those parts or branches, let him referre it to his proper leafe and place. Which course if it bee taken, and these places diligently studied, and now and then reuised and read ouer, wil (in my opinion) much enable a man vpon any occasion to pray with vnderstanding, either alone, or with others to their desired comfort. (sig. CIIr–CIIv)

Parr seems ambivalent about the role of books and reading in the spiritual life: his prefatory remarks regard them as a necessary evil, yet the act of writing his book and the importance he places on the act of reading in his directions for prayer make it seem more than a support for the spiritually dry Christian. Private reading becomes a substitute for official public prayer, a tool for spiritual development, the means by which the reader/prayer becomes his own author, the compiler of a new and personalized book.

Ambivalence about private prayer disappears during the Civil War period, as the Church of England is forced into a posture of defensiveness it had never before had to assume. The arguments for private, unstructured devotion had been propounded by the more radical Protestant sects for several decades in England, and longer still on the Continent, but only after the official church was disbanded and outlawed did private worship become defensible for Anglicans. In 1640 a petition on behalf of 15,000 Londoners urged the abolition of the Anglican episcopacy, "with all its dependencies, roots and branches," and the institution of a government "according to God's word."[42] This petition, known as the Root and Branch Petition, also criticized the "Romish sources" of the prayer book and the likeness of Anglican ceremonies to those of the Church of Rome. In 1645 William Laud, archbishop of Canterbury, was tried and executed. The Solemn League and Covenant of 1643 urged "uniformity in religion, confession of faith, form of Church government, directory for worship and catechizing" in the churches of England and Scotland,the extirpation of popery and prelacy, and the "discovery of all such as have been or shall be incendiaries, malignants, or evil instruments, by hindering the reformation of religion."[43] Anglicans, like the Catholics fifty years before, were under attack.

The political struggles of the 1630s and 1640s were reflected in discussions on the individual person's relationship to God in prayer. The propriety of speaking informally to God, in one's own words, was hotly debated. Private persons would not presume to address royalty without preparation; to a right-thinking Anglican, the same courtesies, of course, extended to God. The idea of greeting God as one would an equal was unimaginable, even disrespectful. Church ceremony mirrored the elaborate customs and manners of courts, where the distance between sovereign and subject was vast (and regarded as appropriate). A defense of traditional devotional practices first published during the Civil War years, Lancelot Andrewes's *A Manual of Private Devotions* (1670, orig. pub. 1648), presents just such an argument.

In the book's preface "To the Christian Reader," Richard Drake presents himself as a reader who is blessed to have held the "Sacred Relique" of Andrewes's original manuscript, an example of "pure and Primitive Devotion." Drake precedes the text of the bishop's prayers with a personal interpretation of Andrewes's text. Andrewes himself offers, not a theology of prayer, but his own private offerings to God. Drake's is a defense of set prayer, a politically useful rereading of the long-dead Andrewes's (1555–1626) own writings:

> From the general inspection of these *His set and sacred Forms,* as you are convinced of *His Piety,* so you may learn *His Judgment* concerning *Ex-tempore Conceptions,* and undigested Prayers.
>
> I am confident He had as great Abilities of Expressing himself to purpose *without Premeditation,* as any Rabby that Pretends to the highest pitch of Inspiration. But his *Devotion* had not taught him to cast off His *Humility;* nor was He so little acquainted with *His God* and *Himself,* as not to know His Distance, and to keep it. It had been a sin to Him to appear before *His God* empty, or with that which cost Him nothing.
>
> There is too much of a Pharisee in him that dares not trust to his Phancy, or Invention, before the Majesty of *Heaven;* when even his most premeditated and Weighted Thought, though cloathed in the best Attire of Language, would be esteemed by himself too unworthy to be offered to his Prince.[44]

This preface, dated 1647, proclaims Andrewes's "Prayers, Supplications, Intercessions, and Giving of Thanks" as "His unquestionable Directory" (sigs. A7r–A7v). *A Directory for the Publike Worship of God* had, in 1645, discarded the Book of Common Prayer and provided only the sparsest of directions for the conduct of public prayer. Drake's preface is a response to that perceived discourtesy to God. He regards the translation of poetic

"Phancy" into prayer as a proper tribute to God, the divine patron for whom only the sweetest inventions will do. Any other approach to God constitutes irreverence and carries with it the possibility of the destruction of social as well as religious order and hierarchies. In the politically charged atmosphere of 1647, two years before the execution of Charles I, Drake is not only defending set private prayer as a replacement for public worship but using it to reaffirm covertly the proper relation of the individual to authority. The ceremonious language of private prayer quietly replaces the public ceremony of church and court for the Anglican believer.[45]

We see, then, that though Puritans, Anglicans, and Catholics approach prayer and spiritual reading from different doctrinal positions, the end results are similar: an increased reliance on the written word and a move toward interior, private devotion. Arguments about reading reconstituted privacy from two directions. The Puritans, though revering the reading of Scripture, regarded total reliance on any book as idolatrous, an interference with the spirit of God. True private prayer was a personal responsibility and had to originate from within. The Anglican practice of reading set and ceremonial prayer was curtailed and redirected both by the necessity of a response to the Puritan attack and by the political conditions of the Civil War and Interregnum. Reading (as for Catholics a few decades earlier) changed in nature, and came to hold an entirely new meaning for the Anglican believer. Without the opportunity to participate in a communal liturgy after the Book of Common Prayer was outlawed, Anglicans were forced to find private times and places for prayer. While Puritans sought autonomy in private interpretation and preaching of the Gospel, Anglicans challenged the parliamentarian government by defining their reading of set prayer as a partnership in the authorship and authority of God.

The Private Spirit and Scripture

The apparent meeting of Puritan and Anglican attitudes toward prayer, however, left unanswered the effects of such privatization of spirituality. What would be the result when total spiritual independence and private reading and interpretation became the norm?

The most crucial sort of reading (in any dispensation) is the reading of the canonical text. Every denomination in England debated the proper method, the proper place, the proper reading audience for the Bible.[46] All disputants, no matter their religious allegiance, recognized that reading Scripture privately placed the reader outside the reach of properly constituted religious authority. An ordained minister reading Scripture aloud in a religious ceremony, or a father reading to his family, was simply assumed to be proclaiming the Word of God before the people of God. But when one read the Bible silently and alone, one moved to a private realm. Whether that realm was the sanctuary of God or of evil spirits was the matter in question. According to Wesley A. Kort, even Calvin would not have regarded solitary reading of the Bible, the basis of the Christian life, as a license for private religion.[47] Isaac Ambrose,[48] in *Prima, the First Things* (1654) ruled for the holiness of solitary Scripture reading, because it provided the occasion for a private audience with God: "The second *Duty* in reference both to secret, private and publike Ordinances, is *Reading the holy Scriptures,* which is nothing else but a kind of holy conference with God, wherein we enquire after and he reveals unto us himself and his will: when we take in hand therefore the Book of *Scriptures,* we cannot otherwise conceive of our selves then as standing in Gods presence, to hear what he will say unto us."[49]

Ambrose proceeds to offer directions for reading Scripture, including writing down pertinent passages. This seems to have been a common approach to reading the Bible; Nicholas Byfield writes an entire book about it (*Directions for the Private Reading of the Scriptures,* 1648).[50] Like Elnathan Parr before him, Byfield suggests that the reader make "a little paper book of a sheet or two of paper" to jot down important "titles" (sig. a2v). The added preface for the fourth edition, by Jo. Geree, sheds some light on reading practices and literacy during the period. (It confirms, for example, that reading and writing were not necessarily allied tasks; one could learn the former without learning the latter).[51] Readers are directed as follows: "Those that cannot write, can yet make marks, and thereby are authentique witnesses in contracts, and effectually ingaged in obligations. . . . And when in reading, they meet with any of these, they may with a pencill of lead (to avoid blotting) note them in the margent with one, two, or more stroaks, according to the number of that head to which they doe belong" (sig. a7v–a8r).[52]

Those who cannot even read are berated for neglecting their Christian duty; they should learn themselves, or, at the very least, have someone read to them. Learning to read, becoming engaged with the text by creating a commonplace book or marking the book, is equivalent to making one's mark in a contract with God. Reading and writing are actions that require individual initiative and autonomy, that reinforce the notion of personal responsibility for one's spiritual life.

In contrast, the well-known Catholic objections to the lay reading of the Bible are expressed quite fully in James Sharpe's *The Triall of the Protestant Private Spirit* (1630). Published abroad at the English College Press in

St. Omer, the title implies a test, a judgment upon the Protestant spirit that was an effect of unfettered Bible reading. Sharpe, a Jesuit, writes as "an *Israelite* among the *Aegyptians,*" a stranger and exile. This book, the second part of two planned, is "a Confutation of the *Priuate Spirit,* the ground of all Protestancy." The implications are obvious: privacy is not a virtue, least of all one on which to base a religion. The author apologizes for the appearance of the second part before the first (which was never published). Like two twins struggling in childbirth, the one more ready receives the "precedence of Birth-right." The first section had been intended to prove "that this *Priuate Spirit* is by the sayd Protestant Doctrine, made not only a Ground, but a sole and whole Ground of their *Fayth* and *Religion.*"[53] The theoretical proof must have come to be seen as unnecessary; what became more urgent for the Catholics was the practical necessity of stamping out this private (read individual) spirit, which was fed by the reading of Scripture.

Protestants, claims Sharpe, firmly reject the tradition of the Apostles, the Holy Ghost, and the Church's "infallible authority" (sig. C4r). Instead, they wholly subject everything to this private spirit.[54] Sharpe makes clear how individualistic he sees this spirit to be: over and over, he identifies it as a personal possession; it is "their owne"; it is "new"; it is not held in common, the property of the entire church. This is to become the crux of Sharpe's argument against Protestantism: that it is not catholic, not universal, and, most importantly, not unifying. The soul of Protestantism is embedded in the salvation of the individual, in personal election, while Catholicism offers hope to all: "For we affirme this grace to be extended, offered, and giuen sufficiently, though not effectually, to all; so that all, and euery one of reason haue sufficient meanes, and ability to know God by Faith, and to loue him by Charity, so afar as is needfull for their saluation. They affirm their spirit, to be restrayned, offered, and giuen, only to the elect, & faithfull (whom they make all one) and that all others neither haue, nor can haue it; but are by the absolut will and decree of God debarred from it, & thereby made incapable of it" (sig. D3v). Deprived of the certainty of divine grace, and unaided by the authority of official church doctrine, Protestants must discern for themselves whether they have received the gift of salvation.

As a Jesuit, Sharpe would have been trained in the "discernment of spirits," the process of discriminating holy inspirations from those begotten by the devil. This methodology was one of the great contributions of Ignatius of Loyola to the theology of the spiritual life.[55] Later in the book, Sharpe even lists the "rules to discerne which are good spirits, which are bad" (sig. L2r *ff.*). Sharpe is not objecting to spiritual discernment between good and evil spirits; at issue, rather, is the agent of discernment: not all individuals possess the gift of discerning good spirits from bad. (He is like the Protestants in his arguments that only elect persons possess this gift; the gift of interpretation of Scripture is granted to only a few.) As proofs of the dangers of private interpretations of God's spirit, Sharpe narrates a brief history of Satan's "inward suggestions" (sig. N2v–N3r), ranging over all of biblical and historical time, from Judas to the Anabaptists to contemporary visionaries "who believe they are inspired by God" (sig. N3v). Acceptance of such interior suggestions is not just sinful—the words of Satan are also likely to be illusions. Words are so easily misinterpreted; even the Bible, the word of God, is difficult and susceptible to misreading: "This sense and meaning of scripture, because it is not facil and easy to be knowne to all, by reason of the great obscurity in the wordes, the great fecundity in the sense, and the great profundity in the mysteries, or articles belieued, (which cannot by euery one, not by any one, without the assistance of the same spirit which penned it, be vnderstood) therefore is necessary some authentical, certain, and infallible authority, for the true vnderstanding of this authenticall, certaine, and infallible sense of the scripture" (sig. P2v–P3r). Sharpe is not just casting doubts on the abilities of new and theologically unschooled readers here. He attributes a certain weightiness to words: their fecundity, profundity, and mystery seem to require very wise, and very careful, interpreters.

Sharpe speaks of the words of Scripture as merely the body, not the soul, of faith; they have, after all, been translated from another language, and therefore, like all translations, do not necessarily convey the exact meaning of the original author:

> For first, as a man consists of body and soule, and the body of it selfe being senslesse & dead, is the inferiour part; the soule being life and giuing life, is the principal part, without which he is not man: So the Scripture consists of the words or text which is read or heard, and is only the body, barke, or couering of Gods word, and of the sense and meaning which is vnderstood & belieued, and is the life, soule and substance of the scripture. Now the words, as they are written or spoken, consisting of letters, syllables, & words, are dead without life. (sig. Q1v–Q2r)

As Sharpe neatly summarizes it in a marginal note, "The Holy Ghost is not inherent in the letter of Scripture" (sig. Q2r). This is oddly like the Protestant argument against church decoration and ceremony: both argue that substance of faith is invisible, ineffable, mysterious, not capable of being represented by externals. Sharpe's argument exists in contradiction to the sacramental stance of most Catholic theology: that signs and sacraments are inherently effective. The Bible presented a dilemma for him and for other Catholic thinkers. While Protestant readers of the Bible believed the common reader could discern the truth in Word, independently of outward guidance, even educated and intelligent Catholic readers of Scripture were to regard priestly ministers as necessary dispensaries of the Bible's truths.

To guard against the possibility that one's readings of the Bible are "the inuentions of ones owne braine" (sig. S2v), Sharpe proposes that his readers think of the church as a spiritual commonwealth, which, in addition to laws, has need of judges to "determine causes, to decide titles, and to punish offenses" (sig. T1r). Sharpe's appeal to a very English notion of political order suits his arguments nicely; he appeals to a desire for unity and order that is slowly disappearing from the contemporary religious and political scene. The private individual cannot be this judge, cannot be this arbiter. Sharpe lists and expounds upon the reasons: its very privacy disallows application to others; it lacks authority, infallibility, certainty, immutability, visibility, unity, and universality.[56] These, of course, are all attributes of the Catholic Church as Sharpe knew it. Most disturbingly, the private spirit tends to divide: "This spirit wants combination, or connexion, by which it may combine all faithfull in one bond of Vnity, and Concord; and so distinguish a true Church from a false; a right belieuing Catholike, from a deceitfull heretike, and a right way to heauen, from an erroneous path to perdition. It is priuate, and particuler in euery man, diuerse and contrary in most men" (sig. Z1r).

For the history of privacy, Sharpe's objections have more significant implications. The divisions deplored by Sharpe and his fellow Catholic apologists begin as doctrinal differences; but religious differences lead to the overthrow of "all this excelle[n]t order" (sig. Aa4r). Because the Catholic Church upheld the doctrine of free will, all laws, even the Ten Commandments, would be unenforceable were the ground of all order placed in the "particuler" conscience: "No prince or Prelate hath any power to make lawes which shall oblige the subiect in conscience; *Ergo* I am not bound in conscience and vnder any sinne to obey them, but may, (so as publicke scandall or punishme[n]t can be auoided) breake them at my pleasure, so it be priuate and unknowne" (sig. Ss4r).

Reading the Bible unguided by church interpretation becomes a first step toward anarchy. No longer bound by official doctrine, the readers Sharpe pictures have no need for outside confirmation of their beliefs.

Centuries of social, political, and religious order and conformity gradually begin to erode with spiritual justifications for a private, individual relationship with God. The interiority produced by direct communion with God by means of a book separates believers (and readers) from one another and from God.[57] Francis Osborne, writing anonymously as "Philolaoclerus" (a lover of lay clergy?) in *The Private Christians Non Vltra* (1656), his defense of private Scripture reading, seeks to redefine the private, to erase its negative connotations. The "private," says Osborne, does not necessarily stand in opposition to the church or to the ordained leaders of the church. Instead, private interpretation is linked to a new humanism, a new emphasis on the individual person:

> *Private* . . . by private interpretation is meant that which is humane and from man, in opposition to that which is from God. So that here is nothing at all directly spoken concerning the interpretation of the Scriptures, when men heare them or read them: and for ought I know, the interpretation of the most learned Dr. when tis erroneous, may be called a private interpretation; when the interpretation of the meanest private Christian being sound and wholesome, must be call'd by a better name. In one word, by private interpretation is meant humane interpretation: the Scripture is not from man, but from God.[58]

Osborne emphasizes that "private" interpretation has little to do with valid religious authority, that even learned doctors may interpet wrongly. Exegesis of Scripture is, in a sense, always private, always circumscribed by the limitations of human thought. All human interpretation is tentative: only the Bible itself originates with God. After over a century of religious turmoil in England, perhaps Osborne is inviting the reader to recognize the distance between God's truth and the claims of the Christian churches of England. When "privacy" is connected with the "humane," and no church—Anglican, Puritan, or Catholic—can demonstrate the strength of its creeds, the individual believer is left quite alone, thrown upon his or her own "private spirit" for sustenance. We have here the potential for the creation of a secular world, a world without a God made manifest by a visible church structure (or a stable government). As one modern legal scholar has noted, "The notion of an ever-present, omniscient God exhibits to some extent a willingness to accept, in some context, life with a total lack of privacy."[59] It may be that, by the end of the seventeenth century, readers could no longer conceive of an existence dominated by an all-seeing, ever-present God.

2

Authoring the Private Self: Reading in Seventeenth-Century Conversion Narratives

"Unconverted persons how many are there, but how few Unconverted Readers?"

—Richard Alleine

The idea of the book of the world, written by that magisterial author, God, has a long history in the Christian dispensation.[1] Dante's *Divine Comedy* ends with a paean to the divine book authored by God:

> O abounding grace whereby I presumed to fix my look through the Eternal Light so far that all my sight was spent therein.
>
> In its depth I saw ingathered, bound by love in one single volume, that which is dispersed in leaves throughout all the universe: substances and accidents and their relations, as though fused together in such a way that what I tell is but a simple light. The universal form of this knot I believe that I saw, because, in telling this, I feel my joy increase.[2]

Dante's book is all-encompassing, unitive, encyclopedic, and authoritative. But the magical powers attributed to books begin to dissipate once the power of the press allow books to proliferate and make their way into more homes in the developing country that was seventeenth-century England.[3] The Bible moves from the local parish church into even the poorest worker's household;[4] news is conveyed by cheap pamphlet, and not simply by royal proclamation; plays can be read within the family, not just viewed in the playhouse. The movement of the book from public relic to private souvenir accompanies this transfer of the book from public spaces to private homes, with the ultimate privatization occurring within the individual reader. Walter Ong has said that "print created a new sense of the private ownership of words." The common ownership of words disappears with the disappearance of an oral culture and its community of listeners. The visualness of the word in print made it more thing-like, made it easier for individuals to imagine a mental space for readerly activity to take place.[5] Printed books (or rather, their increased accessibility) and the practice of devotional reading strengthened the inner life against the exigencies of law, persecution, and religious custom. Moreover, books, which participated in the holiness of the first of books, the Bible, came to be regarded as efficacious instruments of conversion. In the aftermath of the invention of printing, every reader could observe the command given to Augustine, "Tolle, lege." Alongside the social, legal, and public religious pressures to pledge faith with one church or another, printed conversion narratives invited the reader to share in the experience of conversion through personal reading. Public commitment to a church is marked, in these narratives, not by a communal ritual, but by solitary contact with the text. As Michael Ragussis suggests, the site of private reading and the site of conversion are one and the same.[6]

John Wilson saw the printed book as an acceptable substitute for hearing the word of God. His *Zachevs Converted* (1631) is one of the many explications of a biblical story that hope to coax the reader into a conversion of manners: "Amongst other means this is not of the least nor lowest consequence the printing and publishing of good and wholesome bookes, of sound and profitable Treatises. Not onely because if there were not a continuall supply of these, many would reade little; but also because that by these there might bee some helpe reached forth unto such as are either slenderly provided for, or altogether destitute of preaching of the Word where they live."[7]

The seemingly endless supply of new books not only encourages reading—it is a stopgap measure for those Christians deprived of the luxury of a local preacher. Samuel Smith offers another biblical model for his readers' edification in *The Admirable Convert* (1632). Smith expresses much the same sentiments: "It maybee wondred at of many, especially in these daies wherin ther is such a satietie, if not a surfet of bookes, and that vpon this subiect of *Repentance,* that I should thus carry timber to the Wood, or water to the

Sea. And the rather for that my late publication of my exercises of the same subiect, *The Eunuchs Conuersion;* my reasons are ther. First, the good content my hearers had at the publicke preaching of the same, was no small motiue vnto mee to present the same things to their eares, which were so acceptable to their hearts."[8] The printed word, read in private, thus could enhance and reinforce public, sacramental ministry.

Richard Alleine, in his preface to Joseph Alleine's *True Way to Happiness* (1675) sees a direct link between conversion and reading; the latter is not simply *one* means to conversion—it is the primary means:

> To the Unconverted Reader,
> Reader,
> How well were it if there were no more unconverted ones among us, than those to whom this is directed? Unconverted persons how many are there, but how few Unconverted Readers? especially of such Books as this before thee? . . . Friend, know thy self better, or thou perishest without remedy. Thou mayst pray, but what hope is there in thy praying? Thou mayst read, but what hope is there in thy reading. Yet read on, this little hope there is; in this book there's Eye-Salve that may heal thee of thy blindness. In this book there is a Glass that will shew thee thy face. Dost thou know thine own face when thou seest it? Behold thy very Image in those marks that are given of an unconverted person; Read and consider them; and then say, if thou be not the man.[9]

Alleine suggests that reading good books (i.e., spiritual books) and conversion are synonymous. One cannot read and remain blind to one's own faults; one cannot read and fail to know oneself. The book is still talismanic, a magical mirror, a mystic text whose marks reveal the signs of the unconverted person. This self-revelation and self-recognition is the first step toward conversion.

Conversion Narratives and Genre

While reading may serve as the germ for the process of conversion, the supposedly good effects of reading may be differently realized by individual readers, who are sometimes detoured from the "proper" end of reading (i.e., moral improvement) by the pleasures of the story. In the following discussion of four seventeenth-century conversion narratives, I shall explore the role of reading in the experience of conversion and the implications reading has for the creation of a private, autonomous self. This private experience with the text drives the reader in one of two directions, each resulting in a quite different attitude toward traditional authority and each depicting a very different mode of conversion. One type of text leads the reader inward, toward self-examination, a conviction of sin, and then a public confession of adherence to religious authority as expressed in the words of Scripture. (This confession is rooted in the "turning toward" God that the word implies: one journeys into the darkness of one's own soul, and then toward God.) The other leads the reader to an aesthetic and emotional ecstasy, an escape from the self, but an escape that is finally self-centered; this text frees the reader from obedience to any authority. The two kinds of interiority presented in these conversion narratives help, perhaps, to explain our modern ambivalences about the private self—the way in which privacy can enhance self-knowledge but can also elevate individual desires above common needs and concerns. This ambivalence is reflected in these early modern texts: in two stories from 1647 and 1666, the reader acknowledges and returns to the book as the repository and representation of authority; the book and its author, not the reader, are the source and symbol of power. In the second pair of narratives (from 1680 and 1700), the book is no longer the prime authority, with words exerting their power over the reader; rather, the reader takes control, using the book as the means for achieving *independence from* authority. This sort of private reading focuses on the reader, not the text; it liberates the individual, instead of binding him or her to the authority the book represents. In the two earlier narratives, conversion ends in a public proclamation of faith; in the later two, conversion is the vehicle for a personal declaration of independence. While one group of converts reads sacred books in order to coax the self into submission to the divine will, the other group of readers finds books help them to escape the authority, not only of a "false" religion, but of home and parent. In this latter group of stories, even what looks like submission to just another set of religious conventions begin to look startlingly like modern assertions of the autonomous self.

All four narratives share certain devices in common: the reliance on the book, an affective response to the text, a valuing of solitude, the narrator's desire to have the reader share the conversion experience. The two later narratives, though, have a different feel to them, working on the reader in a different way. The first two narratives are public documents of a private spiritual experience that invite the same sort of self-examination and faith commitment; the later ones, however, direct the reader's attention to the private lives of the young women whose subject they are. On reading the latter, one feels almost a voyeur; reading the two sets of narratives is the difference between reading *Robinson Crusoe* and reading *Clarissa.* This is only partly a function of the sex of the protagonists (for one of the earlier two converts is female). The significant difference for the reader has to do with the way in which the texts deal with privacy and publicity and the interplay between personal reading and personal autonomy.

In *The Exceeding Riches of Grace Advanced by the Spirit of Grace, in an Empty Nothing Creature, viz. Mris Sarah Wight* (1647) by Henry Jessey and *Grace Abounding to the Chief of Sinners* (1666) by John Bunyan, the aesthetic pleasures of reading give way to public proclamation, to preaching the word of God. Though conversion may begin as a private encounter between the self and God, or the self and the text, religion cannot, must not, remain a private concern. Perhaps significantly, these two narratives are autobiographical, autobiography being the genre in which the individual consciously and purposefully writes for an audience. Bunyan is straightforwardly autobiographical, while Jessey is the amanuensis of the woman convert whose story he tells. In both narratives, the highest end of reading is likened to preaching, to teaching first oneself, then the rest of the faithful. The reader's role is clear: he or she is to identify with the spiritual struggles of the convert, to aim always for a like moral and spiritual resolution. The text invites, demands, cajoles the reader into a similar holy state; it relies on reason, the intellectual appeal of the apologia to work on the reader's mind. The convert repeats the experience of conversion for her or himself by remembering, for others by the act of writing.[10] Neither narrator nor reader may stray from this purpose by becoming too enmeshed in the intellectual or emotional pleasures of the text. The subject reveals the spiritual and psychological depths that become an essential component of autobiography, the genre into which the conversion narrative eventually develops. The action of the narrative is patently didactic and instructive;[11] the narrator is meant to be seen as an exemplar for the reader. His or her spiritual journey is a "progress" to a holier life, not a contemplation of the goodness of God or his creatures.[12] Though autobiography (and the autobiographical conversion narrative) relate the events of a private life, their goal is self-exposure and publicity. Though the initial movement is internal, highly personal, and dependent on the grace of God, the end result is always public, prophetic, and ritualistic in its final dependence on the efficacy and authority of the Bible.

The second pair of narratives, Gilbert Burnet's *The Conversion & Persecutions of Eve Cohan* (1680) and an anonymous pamphlet, *An Account of the Seducing of Ann, the Daughter of Edward Ketelbey, of Ludlow, Gent. to the Popish Religion* (1700), depict conversion, private reading, and the narrative itself in a more problematic light. While the first type of narrative points to the self as a model of the successful self-made convert (a startlingly Protestant and Weberian notion),[13] the second focuses on plot, on the adventures of two young women who choose a religion different from that of their families. Religious denominations and doctrines appear to have little to do with these conversions (though they must have mattered a great deal to the narrators of these stories). What fascinates is the way in which the authority figures in these conversion dramas finally accommodate themselves to the young converts who have been transformed by their reading. The traditional authority of parents stands directly opposed to the individual conscience, the opposition complicated still more by the fact that the protagonists are female. In the persons of the two young women in these conversion narratives, we see the seventeenth century redefining privacy: personal autonomy becomes possible for every individual and every reader, even the woman reader. This focus on individual experience and personal autonomy leads me to suggest that this form of conversion narrative is a predecessor of the genre whose mode of reading is private, whose primary end is private delight—that is, the novel.[14]

The Exceeding Rich Graces of Sarah Wight

Henry Jessey's *The Exceeding Riches of Grace* precedes the generally accepted urtext of the conversion narrative, John Bunyan's *Grace Abounding,* by nearly twenty years. From the title page of the first edition to the last page and postscript in the seventh edition of 1658, the narrator, Henry Jessey, emphasizes the need to bring light out of darkness, to transform the private experience of Sarah Wight into the published book. Written for "the refreshing of poor souls, by an Eye and Ear-witness . . . Henry Jesse, a servant of Jesus Christ," Sarah Wight is the "Earthen Vessell . . . the CHIEFEST of SINNERS. Who desired that others might hear and know, what the LORD had done for her soul" (t.p.). The emptiness suggested by Wight's name is the sign of her present submission to God's will; Jessey (1601–63), a Baptist divine, serves as the witness, publicizer, framer of her story.[15] It is his role to make public the otherwise private life of the woman, who, he tells his readers in the first preface, is to be a pattern for all other sinners:

> My Spirit rejoyceth in the *Lord,* who hath put such an opportunity as this into my hand, of *Publishing* to you, and to others, and hereby of *Advancing, The Exceeding Riches of the Grace of God,* in such a *Pattern* thereof, as here followeth: The Daughter of a gracious *Matrone,* of mine acquaintance in the *Parish* where I weekly Preach in *London:* who was in as *hopeles* and *desperate* a condition in her selfe, as ever was any. Now often *admiring,* and *uttering* to others, especially to afflicted, despairing, mournfull soules (that resort now to her,) the *unsearchable Treasures of Grace,* to the *ungodly,* and *chiefest* of *lost undone sinners.*[16]

Sarah Wight is important to Jessey because she enables him to perform his proper role as minister and preacher. She is only a private person, a cipher, the nothing her name, "Wight," conveys until her story, and God's grace working in her, is published.[17] Presenting her to the reading public will ratify her experience; Jessey's transcription of her words validates and verifies her conversion. In another preface to Jonathan Vaughan (Wight's half brother) Jessey writes: "The Lord enabled this weak earthen vessell to utter forth ex tempore, in Soliloquies, from April 9. til April 20. when shee knew not that others listened, and heard her, (and wrote it downe, as here followeth:) Neither (to my knowledge) doth shee as yet know to the day of the date hereof, that her words were writ down: much lesse that there is any intent of publishing to the world, what thus was uttered to her own soul, or to others" (sig. A6r). Jessey depicts a woman who is graced with God's spirit, but is yet incapable of writing her "Scripture-phrases" down. She is oblivious to listeners, a naif who does not realize that her words are being recorded or even the day or time of her soliloquies. Jessey takes on what would be inappropriate for a woman: the publication of her private sermons.[18] He edits, fills in lacunae, corrects the reports of the mother and maid who also witnessed the girl's speech, and supports the veracity of the account in one of the book's prefaces.

Sarah Wight's ability to speak is located in her education and her ability to read, and it is a gradual awakening, fostered by private instruction by female members of her family:

> *Touching her Education:* In the time of her Mothers deep afflictions of Spirit, and sore Temptations, shee was *well trained up in the Scriptures,* by her godly faithfull Grand-mother, M[ris] *Wight* of *Daintree.* And when the Lords *time of Love* was, that he vouchsafed

> to manifest his Grace in Christ to her Mothers soule, then the Lord brought her home to her, shee being then about 9 yeares old. Shee gave her selfe much to read and study the *Scriptures:* Which though shee then understood not aright; yet the Lord by his Holy Spirit brought to her *remembrance,* and *opened* to her since her restoring, what formerly shee had read; for great comfort and soul-refreshing to her selfe, and to many others, as hereafter followeth. Which is a great encouragement to all that feare God, to train up their children in the holy Scriptures. (sig. B3v)

The Protestant emphasis on literacy as a means to salvation is reiterated here. Disconcertingly, though, Sarah Wight falls prey to doubts. As a direct result of her reading (which is detailed in the text), she believes herself to be damned: "In the last four yeeres, shee was oft in such extremities, shee could beleeve nothing but Hell and Wrath—to be her Portion; and other times, that there was no heaven, nor hell, but in our Conscience: and that shee was *damn'd already, being an unbeleever:* and therefore if shee could but dispatch this life of hers, there was an end of her sorrows" (sig. B4r).

Wight, who, at the time of the narrative, is "toward 16 years old" (sig. B1v), cannot rely on any other human being, and even marriage seems to be out of the question; her marriage portion threatens to be hell and damnation. Indeed, in later editions of the book, there is no mention of a husband; it appears that she is still unmarried and living with her mother. In her despair and aloneness, Wight attempts suicide, which Jessey points to as a "subtle deceit of the old Serpent." Reading the Bible does not comfort but only seems to confirm the fact of her damnation:

> In her despairing fits, shee severall times would turned to the places in *Job,* and in *Jeremy,* where they *cursed the day of their birth;* and shee said to this effect; *Job cursed the day wherein he was borne, and said, Wherefore hast though brought me forth of the womb? Oh, that I had given up the ghost, and no eye had seen me.* Shee turning to the places, *Job* 3.3. *Job* 10.18. *And* (*Jer.* 20.14. to the end) *Jeremie cursed the man that brought tidings of his birth, with bitter curses, because his mothers womb was not his grave.* . . . But shee said, *Have not I much more cause to say so, then they had? for they were in a blesed condition: but I am curs'd, and must be a fire-brand of Hell for ever.* (sig. B6v–B7r)

Her despair is physical as well as mental and spiritual; she refuses food from March 27 till June 11 (sig. a1r)[19] and seems incapable of using her reading to arm herself against temptation: "Shee told moreover that shee usually every morning formerly was wont to read above twenty Chapters, and so would have still'd her Temptations; but was not a jot the better. That shee could remember nothing of what shee had read, but the *judgements,* and they were laid open to her: But all the *promises* were seal'd from me, *said shee. One day I was tempted to throw my Bible into the fire, and I threw it from me, but it fell not into the fire. But for this I was sore tormented, that I would have throwne it into the fire*" (sig. E6r–E6v). Wight is finally saved, not by more reading, but through divine intervention, her weakness covered over by the grace of God. Reading itself does not save her; belief in what the Bible represents does. The blasphemous desire to burn her Bible is redeemed by the publication of her story; her private temptations can now serve as a lesson to others. The act of publication does not glorify Sarah Wight but God himself; her story becomes a very traditional (and apparently quite popular) exemplar of God's workings in human affairs.

The dangers of publication (perhaps especially because the case involved a woman) are evident from the public reaction to Sarah Wight herself. Jessey's book was published in at least nine editions between 1647 and 1666, and it made Sarah Wight something of a religious celebrity, as Jessey implies in a postscript to the seventh edition (1658). Wight is by that time living quietly, "with her afflicted Mother, attending on her, day and night." Jessey summarizes Wight's present existence:

> Other visiters, that favour not the things of God, but admire, and exalt the Creature, she hath been much troubled at, and grieved by that hinder her soul from better employment. When she had better health, she went to *Alhallows,* and to other places, to partake with others in the Word and Prayer.
>
> But since the death of *Jonathan Vaughan* her Brother, by reason of her own weakness, and attending on her afflicted Mother, she hath been hindered from enjoying the Lord in publick or private Ordinances, in a great measure. But she hopes she shall enjoy him in secret; and longs for Communion with the Lords people."[20]

Jessey's postscript is a caution against ungodly reading. These religious curiosity seekers are readers of Jessey's narrative, and negative examples of the good reader. Instead of replicating Wight's own conversion, reading, and trust in the mercy of God, they have become celebrity-hunters, focused on the cult of personality. Instead of using reading to reform their own lives, they have become fascinated with the life of another. They have created a modern predicament for Wight, who has become a public person. Jessey silently affirms the proper role of the book as the path to God and underlines the difficulty with which women could participate in any aspect of the world of print. For many readers, Sarah Wight's womanhood obscured the message of faith Henry Jessey intended to convey. As we shall see, John Bunyan more successfully establishes the pattern of godly biography, while later examples of the conversion narrative capitalize upon, rather than seek to deemphasize, the gender of the convert.

John Bunyan's *Grace Abounding*

John Bunyan echoes Henry Jessey's proclamation of the graces advanced to Sarah Wight in his autobiographical *Grace Abounding to the Chief of Sinners.* Written while Bunyan was imprisoned for refusing to stop preaching, the book has an uncanny way of publicizing (and therefore sanctifying) a personal and decidedly self-centered experience. Many critics have noted the obliviousness of Bunyan to those about him: we derive few biographical details from the text, know little of his wife, and discover none of the details of his conflict with authorities till the publication of *A Relation of the Imprisonment of Mr. John Bunyan* in 1765.[21] The notes to Roger Sharrock's edition of the book must repeatedly try to explain lapses and inconsistencies in time. Roger Pooley sees Bunyan's work as an example of "the modern splitting on self," the work of a "teacher reflecting on his own earlier, erratic teachability."[22] Pooley goes on to discuss *Grace Abounding* as a prison document and relates it to Foucault's ideas about spectacular forms of punishment. Elizabeth W. Bruss says, with reference to *Grace Abounding:* "The religion of Calvin and Luther had turned hagiography into autobiography, since it was no longer miraculous works which were the sign of a saint, but faith—a private and personal experience."[23] Felicity Nussbaum speaks of the "space of conversion" that Bunyan must enter in order to experience the sweetness of consolation.[24] While these critics focus on Bunyan's journey inward, I argue instead that this journey, seemingly inward, is eventually spectacular (i.e., visible and public) and can be thought about in terms of Bunyan's role as reader. His apparent rejection of, or indifference to, his family, to time and place, to the ordinary events of life, mark Bunyan as a reader whose descent into the self is ever aimed at proclamation of the self and at proclamation of the word of God. One cannot remark on God's transforming powers without speaking of oneself. The autobiographer reads himself, and this reading, as Janet Gunn describes it, is inherently public: "The self who reads, whether it be the autobiographer or the reader of the autobiography, is the *displayed self,* not the hidden self. The displayed self is the self who speaks, who lives in time."[25] The self-reading of the autobiographer, then, becomes always an exposed activity; the context is always public.

Before his conversion, Bunyan, concerned with the "lusts and fruits of the flesh," sees both religion and Scripture as restrictive, an impinging on his independence: "In these days, the thought of Religion was very grievous to me; I could neither endure it my self, nor that any other should; so that when I have but seen some read in those books that concerned Christian piety, it would be as it were a prison to me."[26]

Bunyan recognizes that books can have a double function: to the unconverted (such as he), they are imprisoning, a solitary place in which one has no other company but the unregenerate self. The fearful results of any self-examination are associated with the accusatory nature of books, which would (deservedly, he would later say), enchain him. Then he marries a woman "whose Father was counted godly" and who brings as part of her dowry two devotional books. These Bunyan reads, and they beget in him the desire to practice his religion. (Note that his personal encounter with a woman, in married life, is the impetus for conversion.) Bunyan is not yet ready for an inner conversion, however; these books "did not reach [his] heart" (8), and he is entranced by outward ceremony—the praying and singing of the congregation. Books are always already associated for Bunyan with the public, religious community. And, it is important to note, Bunyan is selective in the reading of Scripture: "I betook me to my Bible, and began to take great pleasure in reading, but especially with the historical part thereof: for, as for *Pauls* Epistles, and Scriptures of that nature, I could not away with them, being as yet but ignorant either of the corruptions of my nature, or of the want and worth of Jesus Christ to save me" (12). Recall that in this period histories were often synonymous with "fiction" and were associated with frivolity and untruth.[27] Bunyan's reading at this stage is not quite serious; reading biblical histories is pleasurable, rather than suitably guilt-inducing.[28] Reading the epistles of Paul, the most well-known early Christian convert, is the goal toward which Bunyan's spiritual life must strain. Several readers of *Grace Abounding* have noted its similarity to the structures of Paul's epistles,[29] but in addition to stylistic similarities, there are the psychological ones. Paul, like Bunyan, undergoes a radical conversion that leads to a life of zealous proselytizing and mission work for the new church. Paul's writings, though written in the first person, sometimes from behind prison walls, are quintessentially public, autobiographical, and self-accusatory. Here is Paul on his own struggles with his conscience: "For we know that the law is spiritual: but I am carnal, sold under sin. For that which I do I allow not: for what I would, that I do not; but what I hate, that do I . . . For I know that in me (that is, in my flesh,) dwelleth no good thing: for to will is present with me; but *how* to perform that which is good I find not. For the good that I would I do not: but the evil which I would not, that I do" (Rom. 7:14–15, 18–19). Paul is advertising his guilt, as Bunyan must; they both have the public audience of a congregation or a reading public before whom to display themselves.[30]

Like Bunyan, Paul is preoccupied with the word of God, from the time he hears the voice of Christ asking, "Saul, Saul, why persecutest thou me?" (Acts 9:4). Paul is likewise oblivious to (or wary of?) the need for another person in his life: "I would that all men were even as I myself" (1 Cor. 7:7)—that is, celibate. Paul's mission requires that he concentrate on the subjugation of his own will and a single-minded dedication to God, and he can do that only by rejecting human ties. He can save others only by preserving his own bodily and psychic wholeness, becoming "all things to all men," but nothing to any particular man or woman. Both Paul and John Bunyan are precariously balanced between their public roles in the Christian community and their private selves, which are steadfastly detached from other human beings.

Bunyan's next serious encounter with the word of the Lord is also sparked by an encounter with women, as though building upon the goodly influence of his wife. Here is Bunyan's narration of the event:

> I came where there was three or four poor women sitting at a door in the Sun, and talking about the things of God; and being now willing to hear them discourse, I drew near to hear what they said; for I was now a brisk talker also my self in the matters of Religion: but now I may say, *I heard, but I understood not;* for they were far above out of my reach. . . .
>
> And me thought they spake as if joy did make them speak: they spake with such pleasantness of Scripture language, and with such appearance of grace in all they said, that they were to me as if they

> had found a new world, as if they were people that dwelt alone, and were not to be reckoned among their Neighbours, Num. 23. 9. (14–15)

Though Bunyan is by now himself "a brisk talker," he admires these women, fluent speakers with an easy command of the language of Scripture, because they seem to dwell apart, alone in a new world with which he is not acquainted. The center of this logocentric world, of course, is the Bible, which, interestingly, the women are not reading but speaking of. The private experience of meeting God in the word has led to their public voicing of their belief and to Bunyan's "great bending of [his] mind to a continual meditating" on the words of Scripture (15). Immediately after this encounter, Bunyan comes upon the books of some Ranters. They have come to him highly recommended by some "Professors" of that sect, but he is unable to make a sound judgment on their teachings. In fact, Bunyan is so reluctant to rely on his own authority that he leaves the decision to God: "O Lord, I am a fool, and not able to know the Truth from Errour; Lord leave me not to my own blindness, either to approve of, or condemn this Doctrine; If it be of God, let me not despise it; if it be of the Devil, let me not embrace it. Lord, I lay my Soul, in this matter, only at thy foot" (16). The fleshly pleasures of the Ranters, who are given "to all manner of filthiness, especially Uncleanness" (16), attracts the young Bunyan, but he is able to resist these temptations. Whereas Paul abjures marriage for a life of dedicated celibacy, Bunyan rejects human love (as the Ranters present it) only because it might be tainted. This is a rejection, a negative choice, not a positive move toward a spiritual relationship with God. As though in compensation for human conversation, Bunyan turns toward the words of the Bible: "And now, me thought, I began to look into the Bible with new eyes, and read as I never did before; and especially the Epistles of the Apostle S. *Paul* were sweet and pleasant to me: and indeed, I was then never out of the Bible, either by reading or meditation, still crying out to God, that I might know the truth, and way to Heaven and Glory" (17). From this time on, Bunyan is continually assaulted by words and succumbs often to spiritual doubt and depression. The possibility that he is not among the elect, that his trust in God is unfounded, comes as a "sentence" that "fell with weight upon [his] spirit." The double meaning of sentence (i.e., judgment and grammatical construct) ties together Bunyan's reliance on the written word with his belief in his own unworthiness and guilt;[31] he begins his habit of searching for confirmation of the oral pronouncements of his soul and for consolation in the words of the Bible, for the saying that will indicate he is truly saved: "I presently went to my Bible to see if I could find that saying, not doubting but to find it presently, for it was so fresh, and with such strength and comfort on my spirit, that I was as if it talked with me" (21). The "saying" that Bunyan seeks is verified by the printed word, which takes on its own voice, talking with him, acting as a substitute for any human one. Bunyan is disconcerted to find that the sentence he is seeking is in Ecclesiasticus, part of the Apocrypha, and therefore "not in those Texts that we call holy and Canonical" (22). Stoically, he accepts it as his "duty" to take the comfort of God's word within an unauthorized text. Bunyan puts the face of duty on his reading of Scripture, even as he derives emotional consolation from it.

The delight is temporary, of course; the path of spiritual progress consists in much moral and emotional backsliding. Bunyan's intensive reading, like Sarah Wight's, leads to despair, and what we post-Freudians would call clinical depression. Christopher Hill remarks that historians have been unable to explain the huge incidence of despair in the mid-seventeenth century; Hill sees suicide, atheism, and conversion as the possible remedies for this condition.[32] My readings of conversion narratives show that the three remedies (but especially suicide and conversion) were closely linked; the intense self-examination that spiritual reading encouraged also engendered (as they were intended to) guilt and a loss of self-worth.[33] For Bunyan, poring "in terrifying isolation over his Bible,"[34] this led to a conviction that he had committed the unpardonable sin, the sin against the Holy Ghost. Convinced of the idolatrous underpinnings of the communal, ritualistic worship of the Church of England, Bunyan finds that his solitary, private reading fosters despair; his only salvation lies in submission to the absolute authority of the book that informs all his reading.

One of the most troubling doubts that Bunyan experiences is over the validity and truth of the Scriptures themselves. What if they are "a Fable and cunning Story," not "the holy and pure Word of God?" (31). They might be no better than the sacred books of the infidels: "How can you tell but that the Turks had as good Scriptures to prove their *Mahomet* the Saviour, as we have to prove our *Jesus* is; and could I think that so many ten thousands in so many Countreys and Kingdoms, should be without the knowledge of the right way to Heaven (if there were indeed a Heaven) and that we onely, who live but in a corner of the Earth, should alone be blesed therewith? Everyone doth think his own Religion rightest, both *Jews,* and *Moors,* and *Pagans;* and how if all our Faith, and Christ, and Scriptures, should be but a think-so too?" (31). Bunyan is obsessed with the thought that the basis of all his creed is fiction, that his beliefs have their foundations in the imagination and not in the real and concrete word of God.[35] His is a belief that requires outside verification; though it originates in the individual soul, it requires some public ratification. The Bible is the instrument that yokes together these disparate needs: the printed text publishes God's word, thereby giving validity to the whole of Christian belief. The ups and downs of Bunyan's spiritual life are dependent upon his reading, the cause of his despair or his delight:

> I say, then I was greatly assaulted and tormented with Atheism; but now the case was otherwise, now was God and Christ continually before my face, though not in a way of comfort, but in a way of exceeding dread and terrour. The glory of the Holiness of God did at this time break me to pieces, and the Bowels and Compassion of Christ did break me as on the Wheel. . . .
>
> The Scriptures now also were wonderful things unto me; I saw that the truth and verity of them were the Keys of the Kingdom of Heaven; those that the Scriptures favour they must inherit bliss; but those that they oppose and condemn, must perish for evermore. (76)

Submission, the breaking on the wheel that leads to bliss, gives way one paragraph later to "O! One sentence of the Scripture did more afflict and terrify my mind, I mean those sentences that stood against me, (as sometimes I thought they every one did) more, I say, that an Army of forty thousand men that might have come against me. Wo be to him against whom the Scriptures bend themselves" (77).

Bunyan's reading of other spiritual books creates the same sort of guilt and conflict. When he reads Martin Luther's commentaries on Galatians, he is pleased, first of all, to have such an old book fall into his hands, "so old that it was ready to fall piece from piece" (40). Contemporary writers, says Bunyan, are too superficial; they do not go "down themselves into the deep." But Bunyan's reading experience of Luther is very different: "I found my condition in his experience, so largely and profoundly handled, as if his Book had been written out of my heart . . . methinks I must let fall before all men, I do prefer this book of Mr. Luther upon the Galathians, (excepting the Holy Bible) before all the books that ever I have seen, as most fit for a wounded Conscience" (41). Luther's old book not only has intellectual depth; it is able to dive into the center of Bunyan's battered psyche. Other writers "studied to answer such Objections as they perceived others were perplexed with" (40); Luther's self-examination matches Bunyan's needs in a way more detached writings do not. Yet his reading of another book, Nathaniel Bacon's *A Relation of the Fearful Estate of Francis Spira, in the year 1548* (1649), does just the opposite. It is salt to Luther's salve: "A book that was to my troubled spirit as salt, when rubbed into a fresh wound; every sentence in that book, every groan of that man, with all the rest of his actions in his dolors, as his tears, his prayers, his gnashing of teeth, his wringing of hands, his twining and twisting, languishing and pining away under that might hand of God that was upon him, was as knives and daggers in my Soul" (49). The intensity of Bunyan's description shows that his experience mirrors Spira's. There seems to be no peaceful resolution for Bunyan the reader; every text has the capacity to raise him up or cast him again into the depths of sorrow. He wants to flee from the torrent of words but cannot escape: "For I did flee from his face, that is, my mind and spirit fled before him; by reason of his highness, I could not endure; then would the text cry, *Return unto me, for I have redeemed thee.* Indeed, this would make me make a little stop, and, as it were, look over my shoulder behind me, to see if I could discern that the God of grace did follow me with a pardon in his hand, but I could no sooner do that, but all would be clouded and darkened again by that sentence" (52). Bunyan's narrative is no *Pilgrim's Progress,* with the safe haven of the Celestial City at the end; it is a continual wrestling within. Words represent unbearable insecurity; they are constantly taunting him with the possibility of damnation on one hand and salvation and pardon on the other. The text proper (para. 264) ends with the biblical vision of Mount Zion, but there is no reason to expect that such consolation will from then on be Bunyan's proper state. As if to stave off any more battles with words, Bunyan appends "A brief Account of the Author's Call to the Work of the Ministry." There, he reports on the invitation to speak to the church assembly. This he does, "in private," but his mission gradually becomes more public: "Wherefore, to be brief, at last, being still desired by the Church, after some solemn prayer to the Lord, with fasting, I was more particularly called forth, and appointed to a more ordinary and publick preaching the Word, not onely to and amongst them that believed, but also to offer the Gospel to those who had not yet received the faith thereof: about which time I did evidently find in my mind a secret pricking thereto: (tho I bless God not for desire of vain glory, for at that time I was most sorely afflicted with the firy darts of the devil concerning my eternal state.)" (83). Bunyan's belief that he should not hide his talents (the "secret pricking") leads him to public preaching of the texts he has experienced privately. Even from prison, after being forbidden to preach, Bunyan continues writing, relying on publication to convey his message; in just five years of confinement, he published five major works.[36] Verbal activity is separated from its "popish" connections with set prayers and private, auricular confession and transformed into public performance: preaching, publication, and subjection to communal judgment and discipline.[37] The Puritan imperative is not spiritual isolationism but communication of the divine wisdom to others; self-analysis and concentration on the self is transformed into a missionary epistle. Autobiography (and Bunyan's work in particular) becomes respectable as a genre, then, not because it is rooted in solitary spiritual struggle, not because it wallows in the subject's private torments, but because it moves into the approved and authorized sphere of public witness.[38] In autobiography the person is offered as an individual within the polis; it is not the solitary individual who eventually matters but the individual within the community.

The Conversion Narrative as Private History

While Wight's and Bunyan's stories depicted their struggles with God and their dark, unregenerate selves, these next two narratives depict two young women at war with religious tradition and the authority of their families. Their stories are antecedents of the novel, which Georg Lukács describes as the "adventure of interiority," the story of a soul that seeks adventure in order to find itself.[39]

Gilbert Burnet, bishop of Salisbury, deals head on with the question of truth and fictionality in his preface to *The Conversion & Persecutions of Eve Cohan, Now Called Elizabeth Verboon, a Person of Quality of the Jewish Religion* (1680). There are so many of these conversion tales about, he says, that one cannot be certain of their sincerity. But even as he attests to the truth (i.e., nonfictionality) of his narrative, Burnet acknowledges that the book may have other functions aside from inspiration and exhortation to conversion: "The particular account of so remarkable a Conversion, and those things which happened upon it, I hope will be no unacceptable entertainment to the Reader; and therefore having gathered the Passages and Steps of it together, upon very good Authority, I now offer them to the World."[40] In short, this narrative, which has all the earmarks of a good story, has been published for the reader's enjoyment. The author's claim of "Authority" is troubling, for the account reads like fiction and signals a break from the works with more clearly religious intent described above. The modern distinction between fiction and nonfiction seems not to be a concern, despite Burnet's claims. Though the genre is ostensibly the same, Burnet's conversion narrative, unwittingly or no, is effective precisely because it teeters on the edge of the fictionality Bunyan abhorred.

The reader's interest in this conversion narrative derives from both the sex and the religion of its protagonist, Eve Cohan.[41] The child of a widowed mother, Eve is a Jewess of marriageable age; she thus inhabits the same perplexing role as that of Jessica in *The Merchant of Venice* and of Abigail in *The Jew of Malta.* As James Shapiro notes, Jewishness is not inscribed in the bodies of women (as it is in circumcised Jewish men), and conversion (and marriage) can erase, or at least mitigate, the otherness of Jewish women.[42]

Eve is the music pupil of a Mr. Shol, who talks with her of Christianity and takes her to a church on the pretext of hearing organ music. There she begins to listen, not only to music, but sermons and prayers. Her attraction to Christianity builds upon this aesthetic appeal when she begins reading in the New Testament:

> And a New Testament being secretly conveyed to her, she took great delight in reading in it. She says, That which first made Impression on her was, that their Nation was not dispersed over the World, no more under the Conduct of any Prophet: . . . When she read the Account of our Saviour's Passion, she felt her self mightily affected with the passage of *Judas's* confesing that he had betrayed Innocent Blood; and his being so transported with the horror of it, that he went and hanged himself. . . . But that which confirmed her in the belief of Christianity, was, what she read of the Resurrection of our Saviour, of which he had given assurance to his Followers before his Sufferings. (sig. B1v–B2r)

Burnet places Eve Cohan's conversion in the context of exile; he reads her change of heart as a call for protection, an escape from the homelessness and constant experience of exile of the Jews. Burnet's description of her reading of the Passion is disturbing in several ways. The secrecy of her reading is one; it proves to be a quiet beginning for a series of demonstrations in the text of Jewish deceit and greed, culminating in the anti-Semitic polemic that ends the pamphlet. A reader sympathetic to Burnet's aims will be properly indignant that the holy book cannot be read openly, as Cohan is driven to clandestine reading of Scripture. The reader can transfer his or her suspicions of private activity (honorable in this case) from the young woman to her family and friends. Cohan herself will be depicted as the prisoner of her Jewish relatives and the Jewish community. Because Cohan's reading in private leads her to the righteousness of Christianity, it cannot be condemned by the Anglican reader who is Burnet's audience. But neither is such reading ideal; hence, the need to blame her "oppressors." The Jews not only prevent her from exercising a choice for Anglicanism: they force her to keep her devotions private.

Cohan also prefigures, despite her role as Burnet's heroine, the helpless females of the popular novel of a century or two later.[43] There is her response to the Passion, for instance. Burnet uses the language of sentimental and Gothic fiction: Eve is "mightily affected by" her reading; Judas is "transported with the horror" of his betrayal. The cult of blood and tears of the metaphysical and baroque poets earlier in the seventeenth century is transmuted into melodrama and sentimentality.[44] Eve is attracted by the doctrine of the resurrection because it seems to offer a sort of catharsis from the emotional onslaught of Christ's (and by extension, her) sufferings.

Eve Cohan is courted by Michael Verboon, a Gentile, though her mother has promised her in marriage to another man. Eve escapes her mother's house (taking nothing with her) and goes to Brussels with Verboon, where they live for a time as brother and sister. Eventually they marry, but not before the villain of the piece, Michael Levi, a Jewish solicitor, spreads the rumour that she is within six weeks of the delivery of a child. The Jews try to make her abandon Christianity and her husband, and have her, and later her husband, arrested for debt and for theft from her mother's house. Burnet depicts Eve Cohan as a modern Christian martyr, persevering in the face of the persecutions of her Jewish enemies. There is even a veiled reference to the popular paranoia about child-stealing and murder: "She knew what she was to expect if she fell in their hands, for *Vandersee* [her mother's choice for her husband] had told her, That if she proved with Child in their hands, she should see it when delivered of it, but never more" (sig. C2v). Burnet disposes of Eve rather abruptly before he begins his diatribe; we are told only that she has been baptized, and that her pregnancy "ended in an Abortion" (sig. E1r). (The death of Eve's child removes from Burnet's and his readers' consideration the discomfiting question of whether her "Jewishness" could be passed on to offspring, despite a conversion to Christianity.) Eve disappears from the narrative in a flurry of anti-Semitic hatred at the end.

This pamphlet departs in significant ways from the two conversion narratives discussed above. The audience for the pamphlet cannot be Jews who might be potential prospects for conversion to Christianity—the view of

Jews is just too unsympathetic. Rather, Burnet's aims are entertainment, as his preface tells us, and a reaffirmation of Anglican religious authority. But Burnet's story can also be read more subversively. While Burnet and other adherents of the Church of England see Eve's conversion as a blessing, they are somehow undisturbed by her rebellion against her family. Eve's break from the prison of her mother's house is significant. We read little of an inner religious transformation, and one might well argue that Eve Cohan has merely exchanged one set of religious conventions for another. Religious conversion, especially in a century when self-preservation often depended upon changing one's religious habits, was not uncommon, but disputing the dominion of parents was another matter. Eve's filial rebellion allows her to abandon her secret reading and indulge in the aesthetics of the Christian religion (music, ceremony, personal piety). Eve moves into the supposedly more open and honest world of the Christian establishment (in which one need not read the Bible in secret), and even symbolically disassociates herself from the old dispensation by taking the new name of Elizabeth, the mother of John the Baptist who first recognizes Christ in the womb of the Virgin. Eve, in short, creates a new identity for herself.

The account of Eve's adventures (one can only read them as such) evokes no desire in the reader to replicate her religious experience. Burnet substitutes the chase for any account of inner reflection and gives the reader ample material for experiencing the easy emotions of revenge, disgust, outrage, and self-righteousness. Even Satan disappears as the spiritual enemy; it is the demonized Jews with whom Eve and the reader must do battle. (A correlate of Satan's disappearance, of course, is the absence and silence of God.)[45] Eve Cohan's emotional reading of the New Testament is to be the model for Burnet's readers; they are to participate vicariously in the sufferings of the story's protagonist, identifying with her, but not undergoing her psychological experience of conversion. Instead, the reader watches as an embattled female is threatened, arrested, calumniated. We share her physical dangers, not her spiritual ones. Nancy Armstrong and Leonard Tennenhouse have located the origins of the English novel in Indian captivity narratives, in which lone women must protect their chastity and their Englishness from the savage and unlettered American native. The literacy of the heroines of these tales was key: it not only distinguished captive from captor but gave these women an identity in print and in the English imagination.[46] Eve is menaced in much the same way, and Burnet's loaded narrative creates sympathy, not for a religious sect, but for a person. Burnet is betting that the reader's sympathy for Eve/Elizabeth will translate into acceptance of the official Church of England, that private sympathies will be transformed into public commitment. But it is the story, not the religious argument, that entrances, and it does so at the expense of all claims to authority. If Eve's family's rightful authority over her can be disregarded, then whose can stand? In my next example, Eve's rebellion is repeated, with a difference, in another young woman.

In *An Account of the Seducing of Ann, the Daughter of Edward Ketelbey, of Ludlow, Gent. to the Popish Religion* (1700), the anonymous author takes aim at the seductive powers of both the Catholic Church and of the printed word. Like the Burnet pamphlet, the *Account* explores the conflicting authorities of Church, parents, the Bible, and the individual conscience. Ann Ketelby, the pamphlet's central character, is a girl of nineteen who is left alone and unsupervised at home. She falls under the influence of "a Popish Family coming Strangers into the Town." They, "with the assistance of a reputed Popish Priest, living with them, (who pretends to Practice Physick now, but in King *James* his Reign shewed himself more open) Seduced her to the Popish Religion; but Instructed her of what dangerous Consequence it might be if discovered, both the Seducer and Seduced being punishable with Death; which made her for a long time disown and forswear her Conversion to Popery."[47]

Here are all the danger signs, the pamphleteer warns: a daughter left to her own devices, acquaintances whom the parents do not know, and a priest who disguises his true profession. The consequence of the daughter's exposure to all these corrupting factors (and, as we shall see, to private reading) is conversion to a venal and secret religion. If private reading in Burnet's story indicated the oppressive nature of the Jews, the Catholic reading in this one is a warning against straying from the proper middle way, from the openness of the Anglican Church.

When Ann Ketelbey's mother returns from the country, she finds her daughter much changed, "disowning her Mother's Power and Authority over her." Not only is the proper order of the family disturbed: the mother discovers her daughter is reading Catholic literature:

> Those Papists often Conversed with the Daughter in private, as 'tis believed, and Conveying Books into her Hands, settled her in that Religion. But the Mother, for some time after she came down, knew nothing of her Daughters new Friends, till coming one Morning early into her Chamber, she found her Reading in a Book in Bed; at which the Daughter being surprized, let it fall into the

> Bed, and denied that she was Reading, or had any Book; but upon search, it was found to be a Book wrote by *Parsons* the Jesuit; which so startled the Mother, that upon Searching the Daughter's Closet afterwards, she found other Popish Books, Pictures, Papers, and other Things relating to Popery. (sig. A1v)

The seduction is complete; the girl is caught in flagrante, reading the works of a Jesuit in bed. For the narrator, reading and seduction are suddenly, problematically linked. If reading can convert, then surely it can also seduce. Even books intended for moral purposes can be seductive because they arouse the sensibilities. Daniel Boyarin has suggested (in a discussion of the Paolo and Francesca episode of the *Divine Comedy*) that reading in the West has moved from the public and liturgical to the private, pleasurable, and erotic. Reading in bed is the final step in this move.[48]

In this particular conversion narrative, the language of reading, seduction, and illicit religious belief are conflated and meant to be condemned, but the author is powerless before Ann and before the implied reader: Ann's right to read and, finally, to choose her own religion, conflicts with the pamphlet's futile call to authority. Even the uncoverers of secret reading eventually find they become coconspirators in its perpetuation.

Ann Ketelbey runs away from home: her disappearance leads to a frantic search by the family for her (including putting offers of a reward into print). The girl is sheltered, hidden in a closet by one Mrs. Rolfe, who intends to carry her abroad to a nunnery, the ultimate enclave of Catholic "vice." In negotiations to return the girl to her parents, the Catholics set the terms: Ann's free exercise of religion, freedom from visits by Protestant clergy, money to buy "Popish Books," and forty pounds a year for maintenance in a Catholic family if she wishes to leave home. These conditions are not met when Ann returns home:

> When she came Home, she was well furnished with *Popish* Books, but these her Parents took from her when she came to Ludlow; and have since permitted no one to come near her but *Protestants.* But she continues Obstinate, refusing to hearken to a *Protestant Divine,* tho' many Ingenious Men have been often with her, insisting upon the Infallibility of the *Popish* Church, and that there is no Salvation in any other. She refuseth also to read any Protestant Book but the Bible; and is so little fond of that, that she says, if the Priests had

> enjoyned her the contrary, she would never have looked into the Bible, but that they have not yet forbidden her that. (sig. B2r)

Books become the symbol of the contest between Ann and her parents. By the end of the story, we discover that she is still at home, imprisoned, only free to write "Complaining Letters to her Friends in *London,* as she calls the *Papists,* of her Father's Correction, burning her Books, and other cruel and severe usage" (sig. B2r). Ann Ketelbey is a sister to the epistolary Clarissa, resolutely but fruitlessly seeking aid from her friends. The punishment seems too severe, even in reaction to the "gross Prevarications, and insolent Boldness" of the Catholic bishops referred to on the title page, and even though the rightful authority of her parents cannot be denied. It is significant that, despite Ann Ketelbey's separation from the hated Catholics, she is permitted two of those activities that led to her imprisonment: reading and writing. Even her parents and the church cannot withdraw such privileges or direct the way in which they might be used. By 1700 (eleven years after the promulgation of the Toleration Act), privacy and the independence of mind generated by reading were permitted, though not especially approved.

Some readers may see Ann's victory over her parents as a pyrrhic one—her books, after all, are burned, and she is confined to home. Her freedoms are only the psychological ones of the prisoner (though we have seen the real potential that prison literature had for encouraging embattled believers of any religious persuasion in seventeenth-century England). Real escape is offered to the reader of the prison narrative, to the reader of Ann's tale, and to the readers of stories of other embattled heroines in later years. Anyone who loves to read knows that its inducements are twofold: reading can engender intense self-scrutiny (accompanied by increased self-knowledge) or its opposite, pleasurable escape from the self and from reality. These four seventeenth-century conversion narratives, treating them as I have in chronological order, seem to move neatly along the continuum from self-examination to escape, from public to private genre, from external authority to internalized power. They share certain assumptions: that reading can lead to a conversion of manners, that the example of others can change one's life, that one meets oneself most directly (and most frighteningly) in solitude. But these two sets of stories also illuminate the seventeenth-century reader's conflicting attitudes toward right reading and privacy and the proper role of the individual within a larger society.

Stanley Fish, in a discussion of a passage from Augustine, claims that "to enjoy the things of the world is to have a *rhetorical* encounter with them; to use them is to have a *dialectical* encounter."[49] The dialectical mode is discursive and rational and in the end points away from itself; the rhetorical mode is antidiscursive and antirational. Fish reminds us of Augustine, converted after reading a line in Paul's letter to the Romans, but also weeping over the death of Dido in his youth. Both events are reported in his *Confessions,* the story of his own conversion. These two types of encounter posited by Fish correspond to our two categories of conversion narrative. Bunyan's and Jessey's narratives are dialectical, fascinated with words and their teaching function; but those readers eventually move away from the initial pleasures of reading and away from the private self. The second group of narratives focuses instead on the rhetorical, on the enjoyment of the text and on the privileges of the individual reader; the authors of these texts seem unable to sustain religious authority as the moral center of the narrative in the face of the choices individual readers are permitted to make.

Autobiographical conversion narratives such as Bunyan's *Grace Abounding* ask readers to examine their consciences, to search for the guilt within. This solitary journey is set into motion by encounters with words, calling the reader to conversion. These conversion narratives ask the reader to be consumed by this "dialectician's art," to sacrifice the self and to look toward a greater goal—in this case, salvation.[50] The private person is to be subsumed into the body of believers. Readers (both the reader within the text and the actual reader) are challenged to entertwine the moral and aesthetic, to refrain from staying with the private pleasures and pains of reading and to assist in the conversion of others. We saw that John Bunyan was able to do so, his book a model of right reading and his life a model for right action; his private agonies are transformed into a vision of Mount Zion and the task of preaching. Sarah Wight's situation is more complex. Like Bunyan, her conversion is presented in print for the edification of others, but the authority of her reading experience is diluted by the third-person narration, and public exposure has a very different effect on her and on her readers. Her status as a female prevents her from becoming the Pauline missionary Bunyan does; even in Jessey's exemplary text, Wight's personal circumstances overshadow the religious message.

In the second group of narratives, the potential problems of concentrating on private experience (or on a central character who is a woman) are erased by abandoning the necessity of moral instruction. The reader need not be consumed by the religious imperative to obey and conform; rather, he or she is meant to indulge in the pleasures of the story, and, perhaps not coincidentally, upon the history of a third person. It is perhaps no accident that increasingly fictionalized conversion narratives permit the reader to enjoy the tales of physically or spiritually endangered women.[51] Centering the narrative on private and domestic affairs changes the meanings of reading and of privacy. The recounting of external events (rather than the workings of the soul) conflict with and supersede the stated desire to present a proper moral, while a trio of observers (author, narrator, and reader) examine and judge the private acts of reading taking place in the narrative. The effect, though seventeenth-century authors and readers did not yet know this, was to create and at the same time invade an incipient privacy.

3

"Extasies in Letters": Reading Personal Letters in Print

> "I make account that this writing of letters, when it is with any seriousness, is a kind of extasie, and a departure and secession and suspension of the souls, wch doth then co[m]municate it self to two bodies . . ."
>
> —John Donne

THE FIRST TWO CHAPTERS of this study have dealt with the implications that reading and literacy had for the development of an autonomous private self during the seventeenth century. My discussions of spiritual reading and the effects of reading conversion narratives demonstrated that reading could ignite the religious imagination, create a private space in the mind or soul, and even encourage and form the seedbed for individual revolts against authority. The independence of mind that reading the Bible and reading about conversions engendered was primarily a psychic phenomenon, a move toward a psychological inner space. In this chapter I wish to focus on something much more tangible: the relationship between personal privacy and the human body. As anthropologist Edward T. Hall has declared: "Man's boundary begins and ends with his skin."[1] Peter Brooks, in his study of the modern narrative, proclaims that "the novel of private life is not only about psychological subjectivity, the inner life of the soul, but as well about what was increasingly coming to be considered as the most private of affairs, the individual's body."[2] The guarding of personal space, the permission to touch or be touched, is of course not solely a physical phenomenon: modern psychologists have shown that individuals vary widely in their tolerance for physical nearness, and personhood itself is deeply connected with the human body.[3] Other authors have dealt with the cultural and social developments that affected common ways of looking at and presenting the physical self to others.[4] Here, however, I should like to explore what printing, publishing, and reading have to tell us about an awakening sense of the private self. More specifically, I will focus on the genre that deals most directly with questions of physical presence and absence, with distances between persons: the personal letter.[5] In an era in which oral literature was being replaced by the printed page, the printed letter could be viewed, not only as a sign of the absent correspondent, but as a symbol of the author, whose thoughts were transmitted, not in person, but by ink marks on a page. The bodies of letters became the metaphorical yet tangible signs of the absent other, and, therefore, the material aspects of letters—the paper upon which they were written, the author's personal hand, and that necessary intermediary, the messenger—assumed a new importance. For seventeenth-century readers (many of them newly literate), the publication of letters became occasions to reflect upon the legitimacy of personal privacy; the ciphered contents of letters and their possibly indecipherable meanings came to be associated with the hidden self, while letters themselves became potent representations of the human person.

I will concentrate on the correspondence of King Charles I and poet John Donne, two individuals whose personal writings became publishing events in the mid-seventeenth century. Charles's personal letters were published against his will after their capture at the battle of Naseby in 1645, while John Donne Jr. edited and published his print-shy father's correspondence in 1651. These two political and religious conservatives (at least as measured against the radical Puritans of the time) become standard-bearers, almost icons, for the private, secret self. Poised against these two letter-writers is the revolutionary John Milton, whose works explicitly fault the king and implicitly accuse Donne's Anglo-Catholic attitude toward the sacramental body and sacramental mysteries. Two theologies face off in the writings of Milton and of Charles and Donne: the first is iconoclastic, devoted to purity in dogma and in language; the second is sacramental, Eucharistic, unashamedly iconophilic, with roots in a patently "Catholic" worldview and political science. Letters become the site for a discussion of the relation between privacy and secrecy, between the individual's legitimate right to prevent disclosure of his hidden self and the public's "right to know" about illicit and illegitimate abuses of power. The letters of Charles and John Donne are linked with ciphers and secrecy; the writings of John Milton, meanwhile, insist on full disclosure, on the stripping away of metaphor, mystery, and intrigue.

The publication of the letters of these two men also has implications for the study of the history of reading, or perhaps for a psychology of self-revelation in print. Writers of intimate letters face the possibility of discovery, of interception, of unauthorized publication and possible misinterpretation.[6] Correspondents' privacy is threatened when letters go astray or are subject to the censor's eye. Charles and Donne, in their letters and in their other writings, insist upon their right to what we would call privacy, their right to psychological and physical integrity. Strangely, publication, and the violation of their wishes by the intrusion of an anonymous reader into the original correspondence, become the means by which the private comes to have value. The late twentieth-century conflict between self-containment and self-expression, privacy and celebrity, are prefigured by the dramas surrounding the letters of Charles I and John Donne. And, as letter-writing becomes an ordinary exercise, done *in secretum,* without the supervision of those in authority who impart the skills of letter-writing,[7] as books of sample correspondence become models for writing, readers develop their own opportunities for self-analysis and self-construction.

Letters: Development of a Genre

During the seventeenth century, the classical epistle was being transformed into a means of personal communication, and letters became a symbol of access to the self, to the inner person.[8] The medieval discipline of *ars dictandi* had codified the method of writing letters, which were usually assumed to be petitionary and public in nature. Based on classical rhetoric and oratory, with their organization into exordium, narratio, and so on, the medieval manuals specified the written form for public and legal matters.[9] A great deal of emphasis was placed on the proper salutation and form of address; eight times more space in Guido Faba's *Summa Dictaminis* was devoted to this apparatus than to all other parts of the letter.[10] The location and length of the "superscription," or salutation, was an indication of the degree of one's inferiority to the person being addressed. Even the physical look of the letter itself was an indication of social and class difference. Jonathan Goldberg quotes a late (1683) letter manual that spells out these rules of decorum: "When we write to persons of quality, we use to leave a great distance between the body of the Letter and the Subscription."[11] The white space on the page between the body of the letter and one's signature was the visible sign of one's deference to authority.

One of the most influential examples of the genre during the early English Renaissance was the *Libellus de conscribiendis epistolis* (1521) of Erasmus.[12] Though written in Latin, it was first published in England for an English pupil of Erasmus and inspired the extremely popular *English Secretorie* (1586) of Angel Day.[13] William Fulwood's *Enimie of Idlenesse* (1568), a translation of a French guide, had been published earlier, but Day's was the first to have included letters written specifically for the book,[14] and of course it lacked the taint of foreignness. These letter-writers were instructional manuals intended for the newly literate, but it was not till Nicholas Breton seized upon the genre that it became apparent that letters could provide entertainment as well as instruction.[15] The original work of Angel Day led to the fictional situations of Breton's work and created a taste in English readers for reading other people's mail. Letters were dropped from mail pouches with suspicious frequency and invited, demanded surreptitious reading. The opportunity to look into anyone's private life was irresistible. Love letters became a staple, and the love letters of women were of especial interest. Women were thought to be especially good letter-writers because they were "unhampered" by the disciplines of a classical education and could thus emote artlessly in their letters.[16]

The extent to which letters became a publishing phenomenon during the seventeenth century can be demonstrated by a rough tally of editions of letters published from 1475 through 1700.[17] The statistics demonstrate the astonishing increase in the number of letters published throughout the seventeenth century. (Some of this increase, of course, may be attributed to the relaxing of the Licensing Acts and an increase in the number of books published overall.) What the numbers do not show is the way in which the character and authorship of letters changes: they become personal, rather than merely political, documents; some even verge on fiction.

Especially as the Civil War years progressed, letters were published with abandon, and often with the unspoken assumption that anyone's letters—even the king's—could reveal hidden secrets about persons or events. There is an air of glee, of knowing irony, in the letters published during the 1640s. Private cabinets of letters contained not just precious philosophical, literary, or spiritual "gems" but political secrets that affected the life of the English nation.[18] Before 1640, letters were overwhelmingly political, religious, and anonymous. Letters from "a soldier of good place," "a Catholic man," "a French Protestant," were written to readers such as "a Lady," "the faithful followers of Christ's Gospel," or "a person of honor." Even when the author is named on the title page, the generic forms of address and valediction invite the reader to identify with the letter-writer solely on the basis of social class or religious persuasion. One rarely has the sense of individual voices; rather, the letters seem to be mouthpieces for ideas. This phenomenon does not disappear after 1640; revolutionary rhetoric, after all, encourages, rather than suppresses, identification with a group or class of people. But letters in the latter half of the seventeenth century exhibit an increasingly personal character and intimacy and begin to move toward everyday experience, even during periods of political crisis. The move toward the publication of personal, familiar letters (and eventually fictive ones) popularizes letter-reading and helps elide public and political concerns with personal, even familial, interests.[19] Gradually, the common reader comes to participate in the invasion of the letter-writers' privacy.

The King's Letter Cabinet

One of the decisive events in the decline of the power of Charles I was his defeat at the Battle of Naseby on June 14, 1645, and the subsequent publication of his personal papers as *The King's Cabinet Opened* not quite one month later. R. E. Maddison has traced the publication history of the pamphlet, and Annabel Patterson has remarked on its smashing of the boundaries between public and private discourse.[20] What had been "meant for the cabinet" wound up a tool for Charles's political enemies.[21] The event is a study in invasiveness, made all the more significant because it touched upon the royal person. The customary deference accorded the king is set aside as a curious process of discovery, of uncovering, goes on. The public investigation of the private Charles is especially ironic, given Charles's predilection for aloofness and secrecy, for restricting access to his person.[22] The rifling of his personal belongings, the opening of his letter-cabinet, and the reading and deciphering of his letters force Charles into the public in a new way, into the self-revelation of *Eikon Basilike* (1649). Charles (or his amanuensis John Gauden, the likely author of the "King's Book") answers public charges with personal prayer and meditation; ironically, though the publication of his letters leads to his destruction, it also creates the environment for his canonization.[23] The violation of the royal person (and of his intended royal reader in this case, Henrietta Maria) became the catalyst for, and the symbol of, a shift in seventeenth-century perceptions. The first of these perceptions (acknowledged by astute observers and entrepreneurs of the period) was a recognition of the role of the printing press as the social intermediary between writers and their readers; the second, less easy to isolate but more profound, was the simultaneous development of psychological boundaries between the public and private and the realization that print could (and would) erode them. The publication of the king's letters became the focal point for a meditation on the king's two bodies; the discussion of the king's private person became one step toward the commonplace that everyone, not just the king, had a private self. While Charles's letters exposed public and political matters (his negotiations with the Irish army, his willingness to repeal the penal laws against Roman Catholics, his failure to recognize the Parliament), the letters themselves became a vehicle for the examination of interiority.

In their prefatory remarks, the editors of Charles's letters present their publication as a religious and civic duty: "It were a great sin against the mercies of God, to conceale those evidences of truth, which hee so graciously (and almost miraculously) by surprizall of these Papers, hath put into our hands; nor dare we smother this light under a Bushell, but freely hold it out to our seduced brethren, (for so in the spirit of meeknesse labouring to reclaim them, we still speak) that they may see their errors, and return into the right way."[24] Charles is "a Prince seduced out of his proper sphear"; the editors imply that Charles has engaged in an adulterous or idolatrous relationship, that he has hearkened to false gods. Defending themselves against their "Cabalisticall adversaries" at court and among the papists, the Parliamentarians avow the authenticity of the letters, insist that they are not forgeries. They not only build upon the biblical metaphor of the light under the bushel-basket but associate the letters specifically with the king's body: "He cannot disavow either his own hand writing, or the matters themselves here written. All the Ciphers, Letters, all circumstances of time, and fact, and the very hand by which they are signed (so generally known and now exposed to the view of all) will averre for us, that no such forgery could be possible" (sig. A3v). The king's actions, his letters, and his hand are here exposed; his "hand writing" is curiously detached from his body, much like the dismembered hands Goldberg has found in Renaissance writing manuals.[25] This image of a severed hand is perhaps a premonition of the violence of 1649, the year in which Charles is beheaded.

Charles derives the basis for his self-defense from the thought of his father, James I, and the medieval doctrine of the "king's two bodies." In *Basilikon Doron,* (addressed to the prince, Charles's older brother, Henry), James outlines his duties as a Christian and as a king: "He made you a little GOD to sit on his Throne."[26] Henry/Charles is required to rule in "godlinesse and vertue": "Let your own life be a law-booke and a mirrour for your people" (30). The image of "law-booke and mirrour" is allied to the medieval notion of the book: both are talismanic, tokens of a higher power. One did not so much read the medieval book as reverence it, marvel at the knowledge and power it represented. Patterning himself after God, James deigns to bridge the distance between ruler and ruled by taking on the incarnational role of Author. George Herbert, as University Orator at Cambridge, had among his duties the writing of letters; his first official letter was a thank-you for James's gift of his *Opera Latina* to the university library. Herbert exploits the notion of the king's ineffability; as Michael C. Schoenfeldt phrases it, James "displays a Christlike condescension toward his creatures" by publishing his writings.[27] Herbert, an author acutely conscious of the distance between himself and God, praises James in these words: "Laying aside thy majesty, thou dost offer thyself to be gazed upon on paper, that thou mayst be more intimately conversant amongst us. O astonishing benignity."[28] Herbert is reflecting back upon James the image of a gracious ruler who permits the intimacies of the gaze and conversation. James's "duplication of the divine glance" marks him as possessing a "special individuality," the ineffable mystery of the gods residing in the body of the earthly ruler.[29] James is emulating at least two persons of the Trinity here: he is God the Father, the creator-author, while the text itself is the incarnation of his royal self. (Such unseemly aspirations to dignity will form the kernel of Milton's attack on the *Eikon Basilike.*) This princely dichotomy between physical body and divine state prefigures the modern split between the public and private persona that we take for granted and that seventeenth-century Englishmen and women were just beginning to articulate.

The notion of the king's two bodies is important here and helps explain some of the vehemence with which Milton and other Parliamentarian radicals later attacked Charles, for Charles and his supporters used a "papist" theology to shore up, not only royal prerogative, but new concepts of the self. Ernst Kantorowicz traces the political principle of the king's two bodies to medieval theology: the mystical body of the king had its roots in Catholic views of the mystical body of Christ. Jurists spoke of royalty in christological or Eucharistic terms: the king was head of state just as surely as Christ was head of his church.[30] The language of sacramentality and corporal presence came to be applied in the secular realm as much as in the political (199). The king's power was even modeled upon that of the pope: where the pope was, there was the *corpus mysticum;* where the emperor was, there was the empire (225).

Nothing, then, could have enraged the Puritan factions of Parliament more than the publication of the *Eikon Basilike.* Its frontispiece, depicting a suffering, Christ-like Charles as martyr, reinforced the popular notion of king as icon and bore too close a likeness to Catholic ideas about the sacraments, the real presence, and saintly relics.[31] Available on January 30, 1649, the day of Charles's death, it had the effect of a deathbed utterance, unpremeditated musings from the "secret cabinet of the king's heart."[32] Just as Gauden substituted as author for the king, this text stood in the place of his absent body.[33]

It was no wonder that so many Puritans mocked and were horrified by the frontispiece to the *Eikon Basilike:* it confirmed their worst suspicions of Charles's idolatry, his connections with Catholicism, and the political intrigue that could be cloaked by appeals to royal privilege. The publication of Charles's letters is a crucial signpost of the modern era, for here the language of King James's "divinity" is transformed into the idiom of personal and psychological privacy and bodily integrity.

Charles not only assumed James's mantle of mystery but transformed the theology of the king's body into a theology of the secret person; in fact, secrecy, mystery, and the transcendental meaning of private places became part of the royalist project during the years of the Civil War and the Interregnum.[34] In the *Eikon Basilike,* Charles counters the metaphorical language of his accusers by insisting on his "integrity," his wholeness. (As we shall see, this notion of integrity, both physical and psychological, will be an important one for John Donne as well.) Charles does not so much defend himself as make his psyche visible, open himself up to public observation in the prayer ending chapter 21 of *Eikon Basilike,* "Upon His Majesty's Letters Taken and Divulged": "As Thou didst blast the counsel of Ahithophel, turning it to David's good and his own ruin, so canst Thou defeat their design who intended, by publishing my private letters, nothing else but to render me more odious and contemptible to my people. I must first appeal to Thy omniscience, Who canst witness with my integrity how unjust and false those scandalous misconstructions are which my enemies endeavour by those papers of mine to represent to the world."[35] Charles is suggesting that print can be used to misrepresent the facts, that it has, in this case, impugned his integrity, divided him, and opened him up to the contempt of his people. Charles's supporters followed the king's lead and chose to defend the King's person, his right to royal privacy:

> Our Thoughts no Commons, but Inclosures are:
> What bold Intruders then are they, who assail
> To cut their Prince's Hedge, and break his Pale?
> That so Unmanly gaze, and dare be seen
> Ev'n then, when He converses with his Queen.[36]

Charles's defenders go beyond the traditional notion that physical distance (like the distance between the body of a letter and one's signature) measures the respect one has for the king. Charles, seen here in personal conversation with his queen, merits a separate psychological space where his thoughts can be "inclosed." The metaphorical hedge, like the king's body, is the boundary beyond which outsiders may not stray. Moreover, the public's intrusion upon "their Prince's Hedge" is defined as effeminate, or perhaps androgynous and monstrous.[37] (Both sides in the rebellion charge their opponents with susceptibility to supposedly "female" traits; both insist upon their opponents' inability to contain their thoughts or their gaze.) The "Unmanly gaze" of the reader of Charles's letters pierces the imaginary boundary surrounding the king. The locus of control is reversed as the untouchable, godlike king becomes susceptible to public opinion in the person of the reader. (The "unmanliness" of the observer-reader also prefigures the maligned female reader of novels in later centuries; unable to maintain custody of the eyes or senses, women readers supposedly feel no compunction about prying into the private lives of fictional people.)

Charles appeals to his people's affection and sense of honor, insisting that "a civility from all men not wholly barbarous" would prevent gentlemen from publishing his letters. He passes over the political implications of his letters and emphasizes instead the impudence of those who made his private letters public. Since he realizes that further distribution of the letters is beyond his control, he astutely chooses to offer his private life as a sacrifice in the public service. He aligns his experience with that of his readers; he becomes a "private" person like them and emphasizes that the letters are a picture of his true heart: "Yet since Providence will have it so, I am content so much of my heart (which I study to approve to God's omniscience) should be discovered to the world without any of those dresses or popular captations which some men use in their speeches and expresses. I wish my subjects had yet a clearer sight into my most retired thoughts, where they might discover how they are divided between the love and care I have, not more to preserve my own rights than to procure their peace and happiness, and that extreme grief to see them both deceived and destroyed" (129–30). With studied graciousness, Charles offers the opportunity to glimpse his "retired thoughts," to share in the life of the pious believer and devoted husband. To read the letters as evidence of political chicanery is simply perverse, "sucking poison." The subsequent popularity of the *Eikon Basilike* proved Charles (or rather, his ghostwriter) was more psychologically and politically savvy than were the Parliamentarians. By permitting revelations of his personal self, Charles establishes his readers as his allies. Even as he eschews the prerogatives of a divine and absolute authority and uses publication to valorize his virtues, Charles reinforces his special status as king and martyr. Book, image, and words succeed where John Milton's reasoned attack on idolatry will not.

Milton attempts to demythologize Charles and deconstruct his words in *Eikonoklastes* (6 October 1649); he works to disabuse the English people of the sanctity of kings, and this king in particular. The chapter answering the *Eikon*'s chapter 21 focuses on the necessity of discovery, of revealing to all right thinkers the hypocrisy of the king and the emptiness of his promises:

> The Kings Letters taken at the Battell of *Naesby,* being of greatest importance to let the people see what Faith there was in all his promises and solemn Protestations, were transmitted to public view by special Order of the Parlament. They discover'd his good affection to Papists and Irish Rebels, the straight intelligence he held, the pernitious & dishonorable peace he made with them, not solicited but rather soliciting, which by all invocations that were holy he had in public abjur'd. They reveal'd his endeavours to bring in forren Forces, Irish, French, Dutch, Lorrainers, and our old Invaders the Danes upon us, besides his suttleties and mysterious arts in treating: to sumn up all, they shewd him govern'd by a Woman. All which though suspected vehemently before, and from good grounds beleev'd, yet by him and his adherents peremptorily deny'd, were, by the op'ning of that Cabinet, visible to all men under his own hand.[38]

Charles's and Milton's responses to the publication of private letters reveal a paradox about the proper uses of and responses to the relatively new medium of print. While Charles laments the incivility of Parliament in publishing his personal papers, Milton homes in on the public service done by Parliament: the letters have been "transmitted to public view" and Charles's private actions are "discover'd," and "reveal'd" as "suttleties and mysterious arts." Milton must convince his readers of the theatricality and idolatry surrounding Charles: "But the People, exorbitant and excessive in all thir motions, are prone ofttimes not to religious onely, but to a civil kinde of Idolatry in idolizing thir Kings; though never more mistak'n in the object of thir worship" (343).

The newly created iconography attached to the dead king in the frontispiece to the *Eikon Basilike* hearkens back to the notion of the king's body as sacramental and Christlike; Milton was quick to attribute the effectiveness of that picture to the tendency of the people to backslide into idolatry. He attacks the notion of the king at prayer as the enticement and enchantment of an "inconstant, irrational, and Image-doting rabble; [that like a credulous and hapless herd, begott'n to servility, and inchanted with these popular institutes of Tyranny, subscrib'd with a new device of the Kings Picture at his praiers, hold out both thir eares with such delight and ravishment to be stigmatiz'd and board through in witness of thir own voluntary and beloved baseness]" (601). Milton insists that the theatrical props of kingship and godliness be stripped away, that the self be transparent, always open to the gaze of others. But, as Marshall Grossman has pointed out, though the Parliamentarians saw the need to tear down the stage curtains surrounding the king and his plots, supporters of the king would have thought the destruction of the king's privacy as portentous as the renting of the curtain in the Temple at Jerusalem at Christ's death.[39] Perhaps Milton's *Eikonoklastes* did not take hold as strongly as the king's book because it discounted the human need for icons, for celebrities, and for a certain amount of theatricality in most people's dull existence. Milton could not rely on the "hapless herd" reading his book—it is much more likely that this sheepish mob would have seen (and worshiped) Charles's printed icon.[40] Even Milton the revolutionary falls into a bit of the same trap; he is, after all, as Lana Cable has pointed out, an icon-user as well.[41]

Milton further buttresses his claim against Charles's special and divine privilege by linking his secrecy and supposed deviousness to rule by his wife, Henrietta Maria. His letters reveal not a godlike but a deplorably weak and feminine Charles. Indeed, the editors' annotations on *The King's Cabinet Opened* name susceptibility to the queen as Charles's chief failure: "It is plaine, here, first, that the Kings Counsels are wholly managed by the Queen; though she be of the weaker sexe, borne an Alien, bred up in a contrary Religion, yet nothing great or small is transacted without her privity & consent" (sig. G2r).

For Milton, as for Parliament, this aspect of the king—his uxoriousness—must be made visible to all for the good of the Commonwealth.[42] The king's private actions, so at odds with his public self-presentation, must be examined in the public discourse of print. There could be none of the ambiguity about the sovereign's two bodies that showed itself most forcefully in the person of Elizabeth I, who embodied both masculine and feminine, public and private. The Virgin Queen sought to overcome the common perception of feminine weakness by insisting on the strength of her kingly heart and the unity of her chaste person, whose spouse was England.[43] The Parliamentarians' association of the king's private life with an unnatural submission to his wife, to the feminine, complicates our picture of a growing sense of privacy in the mid-seventeenth century. While the king and his supporters see the exposure of the king as monstrous and unmanly, the revolutionaries' actions seem to indicate their resistance to the protection of a "feminine" private self. Both sides attach the stigma of femininity to the private self.

One telling manifestation of this opposition between Charles's self-concealment and Parliament's call for public "discovery" is the growing use of ciphers or codes in both personal and political correspondence. Ciphering became, during the Elizabethan era, a tool for spies and even official ambassadors. The British Public Record Office alone holds 180 to 200 cipher-codes from this period.[44] Henry Wotton, intimate of John Donne and ambassador to Venice and The Hague, was familiar with the *Steganographia* (pub. 1606) of Johannes Trithemius, the first important book on cryptography, and practiced secret writing himself.[45] (In a 1623 letter to Sir Albertus Morton, Wotton furnishes Morton with what is apparently the key to a cipher and asks that a fair copy be kept with the Dean of St. Paul's, John Donne.)[46]

In *The Qveen's Maiesties Gracious Answer to the Lord Digbies Letter* (1642), it was revealed that the queen herself used ciphers.[47] This pamphlet not only cast further suspicion on the queen's loyalty but also indicated that privacy and secrecy were inextricably connected with faithful service to the king. This early report of the queen's use of ciphered texts (three years before the capture of Charles's papers at Naseby), certainly inflamed public opinion against the queen, but it was not until Naseby that the king was irremediably implicated. Parts of the king's captured letters had also been written in cipher, in a code so enigmatic that *The King's Cabinet Opened* was published without all the ciphers being decoded.[48] To opponents of the king, the unsolved mysteries represented by magical ciphers simply confirmed the devilish intent of their enemies.

It became quite the fashion to learn to write in cipher, just as it became the fashion to write fine letters based on the models presented in letter-books. John Wilkins's *Mercury, or the Secret and Swift Messenger* (1641) was a cryptographer's manual written to suit "some occasions that are incident to *Statesmen* and *Souldiers.*" The "secret method of writing love letters" explained by John White in *A Rich Cabinet with Variety of Inventions* (1653) required the use of ciphers. By 1653 writing in code had evidently become a parlor trick, though the continued political uses of cryptography are evident in works such as G. B.'s *Rarities: or, The Incomparable Curiosities in Secret Writing* (1665) and John Falconer's *Cryptomenysis Patefacta* (1685). The target audience for these letter-books and cipher keys was wide, ranging from the upwardly mobile soldier to the pining lover. Letters, inextricably linked with ciphering in the case of Charles and Henrietta Maria, become the common carriers of private meaning; ciphers and letters became the conveyors of everyday life and familiar relationships for commoners as well as kings.

John Donne and the Familiar Letter

In comparison with the tragical end of Charles I, the case of John Donne would hardly seem to warrant a great deal of concern about invasions of privacy. Though a respected and well-known poet and preacher, the posthumous publication of his letters by his son in 1651 certainly did little damage to him or to his reputation. But, like Charles's letters, Donne's are important, not only because they constitute one of the first major collections of letters published during the period but for what they tell us (and may have told contemporary readers) about a burgeoning sense of self. Donne, the man who likens himself to princes in his poetry, articulates his anxieties and concerns about the integrity of his body in his letters, sermons, and poetry. Like Charles, Donne expresses his belief in the importance and inviolability of his physical body. Letters are the vehicle by which he delivers that self over to those whom he loves; for Donne, books and words are as substantial as physical presence. This is, perhaps, a remnant of his Roman Catholic education—the notion that ideas and feelings cannot be realized without some physical incarnation of them.[49]

As with Charles, the publication of Donne's personal letters illustrates the consequences of the purposeful readdressing of private letters to a larger audience. As Janet Gurkin Altman has put it, with the publication of private letters, the author of a letter is "autobiographically *undressed,*" "rhetorically addressed" to the original recipient, and then is "readdressed" to a new reader, who sees the original "redressed" by a publisher or editor.[50] Publication inserted two additional elements into the letter-writing dyad: the publisher, and the book-buying reader. The original inditing of the letters by Donne and the subsequent editing and publication of Donne's letters in 1651 by the younger John Donne exemplify the problems of inserting a new audience into the "epistolary situation."[51] That situation positions letter-writer and letter-reader in, and leaves both vulnerable to, contingencies of time and space.

Some of Donne's letters were published in the first edition of his poetry (1631) as examples of "epistolary elegance."[52] The close connection between Donne's verse and letters in general is exhibited by the inclusion of some of his poetry in John Gough's popular (and frequently reprinted) letter-writer *The Academy of Complements* (1645). In another example of the letter sample-book, *The Marrow of Complements,* Samuel Sheppard even transformed the elegy "The Expostulation" into a model letter.[53] But the 1651 collection of letters was another matter altogether. It is generally agreed that the younger Donne, in an attempt to curry favor with the dedicatee of the volume, Bridget Dunch, took vast liberties with the order and addressees of the letters.[54] The letters do not appear in chronological order; many of the letters were readdressed from the then-unremembered Henry Goodyere to members of Bridget Dunch's more influential family; finally, there is evidence of omission and synthesis of several letters. Aside from the biographical and bibliographical significance of these changes for students of Donne's work, the case of Donne exhibits, in exaggerated fashion, what happens when personal letters get into print. The younger Donne felt no qualms about confusing now and then or about violating the original correspondents' privacy by resending letters to new correspondents—especially disturbing because the prompt and secure delivery of his letters to their intended readers was one of Donne's constant concerns, as we shall see from the letters themselves.[55] His son anticipates the epistolary novel of the eighteenth century with his "resending" of the letters; his cavalier treatment of content, correspondent, and correspondence already begin to erase the distinction between fictive and real. The reader (albeit unknowingly in the Donne case) is continually skirmishing at fictional boundaries.

It is not impossible to imagine that Donne, who circulated his poems in private coteries, also envisioned a wider audience for his letters.[56] But it is difficult to imagine that Donne would have approved of his son's appropriating his work for a new audience. His letters show him continually worried about unauthorized readers of his letters: he worries lest his or his correspondents' letters "perish," "miscarry," or come by "hazardous waies" and is dependent on an unreliable post and third, or even fourth, parties to post his letters.[57] In a letter to Henry Goodyere (but assigned to Henry Wotton by the younger Donne), Donne alludes, ironically, to some unintended readers of his letters: "When it shall not trouble you to write to me, I pray do me the favour to tell me, how many you have received from me, for I have now much just reason to imagine, that some of my Pacquets have had more honour then I wished them: which is to be delivered into the hands of greater personages, then I addressed them unto" (126). It is appropriate that his son sends this to Wotton, who, in his role as ambassador, felt no qualms about intercepting letters. Wotton prided himself on furnishing King James with "the knowledge of the secretest practices out of the very packets of the Jesuits themselves" by opening, reading, and then sending on their letters.[58] Wotton claimed "a special appetite" for these packets,[59] and the king was so pleased with Wotton's efforts that he was willing to fund Wotton's mail-tampering projects.[60] Donne would have been familiar with Wotton's methods, and knew that his own letters could be subjected to the same treatment. He had some competence in this area himself, as an aside in one his letters hints: he complains that his friend's letter lacks a precise date, and he "is not so good a Cabalist, as to finde in what moneth it was written" (246). In one letter detailing news of court and references to imprisonments and religious tumult, Donne sees "small hope" of recovery from the Inquisition for one L. Rosse and expresses interest in a newly open position as secretary in Ireland. He hopes, but cannot be certain, that the letter will reach its intended reader, and remaining anonymous, dispenses with a signature: "It is extreme late; and as this Letter is nothing, so if ever it come to you, you will know it without a name, and therefore I may end it here" (146). Donne, the ambitious apostate who figures in John Carey's study, seems to revert to the cautiousness of his Catholic youth, when, as a member of an underground religion, anonymity and secrecy were *de rigeur.*[61] Another letter, reporting on some incident involving the earl of Salisbury, Herford, and the king, is signed: "Yours intirely, You know me without a name, and I know not how this Letter goes" (217). He "importunes" Goodyere to burn a letter referring to the Lady Bedford, "for I would say nothing of her upon record, that should not testifie my thankfulnese for all her graces" (218).

The reasons for Donne's reticence about his letters were not based solely on their political content. Donne regarded letters as special forms of communication, like his poetry, which he regarded as a form of "private speaking."[62] Circulation among more readers would destroy the intimate quality of the relationships engendered and supported by letters: "If you were here, you would not think me importune, if I bid you good morrow every day;

and such a patience will excuse my often Letters. No other kinde of conveyance is better for knowledge, or love; . . . they are also the best conveyors of love" (105–6). Letters, like the books in his poems, are vehicles for communion.[63] Donne's verse letter "To Sir Henry Wotton" opens with lines that link letters and absent friends:

> Sir, more then kisses, letters mingle Soules;
> For, thus friends absent speake. This ease controules
> The tediousnesse of my life: But for these
> I could ideate nothing.[64]

Better than kisses (which, according to Renaissance doctrine, allowed lovers' souls to merge), letters connect the spirits of distant friends.

Letters also have incarnational meaning; like bodies, they can be mutilated, lost, or decayed. Donne speaks of "sacrificing" one of his letters (141), of "burying" another (224). Like persons, letters do not consist only of bodies. Their nature is mixed, as that of human beings is: "In the History of style of friendship, which is best written both in deeds and words, a Letter which is of a mixed nature, and hath something of both, is a mixed Parenthesis: It may be left out, yet it contributes, though not to the being, yet to the verdure, and freshnesse thereof" (114). For Donne, the double nature of letters means that they can overleap distances of time and space—even should the intended recipient never receive the letter: "When we thinke of a friend, we do not count that a lost thought, though that friend never knew of it. If we write to a friend, we must not call it a lost Letter, though it never finde him to whom it was addressed: for we owe our selves that office, to be mindefull of our friends. In payment of that debt, I send out this Letter, as a Sentinell Perdue" (286). The physical act of writing, the effort of remembrance of a friend, the posting of the "Sentinell," is a ceremony that binds the friends. A simple remembrance of the friend will not do; the friend must give life to a letter, which, anthropomorphically, must attempt to find its recipient.

All this seems of a piece with Donne's support for outward ceremony, for the use of images to instigate prayer and devotion.[65] The incarnational value of letters and their earthly insufficiencies should be viewed in tandem with the themes of Donne's sermons, several of which focus on the resurrection of the body and the final reunion of soul and body. In Carolyn Bynum's recent study of medieval thought on the resurrection of the body, she notes that "only embodied souls can fully love."[66] This theology (derived from both medieval mystics and the church fathers) helps explain Donne's fascination with the mixture of body parts and the decay that must precede individual resurrections.[67] Resurrected, Donne will not only be more like Jesus Christ and the angels (*Sermons* 4:46–49, 327)—but he will experience a bodily reintegration that is paralleled by a seemingly new psychic integrity: "And yet, *Ego,* I, I the same body, and the same soul, shall be recompact again, and be identically, numerically, individually the same man. The same integrity of body, and soul, and the same integrity in the Organs of my body, and in the faculties of my soul too; I shall be all there, my body, and my soul, and all my body, and all my soul" (*Sermons* 3:109–10). Donne cannot seem to contain his excitement at the prospect of this undivided self that will exist after the resurrection. This excitement is not a simple rejoicing in having all the parts of his body rejoined into a glorious one; the integrity of his body seems bound up with his very person. In some uncanny way, the reunion of body and soul, of Donne with his wife and friends, confirms Donne's individuality; the resurrection somehow resolves the conflicts between Donne's desire for individuality and for a union of souls. Perhaps it is not too great a leap to conclude that, in Donne's earthly existence, letters were the means for staving off separation from others and for resolving his own internal divisions.

All of the observations above about Donne's awareness of the body, and the burden he placed on letters to act as a substitute for friends and lovers (separated for now), make one aspect of Donne's writings a bit puzzling. The intimate quality of expression and the glimpses of ecstasy lend the letters a peculiar air—precisely because the reader acts in the invasive role of observer and unintended correspondent. How does the reader's role compare with those who, with "unmanly gaze," stripped King Charles of his privacy?

It has long been recognized that Donne's poetry exploits the triangular situation of lovers and observer.[68] Sometimes the reader shares in the lover's paranoia; with the ghost-lover, the reader spies on the faithless woman exhausting her latest lover in "The Apparition," shares in the lover's defense of his beloved in "The Canonization," mocks the suspicious husband in "Jealosie." At other times, the reader is the uninvited intruder into a happy kingdom. The "you" of the opening invocation in "The Sunne Rising" is both the "Busie old foole, unruly Sunne" and the reader; the effect of "The Relique" is to exclude the reader from the community of holiness by placing the lovers in a hallowed grave, the reader outside it. In "The Extasie," the souls of the two lovers, "to advance their state," leave the bodies and "interinanimate"—mingle souls, as letters and kisses do. The reader of the poem observes the bodies of the lovers below, but the reader does not feel himself to be an intruder, precisely because of the poet's invitation, nay, command, to "mark" the lovers. Self-consciousness is the malady of the spied-upon, the condition of the adolescent who feels the world judging and observing him. Ecstasy (an out-of-body experience) is the correlate freedom from one's surroundings, a satisfying oblivion. "The Extasie" is an object lesson in what love, or letter-writing, can do. This is what Donne hoped for in his letters—freedom from observation. Consider Donne's prose expression of "literal" ecstasy, in a letter to Goodyere (not Thomas Lucey, as the 1651 edition indicates): "I make account that this writing of letters, when it is with any seriousness, is a kind of extasie, and a departure and secession and suspension of the souls, wch doth then co[m]municate it self to two bodies: And as I would every day provide for my souls last convoy, though I know not when I shall die, and perchance I shall never die; so for these extasies in letters, I oftentimes deliver my self over in writing" (11). Surely, after reading this letter, one knows that Donne would have felt as strongly about the publication of his letters as he did about the printing of his poetry. What is it but a kind of denuding of Donne to know of his special affection for Goodyere, expressed here: "I am not weary of writing; it is the course but durable garment of my love, but I am weary of wanting you" (42).

When one finds Donne closing a letter by wrapping up his heart in its paper (41), one is reminded of the absolute impossibility for Donne of separating body from soul, letter-paper from feeling, writing from friendship. Bodies and letters and angels are one: they are all revelations of love. They "make up, and they nourish bodies of friendship" (74). Letters, then, do not have as their purpose the conveying of news—hence, Donne's "newsless letters."[69] Donne's thoughts occupy the body of most of his letters, while news is often relegated to a postcript. As in Donne's love poems, knowledge and love are communicated in quite physical ways; letters, though, have a more serious burden than the reporting of facts:

> Such Letters as mine, which (perchance out of the dulnesses of the place) are so empty of any relations, . . . You (I think) and I am much of one sect in the Philosophy of love; which though it be directed upon the minde, doth inhere in the body, and find piety entertainment there: so have Letters for their principall office, to be seals and testimonies of mutuall affection, but the materialls and fuell of them should be a confident and mutuall communicating of

> those things which we know. How shall I then who know nothing write Letters? Sir, I learn knowledge enough out of yours to me. (120–21)

Donne insists on the efficacy of words, on the power of letters to bind souls and to confer upon loving correspondents sanctity, power, a self-contained and protected world. He is also, however, supremely aware of the dangers of self-revelation and of the limits of that self-created world. Political or emotional betrayal are always possibilities. Because of this awareness, Donne is especially sensitive to others' privacy (though he does not yet have the word for it): "I would not open any doore upon you, but look in when you open it. Angels have not, nor affect not other knowledge of one another, then they lift to reveal to one another. It is then in this onely, that friends are Angels, that they are capable and fit for such revelation when they are offered. If at any time I seem to studie you more inquisitively, it is for no other end but to know how to present you to God in my prayers, and what to ask of him for you" (109–10). Donne is reassuring his friend and subtly correcting himself, but he is also reaffirming the attitude that he so frequently displays in the poetry: that friends, like lovers, are in a special category. They are centers of their own universe (one little room can be an everywhere, a place where lovers are "States" and "Princes"). Like the persons of Kings James and Charles, the ordinary lover or friend merits a kind of veneration, and this exalted condition is not available to the uninitiated.

But Donne's cautions are disregarded in the middle of the seventeenth century. Publishers and editors begin to act as authorized letter-openers, as socially acceptable kinds of literary spies. Consider the many prefaces to the reader from publishers, printers, and authors, which, in the manner of letters, begin with salutations "To the Reader" and bid farewell in their closings. The printed book, that strange mix of public and private medium, seems, contradictorily, both to shelter and to expose the private self.

I close with a long quotation from a recent essay by Czech novelist Milan Kundera:

> I am looking at a window across the way. Toward evening the light goes on. A man enters the room. Head lowered, he paces back and forth; from time to time he runs his hand through his hair. Then, suddenly, he realizes that the lights are on and he can be seen. Abruptly, he pulls the curtain. Yet he wasn't counterfeiting money in there; he had nothing to hide but himself, the way he walked

> around the room, the sloppy way he was dressed, the way he stroked his hair. His well-being depended on his freedom from being seen.
>
> Shame is one of the key notions of the Modern Era, the individualistic period that is imperceptibly receding from us these days; shame: an epidermal instinct to defend one's personal life; to require a curtain over the window; to insist that a letter addressed to A not be read by B. One of the elementary situations in the passage to adulthood, one of the prime conflicts with parents, is the claim to a drawer for letters and notebooks, the claim to a drawer with a key; we enter adulthood through *the rebellion of shame.*
>
> An old revolutionary utopia, whether fascist or communist: life without secrets, where public life and private life are one and the same.[70]

Kundera goes on to describe the surveillance of a Czech political leader by the Russians after the invasion of 1968: people "realized (as if by electric shock) that private and public are two essentially different worlds and that respect for that difference is the indispensable condition, the sine qua non, for a man to live free; that the curtain separating these two worlds is not to be tampered with, and that curtain-rippers are criminals" (24).

It is interesting that a late twentieth-century writer should express his concerns about the need for privacy in much the same terms as our correspondents of the seventeenth. Kundera's "epidermal instinct" is to defend the body from observation, to hide one's letters and thoughts in secret cabinets. He feels disgust and repugnance toward the curtain-rippers who demand full disclosure; he insists that one can only be free if the private self is allowed to remain hidden and flourish. He fears that this self is being erased with the incursions of modern technology and that the survival of the individual is at stake.

Charles I and John Donne, living at the cusp of the modern era that Kundera thinks is now disappearing, begin to frame themselves in modern terms. Though each has roots in traditional thought on the role of the body, on kingly prerogative, and on the sacredness of private communications, they articulate for their readers, both now and long ago, the ways in which publication can both confirm and conflict with the physical and psychological realities of the private self.

4

Margaret Cavendish and the Virtues of Publication

NOWHERE IN THE seventeenth century is the changing sense and status of "privacy" more apparent than in the life of that writing (and publishing) woman Margaret Cavendish, duchess of Newcastle.[1] Her contemporaries saw her as an egregious example of the world turned upside down: a married woman, a member of the upper classes, who not only insisted on publishing her work but made the pursuit of fame her life's goal. Cavendish was challenged by her lack of a serious education, by the political conditions in mid-seventeenth-century England that led to the royalist exile from home, and by the "anxiety of influence" of such illustrious predecessors in the drama as Ben Jonson and William Shakespeare. Her temerity in releasing her works in folio format (a form that had traditionally been reserved for classical and theological works and had only recently been used for the works of lyric and dramatic poets) astounded her contemporaries.[2] This writing woman appeared to overstep the gendered boundaries between public and private by publishing her work.[3] This, as well as her reputedly curious mode of dress, indicated to her contemporaries her complete lack of female propriety.[4] Cavendish's challenge was to reconcile her life of writing with her feminine self, her domestic role with her public persona. She had to redefine the public in publication, to erase the negative connotations of being a public, publishing woman. Cavendish had to test her readers' gendered conceptions of the moral life, which presumed that female virtue depended upon confinement to the domestic, private sphere. Instead, she reframed the meaning of privacy for both men and woman by appropriating all its positive, elitist (and male) aspects and by casting suspicion on those aspects of privacy that endangered public virtue.

The Civil War had precipitated a period of solitude and exile for the Cavaliers, leading their poetic spokesmen to find "transcendental meaning" in the hidden life.[5] This stereotypically "feminine" lifestyle became an option for men, but the reverse—the public life—was still not available to women. Margaret Cavendish's response was double-pronged: first, as a woman, she aimed to erase gender differences, to obtain for women the same privileges and autonomy as men. Secondly, as a royalist, publishing after the Restoration (when Puritan dissent was associated in royalist minds with a dangerous private spirit), she reminded her readers of the dangers of too much solitude, and of the necessity for private thoughts always to resolve themselves into public displays of virtue. In her *Playes,* published in 1662, Cavendish creates a series of characters and situations that support these seemingly contradictory needs of hers. She depicts women who share in the privileges of men, and she insists on the necessity of their participation in public life, whether as soldiers, orators, or authors.

Cavendish sees solitude and contemplation—the retired life—as the ideal.[6] (She still had to use an old word, *contemplation,* for what we would call "privacy"). But she knows that, for women, the retired life is only a pale imitation of that of men. Marriage and domesticity *restrict* women to the private sphere; it does not free them from authority as it does men. Submission to a husband meant loss of personal autonomy, loss of a private self. Cavendish's solution is simple: she proposes that women remain unmarried. The celibate life is the closest a woman can come to sharing in the freedom of men; it is what supports Cavendish's fighting, studying, orating, writing, and publishing female characters. Virginity allows for independence, the proper pursuit of "self-love" (what we might call self-esteem), and the cultivation of virtue. However, marriage is inevitable for most of Cavendish's female creations. Only Cavendish herself (as she reminds the reader over and over again in her writings), seems graced with the ability to maintain her personal and artistic autonomy within the social structure of marriage. Her exceptionality is evident in the author's idealized husband-wife pairings, in which her heroines combine romantic love unions with intellectual and emotional independence.

Despite her professions of uniqueness, Cavendish felt compelled to justify her literary activities to her readers and to her critics. This she does by recreating her female identity, which, in the seventeenth century, consigns her to domesticity, silence, and obedience, but certainly not to the male-gendered privileges of solitude and autonomy. By refining commonplace notions of solitude and private life, she frees herself to publish and to pursue the fame she so wholeheartedly desired.[7] "Privacy," as it was defined in the seventeenth century, was suspect; it covered over all sorts of vice: adultery, political intrigue, flattery. For Cavendish, the proper result of her lived solitude was publication, revelation. Publication meant not only the printing of her writings and public oratory but the construction of a literary monument to her fame. In the late twentieth century, fame has unpleasant associations with publicity, voyeurism, and the invasion of private life, but for Cavendish, fame guaranteed the proclamation, dissemination, and continuance of both literary and moral virtue.[8] One could only know the fruits of private reading and writing by their display.

The 1662 *Playes,* written during Cavendish's exile with her husband on the Continent during the 1650s, are her description of the proper relation between private and public life for both men and women.[9] The plays are simultaneously an answer to those who find the theater immoral, her way of staging her dramas despite the closed theaters, and an accommodation to her slim options as a female playwright. And even though the theaters had been restored, along with Charles II, by 1662, the print medium became instrumental in defining the public and private for Cavendish.[10] While the dramatic form implies ostentation and presentation, the presence of an audience, print restricts the drama to the gaze of a single person, the reader.

In this chapter, I examine the *Playes* as a physical object (because this tells us something about Cavendish's own dealings with her publishers and her public) and analyze the ways in which they thematize her opposing desires for personal autonomy and social respectability, for the contemplative life and for fame, for authorial freedom and for her readers' acceptance. The book and the plays themselves demonstrate Cavendish's ideal and lived experience of transforming solitude into virtue, of reconciling the private and public through reading, writing, and publication.

The 1662 *Playes*

Playes Written by the Thrice Noble, Illustrious and Excellent Princess, the Lady Marchioness of Newcastle was printed in London by A. Warren for John Martyn, James Allestry, and Thomas Dicas at the Bell in Saint Paul's Church Yard in 1662.[11] The reader opens the volume to find Cavendish, set upon a pedestal, gazing back at the reader from the frontispiece (fig. 2).[12] The poem engraved on the pedestal invites us:

2. Frontispiece, Margaret Cavendish, *Plays, Never Before Printed* (by permission of Rare Books & Special Collections Library, University of Illinois at Urbana-Champaign)

Here on this figure Cast a Glance,
But so as if it were by Chance,
Your eyes not fixt, they ought not Stay,
Since this like Shadowes to the Day
It only represent's; for Still,
Her Beauty's found beyond the Skill
Of the best Paynter, to Imbrace,
Those lovely lynes within her face,
View her Soul's Picture, Judgment, witt,
Then read those Lines which Shee hath writ,
By Phancy's Pencill drawne alone
Which Peece but Shee, Can justly owne.

When we examine this figure, we see what is in some ways a typical seventeenth-century title page: the engraved illustration, the architectural setting, the classical motifs—all, perhaps not incidentally, also characteristic of the book illustrations drawn by Peter Paul Rubens, whose home in Antwerp the Cavendishes occupied after his death.[13] According to Margery Corbett, architectural settings on titles pages conveyed three distinguishable meanings: that of the triumphal arch, the stage for an allegorical tableau, and a monument to celebrate the living or commemorate the dead.[14] As we read Cavendish's plays, we will see that all of these interpretations of the decoration suit Cavendish's various incarnations as lady-general, playwright, and famed author. The full-length depiction of the author is nothing like the discreet and rather petrified busts of Shakespeare and Beaumont and Fletcher in the folio editions of their collected works. Instead, we find Cavendish, dressed in classical style, barefooted, with more than a little décolletage, wearing an ermine-lined cloak, and crowned with a coronet which sits jauntily at the back of her head. Ermine, the traditional emblem of purity and female virtue, is a token of the themes of Cavendish's plays; not only does its use recollect Elizabeth I in the Ermine Portrait (1585)[15] but ermine was the symbol of St. Ursula, patroness of the Ursulines, a Catholic order of nuns founded in 1535 and dedicated to the education of girls.[16] (Cavendish could have known of their work from her time spent in France as lady-in-waiting to Henrietta Maria.) The coronet indicates, not only Cavendish's "thrice-noble" status, but her desire for the crown of artistic fame. To Cavendish's left is Apollo, the god of music and poetry. Wearing the laurel that reminds us of his poetic prowess as well as his pursuit of the nymph Daphne, he holds his traditional implements, the lyre and a scepter topped with the sun. To Cavendish's right is Pallas Athena, the virgin goddess who sprang full-grown from her father's head. The shield decorated with the Medusa's head and the spear symbolize her wisdom in military matters. Margaret is in most illustrious company: the inspirer of poetry and the goddess who visited with the Muses on Mount Helicon. The cornucopias at the feet and head of the divinities only serve to emphasize their gifts to this unusual woman, an author like and unlike the classical (and male) authors of old.[17] Not just a sculpture in vivo of the author, the title page serves as a sort of monument to Cavendish herself. Disconcertingly reminding the observer of funerary sculpture, it is intended to be the paper equivalent of the statues, monuments, and mausoleums that pepper Cavendish's plays. Tomb sculpture of the Renaissance, claimed Erwin Panofsky, sanctioned the commemoration of individual persons, rather than families. It revived classical symbolism and readmitted the biographical element that had been eliminated in the medieval period. The Virtues appeared as character witnesses to the deceased, and the effigy represented the deceased as a living being, rather than as a *reprecentacion de la mort.* The only aspect of Panofsky's model missing from Cavendish's portrait is the motif of "the Arts Bereft"—the Arts mourning the death of their patron;[18] its absence is appropriate, for Cavendish expected to live forever in her writings. Her prefatory poems and the plays themselves will illustrate this point.

Despite the confidence Cavendish displays in the visual opening to the book, the complicated binding of the prefatory matter to the *Playes* gives some indication of Margaret Cavendish's practice of revision and her need to apologize for her work. The bibliographical format of the book indicates the author had second (and third and fourth) thoughts about the introductions to her plays. The insertion of four separate leaves into the initial gathering (that containing the books' prefatory matter) and the duplication of signature marks likely indicates that Cavendish supplied the printer with more material after her manuscript had been set in type.[19] Each preface must have been a new opportunity, more space in which Cavendish could explain her role as a woman writer, cajole the reader, or theorize about literature and the theater.

This introductory matter includes two dedications, nine prefaces "To the Readers," an unaddressed preface, a dedicatory poem by her husband, a "General Prologue," and an introduction in the form of a dialogue.[20] The initial dedication in Cavendish's book of plays neglects to specify the dedicatee by name—but it is clearly addressed to the general reader:

To those that do delight in Scenes and wit,
I dedicate my Book, for those I write;
Next to my own Delight, for I did take
Much pleasure and delight these Playes to make;
For all the time my Playes a making were,
My brain the Stage, my thoughts were acting there. (sig. A2r)

The verse sets the theme for the volume. The implied reader (addressed as "noble" or "worthy" in the next nine prefaces) does not so much read as watch the scenes unfold, as Margaret, the author, focuses on her pleasure in writing and signals to the reader her willingness to open her creations to public display. The theatrical metaphor indicates that her works are meant for presentation, even though political circumstances forbade staging them in England at the time she was writing.[21] Cavendish's stage and her brain, like her poetic atoms, are both infinitely small and infinitely vast, containing worlds within worlds.[22] The reader, though he or she might be reading in a closeted room, can enter into the public new worlds created by Cavendish's imagination. The printed page simply sets the scene for the dramatic action. Cavendish combines her dual role as author and director of plays throughout the book: readers are spectators, and in play after play, prologues and epilogues ask the audience to applaud, even though Cavendish acknowledges from the first that her plays will never be produced. "The Epistle Dedicatory," addressed to her husband, recognizes the influence of his own dramatic writing on hers but claims that hers is the inferior. While some of her husband's plays were actually produced,[23] the Lady Cavendish sees no such hope for her own:

> And as for this Book of Playes, I believe I should never have writ them, nor have had the Capacity nor Ingenuity to have writ Playes had not you read to me some Playes which your Lordship had writ, and lye by for a good times to be Acted, wherein your Wit did Create a desire in my Mind to write Playes also, although my Playes are very unlike those you have writ, for your Lordships Playes have as it were a natural life, and a quick spirit in them, whereas mine are like dull dead statues, which is the reason I send them forth to be printed, rather than keep them concealed in hopes to have them first Acted; and this advantage I have, that is, I am out of the fear of having them hissed off from the Stage, for they are not like to come thereon; but were they such as might deserve applause, yet if

> Envy did make a faction against them, they would have had a publick Condemnation; and though I am not such a Coward, as to be affraid of the hissing Serpents, of stinged Tongues of Envy, yet it would have made me a little Melancholy to have my harmless and innocent Playes go weeping from the Stage, and whipt by malitious and hard-hearted censurers; but the truth is, I am careless, for so I have your applause I desire no more, for your Lordships approvement is a sufficient satisfaction to me. (sig. A3r–A3v)

Cavendish is performing a neat trick here: the "honest Wife" and "faithfull Servant" who signs this dedication is acknowledging her subservient role in the domestic sphere. Though she proclaims her husband's superiority, her modest judgment of her own plays is simply a pose; one can see that she intends these "dull dead statues" to have a long life, the printed book having greater substantiality than the fleeting stage-play. Recall the frontispiece, in which Margaret is dressed as a classical author. Statues may represent the dead, but they are enduring, just as printed plays outlast stage performances. She will neither "conceal" her work (i.e., be secretive about it) nor dare the censure of a live performance, which, being public, will elicit "publick Condemnation." By publishing her plays, Cavendish strikes a middle ground between public and private: she abjures the secrecy of the modest closet dramatist yet uses her plays to assert her social role as dutiful wife and contrasts her moral virtues to those of her potential detractors, the "hissing Serpents" and "Envy." Publishing plays is not immodest but the real sign of her wifely virtue. Ironically, the proclamation of her virtue gives her an audience who, though it may read her plays in private, provides her with a stage for the dramas teeming in her brain.

Cavendish even attaches an aura of virtue and industry to her much-derided desire for fame. In "A General Prologue to all my Playes" (sig. A7r–A8r), she compares her work to that of the master playwrights Ben Jonson, William Shakespeare, and Beaumont and Fletcher. The first sixteen lines of this verse prologue praise Jonson, whose plays were learned and polished and appeared about as infrequently as did foreign emperors to their subjects.[24] Cavendish's plays, though, gather in throngs, are quickly written, and lack "Learning, Reading, Language, wit." Unlike the plays of her illustrious predecessors, her plots are not derived from Plutarch, Greek romances, or *Don Quixote.* Hers are all new inventions, springing forth from her "poor brain." Cavendish values individual inspiration; any borrowing or imitation is plagiarism or simple theft. This notion springs up repeatedly in the plays and reminds the reader how protective Cavendish was of these children of her mind. For a woman writer, ownership of one's texts might be one of the few real chances to own property in seventeenth-century England.[25]

The authors Cavendish admires are monumental: their works are the foundation of the modern English language. Cavendish chooses to build a different sort of monument, however. Here is how she describes her work:

> But I upon my own Foundation writ;
> Like those that have a little patch of Land,
> Even so much whereon a house may stand:
> The Owner builds a house, though of no shew,
> A Cottage warm and clean, though thatch'd and low;
> Vitruvius Art and Skill he doth not take,
> For to design, and so his house to make;
> Nor Carpenters, nor Masons doth not hire,
> But builds a house himself, whole and intire: . . .
> Just so, I hope, the works that I have writ,
> Which are the buildings of my natural wit;
> My own Inheritance, as Natures child,
> But the Worlds Vanities would me beguild:
> But I have thriftly been, housewiv'd my time,
> And built both Cottages of Prose and Rhime;
> All the materials in my head did grow,
> All is my own, and nothing do I owe:
> But all that I desire when as I dye,
> My memory in my own Works may lye:
> And when as others build them Marble Tombs,
> To inurn their dust, and fretted vaulted Rooms,
> I care not where my dust, or bones remain,
> So my Works live, the labour of my brain.
> I covet not a stately, cut, carv'd Tomb,
> But that my Works, in Fames house may have room:
> Thus I my poor built Cottage am content,
> When that I dye, may be my Monument. (sig. A7v–A7^{2}r)

Cavendish orchestrates the imagery here in the same way she did her dedicatory letter to her husband. She contrasts her humble cottage (built with her own hands) to the palatial works of the great poets. There is a peculiarly domestic and nationalistic ring to Cavendish's verse; one is reminded of Jonson's call to Robert Sidney in "To Penshurst" to return to a true simplicity of life, rooted in English tradition. Her gifts are "native" in a double sense of the word. She casts aside foreign materials and the classical architecture of a Vitruvius for building materials garnered from her own property. The privatizing of the household I described earlier reaches its ultimate end in Margaret Cavendish's solitary cottage. Cavendish emphasizes her own contribution to the building of the English verse tradition but deflects possible criticism by setting herself apart from the monumental work of her male counterparts. A bit disingenuously, considering the self-portrait facing the title page of the book, she rejects marble tombs for the more enduring fame her prose and verse will bring.

By comparing herself to established male authors, Cavendish invites the mockery of those who regard female authors as vain, vainglorious, immodest, and foolish. In the fourth preface to the readers, she acknowledges these possibilities, even seeming to be criticizing members of her own sex: "But the greatest talkers are not the best writers, which is the cause women cannot be good Writers; for we for fear of being thought Fools, make our selves Fooles, in striving to express some Wit, whereas if we had but that power over our selves as to keep silence, we perchance might be thought Wits, although we were Fools, but to keep silence is impossible for us to do, so long as we have Speech we shall talk, although to no purpose" (sig. A5r–A5v). Good writing for Cavendish is connected with the proper balance between speech and silence and with self-discipline (that "power over our selves"). She sees both writing and wit as desirable in themselves, but they are displays that deserve to be made public only after fulfilling the prerequisites of silence and self-control. Women, Cavendish stipulates, lack these characteristics and hence make poor writers. But no more so than men, as she turns her own seemingly misogynist argument against them, continuing: "But to speak without partiality, I do not perceive that men are free from this imperfection, nor from condemning us, although they are guilty of the same fault; but we have this advantage of men, which is, that we know this imperfection in our selves, although we do not indeavour to mend it; but men are so Partial to themselves, as not to perceive this imperfection in themselves, and so they cannot mend it; but in this, will not or cannot is as one" (sig. A5v). Somehow confinement to the private sphere has made women more aware of their imperfections—an awareness that seems to have escaped men blinded by the bright lights of public life. That last flourish of "will not" and "cannot" frees Cavendish to write as well or as poorly as any man. The burden of self-control and judicious speaking should not be unfairly placed on women: both sexes must have the same freedom to appear foolish in public.

In "An Introduction," the last prefatory remarks before the plays themselves, Cavendish again picks up the themes of foolishness, wit, and male and female authorship. But she craftily transfers her arguments to three gentlemen, who present a dramatic prologue to the plays themselves. Without putting her signature to the introduction, Cavendish insinuates herself into their dialogue. (Each of the prefaces is signed with her initials, M.N.; the dedicatory poem by her husband is signed more fully, W. Newcastle, but Margaret's name disappears with the "General Prologue" and this dialogue.) The three gentlemen, and then her characters, take over for the female author.

One of the gentlemen, on the way to see a play, invites another to accompany him. The second refuses, complaining of the large number of words and small amount of wit in most plays. All three agree that the length of plays, the authors' insistence on treating of only one humour, a general lack of variety, and poor acting are reason enough not to attend the theater. The first gentleman is hopeful, however, that this play will be different, for it is written by a lady—and one with "native and naturall" talent. The second gentleman responds that women's wit is too weak and "conceited" to allow any of them to write well. Should such an impossibility occur, he remarks: "Why I will say no body will believe it, for if it be good, they will think she did not write it, or at least say she did not, besides the very being a woman condemnes it, were it never so excellent and rare, for men will not allow women to have wit, or we men to have reason for if we allow them wit, we shall lose our prehemency" (sig. B1v). The double literary standard tells against women and protects men's preeminence, as Cavendish herself knew. In the preface to her life of William Cavendish, she reminds him that people have both attributed her work to a man and at the same time complained of her lack of learning.[26] Cavendish's writings are excellent and foolish at the same time—"good enough" to be the work of a man (and therefore challenge male literary supremacy) and weak enough to link them to a woman author. The question of male and female authority will be resolved in Cavendish's plays by obliterating the sex of the female author: chastity, cross-dressing, and participation in traditionally male activities such as education and war become the means by which women can share in the rewards of a male-dominated public life. The issue is almost a religious and moral crusade for Cavendish, as we shall see when we examine her choice of imagery and the moral colorations of her plays. The gentlemen close their conversation in just such religious tones, as all three agree to attend the play:

> *2. Gentleman.* Nay stay, I will go with thee, for I am contented to cast away so much time for the sake of the sex. Although I have no faith of the Authoresses wit.
>
> *3. Gentleman.* Many a reprobate hath been converted and brought to repentance by hearing a good Sermon, and who knowes but that you may be converted from your erroneous opinion; by seeing this Play, and brought to confesse that a Lady may have wit. (sig. B1v)

The gentlemen stand in for readers, who, because the theaters are closed, cannot attend the play themselves. Like Catholics throughout the century, and Anglicans during the Interregnum, they are forced to worship at home, to read in private. The many small sermons in Cavendish's plays will convert her readers to belief in women's wit and power.

In other addresses to the reader, Cavendish expands upon the theme of the moral life. In the fourth preface "To the Readers," she begins her defense of the theater, and even of acting by the nobility. It is her answer to the Puritans.[27] "Noble Readers," writes Cavendish, the noble youth among the Romans—and even emperors—acted upon the stage: "for certainly there is no place, wayes, or meanes, so edifying to Youth as publick Theatres, not only to be Spectators but Actors; for it learnt them gracefull behaviours and demeanors, it puts Spirit and Life into them, it teaches them wit, and makes their Speech both voluble and tunable, besides, it gives them Confidence, all which ought every man to have, that is of quality" (sig. A4^{2}r). Cavendish interrupts this testimonial to the theater to explain the absence of such effects on the professional actor: he acts from mercenary motives, "for the lucre of gain." Since he learns his lines "as Parrots speak, by wrote," there can be no true learning, no education, no moral improvement. The graces pretended by professional actors desert them once they leave the stage. Cavendish here responds to the detractors of stage-plays by silently conceding that the offstage behavior of actors is less than honorable but also suggests that noble actors (and noble readers?) are best suited to creating and acting in plays.[28] The public nature of the theater mirrors the public roles to be assumed by the ruling elite. More than book learning, the theater educates: "A publick Theatre were a shorter way of education than their tedious and expensive Travels, or their full and solitary Studies, for Poets teach them more in one Play, both of the Nature of the world and Mankind, by which they learn not only to know other men, but their own selves, than they can learn in any School, or in any Country or Kingdome in a year; but to conclude, a Poet is the best Tutor, and a Theatre is the best School that is for Youth to be educated by or in" (sig. A4^{2}r). Cavendish is not condemning studies outright, as we shall see when we visit with the characters she most admires; rather, it is pedantry to which she is opposed. And the problem with pedants is that they insist on classifying, on "Rules, Forms, and Terms," rather than permitting themselves to succumb to the creations of the author. In the very next preface, Cavendish challenges the adherence to allegorical forms demanded by scholastics and pedants. Her example is related specifically to gender: she claims the right to decide for herself, the author, whether virtues and vices should be gendered masculine or feminine:

> I Know there are many Scholastical and Pedantical persons that will condemn my writings, because I do not keep strictly to the Masculine and Feminine Genders, as they call them as for example, a Lock and Key, the one is the Masculine Gender, the other the Feminine Gender, so Love is the Masculine Gender, Hate the Feminine Gender, and the Furies are shees, and the Graces are shees, the Virtues are shees, and the seven deadly Sins are shees, which I am sorry for; but I know no reason but that I may as well make them Hees for my use, as others did Shees, or Shees as others did Hees. (sig. A4^{2}v)

She aims for clarity of meaning, rather than metaphorical obscurity, as "to be understood is the end of all Speakers and Writers." Defending her right to literary independence from the rules that govern other authors, Cavendish claims indifference to literary niceties and the censorious readers who subscribe to them: "And if any dislike my writings for want of those Rules, Forms, and Terms, let them not read them, for I had rather my writings should be unread than be read by such Pedantical Sholastical persons" (sig. A4^{2}v).

Cavendish grants her readers a great deal of freedom, seems at times even deferential to their habits. In the second preface "To the Readers," she explains again her reasons for having plays printed rather than acted. With a sly bit of irony, she notes that her plays happen to be written in English, even though plays could not, at the time of her writing, be staged in the Commonwealth: "England doth not permit, I will not say, of Wit, yet not of Playes" (sig. A3^{2}v). But the chief reason appears to be the nature of the plays themselves: they are too long for acting (though not "so long as Ben. Johnson's Fox, or Alchymist, which are somewhat too long"). Her plays are meant for reading.[29] Spectators of plays are forced by custom and courtesy to sit through entire plays, even bad ones; readers need suit only themselves: "But for the Readers, the length of the Playes can be no trouble, nor inconveniency, because they may read as short or as long a time as they please, without any disrespect to the Writer" (sig. A3^{2}v). Though the permanence of print has its advantages for readers (and for the sustenance of the author's fame), Cavendish seems to lament her plays' unsuitability for the stage. Audiences desire novelty, and books, once read, preclude surprise for the audience. Perhaps Cavendish's mixed feelings about print, rather than production, explain her constant melding of spectator and reader in the 1662 *Playes,* as in the ending to this preface: "But the printing of my Playes spoils them for ever to be Acted; for what men are acquainted with, is despised, at lest neglected; for the newness of Playes, most commonly, takes the Spectators, more than the Wit, Scenes, or Plot, so that my Playes would seem lame or tired in action, and dull to hearing on the Stage, for which reason, I shall never desire they should be Acted; but if they delight or please the Readers, I shall have as much satisfaction as if I had the hands of applause from the Spectators" (sig. A3^{2}v).

In one preface, Cavendish gives specific instructions on how to read plays. Cavendish's ideal reader must be an actor as well as an interpreter of her plays:

> For Scenes must be read as if they were spoke or Acted. Indeed Comedies should be read a Mimick way, and the sound of their Voice must be according to the sense of the Scene; and as for Tragedies, or Tragick Scenes, they must not be read in a pueling whining Voice, but a sad serious Voice, as deploring or complaining: but the truth is there are as few good Readers as good Writers; . . . but when as a Play is well and skillfully read, the very sound of the Voice that enters through the Ears, doth present the Actions to the Eyes of the Fancy as lively as if it were really Acted; but howsoever Writings must take their Chance, and I leave my Playes to Chance and Fortune, as well as to Censure and Reading. (sig. A6v)

The presumption is made that oral reading is the norm, and this implies an audience. Reading Cavendish's plays aloud enables them to be simultaneously private and public acts; though not presented on the public stage, nor even in the private theaters, they will come alive at home, perhaps the perfect setting for Cavendish's quite undomestic dramas, which straddle the line between public and private concerns. Cavendish is not the first to send forth her works for potential condemnation or ridicule, but she may be unique in requiring the readers of her plays to assume the triple roles of reader, actor, and spectator. Perhaps such roleplaying was a given with the closet drama of this period. The preface certainly illustrates the fact that oral reading in small groups was still a common practice, but it also undoes neat distinctions between private and public. Reading itself becomes a public act, readers are actors, and writing (and publication) seems the more private and discreet activity.[30] The habit of oral reading presented Cavendish with the opportunity to unsettle her readers' assumptions about private and public; those scenes acted out before "the Eyes of the Fancy" not only presented the audience with pictures of virtue, but guaranteed that of their author.

The *Playes* of 1662 include fourteen plays, seven of which are presented in two parts because of their length. Nearly all these plays are comedies (i.e., they end in marriage). Two are unrelievedly tragic (*Youths Glory and Deaths Banquet,* and *The Unnatural Tragedy*), and *The Matrimonial Trouble* is, as its subtitle indicates, a "come-tragedy." Cavendish's treatment of the traditional marriage plot is significant, because it illuminates her ideas about the role of women, about personal privacy and the choices available to men and women, and about the place of women in the world of publishing. She does not focus on romantic attraction, thwarted physical desire, and star-crossed love but on the limitations marriage places on individuals, particularly women. Marriage, says Cavendish, prevents the realization of a life of solitude, contemplation, and the creative imagination. It destroys personal autonomy and enforces a narrow definition of the social roles men and women may inhabit. Both men and women in Cavendish's plays express their desire to remain single, but their reasons are quite different. The men, rather stereotypically, lament the loss of their freedom for sexual adventure; lustful women, on the other hand, prefer the cover of marriage. The admirable women who express a preference for a chaste or virginal life are much more numerous and regard marriage as a pall cast over their active imaginative and intellectual lives. Each of the plays depicts female characters who at one time or another express the wish not to marry. In the comic plays, most of these women reconcile themselves to marriage through the selection of a partner who accepts this aspect of the women's lives, just as William Cavendish did Margaret's.[31]

An alternative course lies open for some: the life of an anchoress, a sort of secular nun, sometimes even in partnership with a like-minded male. This drive toward chastity and total sexual abstinence is, for most of the women characters in the plays, the only way to erase their female identity and participate in the public world open to men. For Cavendish, privacy is defined by the sort of personal autonomy that virginity guarantees; it frees her women from their female bodies, making them "men" in body, spirit, and opportunity.

Cavendish's desire to imitate the "humorous" drama of Ben Jonson resulted in the creation of a great number of flat characters whose names immediately give away their moral stance, but if we read these characters as different aspects of a whole person (perhaps even of Cavendish herself),[32] we can perhaps draw a picture of Cavendish's own view of real and ideal possibilities for women's lives and for publishing women in particular. If we read the plays as individual, coherent efforts to imitate life, we shall be disappointed. But taken together, the plays represent a range of possible worlds, from visionary to pessimistic to realistic. I have selected three plays for discussion: *Loves Adventures, Youths Glory and Deaths Banquet,* and *Bell in Campo.* These are not only the best and most dramatically coherent of her plays; their arrangement in the collection also, perhaps coincidentally, represents a thematic progression in Cavendish's thoughts about privacy and fame.

Loves Adventures

Loves Adventures, the first play in Cavendish's collection, is a preparation for those that follow. In this two-part invention, she presents a female protagonist who, though she does not write and publish, succeeds in traditional male roles. Cavendish needs to establish the requirements for female success in public life and for the publishing women of the later plays; she does so by focusing on a woman who is independent, autonomous, competent on the battlefield as well as on the podium, and who also has a private life that sustains and supports her public life. Cavendish blurs gender differences, cross-dresses her heroine, and almost allows her main character to relinquish marriage in order to make her point about the proper balance between public and private selves. The Lady Orphant/Affectionata is a woman of action, a public woman, who depends on secrecy, pseudonymity, and disguise to retain her autonomy.

Loves Adventures opens with a conversation between a young man, Lord Singularity, and his father, appropriately named Lord Fatherly. They argue over a proposed marriage to a young (and rich) girl, the Lady Orphant. Singularity has no desire to marry at all, and he trots out the usual arguments against marriage: the danger of cuckoldry, women's inherent lightness, the threat of a "womans management"; in this particular case, there is also a great age disparity between the couple. One of the father's arguments in answer to his son is one that signifies in play after play (though this is perhaps the only instance in which it is used by a man). The father accuses his son of wishing to lead a profligate life with his mistress:

> *Lord Father.* . . . but howsoever Son, if all Men should be of your mind, there would be no Marring [*sic*] nor giving in Marriage; but all must be in Common.
>
> *Lord Singularity.* That were best Sir, for then there could be no Adultery committed, or Cuckolds made. (5)

The parent here conflates two biblical passages, the words of Jesus Christ on the condition of the resurrected in Mark 12:25: "For when they shall rise from the dead, they neither marry, nor are given in marriage; but are as the angels which are in heaven"; and the description of the early Christian community in Acts 4:32: "But they had all things in common." Lord Fatherly, as a representative of the human familial and social order, cannot fathom holding everything and everyone in common; the father's view is of the here and now, where property (and sexual partners) must be duly portioned out. The son picks up on the biblical allusion, recognizing that the abolition of property rights would end the possibility of sin and transgression. No marriage, no adultery, no cuckoldry and embarrassment for the husband. Singularity's appropriation of the eschatological view guarantees his freedom, both theoretically and in actuality: his father does not force him into marriage. But the double (and conflicting) view of marriage remains. The demands of an ordered society exemplified in the marriage contract are opposed to notions of personal independence. The religious imagery stands in for (and quietly supports) the drive for the exercise of private choice amid society's demands. This exchange has echoes in other Cavendish plays and characters; marriage is often discarded in favor of the spiritual and emotional independence of the single and virginal life.

Seven years pass, and although the Lady Orphant has never met nor even seen Singularity, she falls in love with him at the sight of his picture. Her flighty companion, Mrs. Acquaintance, expresses some reservations about his appearance, but Lady Orphant replies: "You mistake lust for love, ambition, for merit, I love not for the bodyes sake, but for the soules pure spirit" (11). As a sign that Orphant's love is driven by spiritual rather than physical concerns, Cavendish obliterates the signs of Orphant's femininity (though not her sexuality) through the dramatic convention of cross-dressing.[33] Despite her guardians' objections, Orphant decides to dress like a vagabond (that is, as a man) in order to travel to Lord Singularity and offer proof of her constancy, affection, and service.[34] She adopts the telltale feminine name of Affectionata. Dressed as pilgrims, Orphant/Affectionata and her foster father travel to the army encampment where her lover is the general in command. She volunteers to be his page, and Singularity agrees, so immediate is his attraction to her. Singularity finds such solace in Affectionata's company that he adopts "him" as his son, and even resolves to find him a wife. He seems not to notice the implications of the feminine pseudonym, Affectionata, though jealous soldiers suspect the young "boy" of pimping and conveying love letters, of being a Ganymede, and even a spy. The necessity for secrecy becomes Affectionata's central concern. Singularity, burdened by his secret excesses with a mistress, wishes to confide in Affectionata, because "to conceal them, is to be an Actor" (39). Cavendish's Singularity argues for the cleansing powers of revelation, but Affectionata fears revelation will bring only disillusionment. Some things—especially scandalous and immoral actions—are better kept private. The accusations of treachery against Affectionata are even more troubling to her: the possibility of torment while under interrogation means also the likelihood of revelation of her real sex. Secrecy is the sine qua non for her independent life as a man. As a man, Affectionata, unlike many accused heroines, is permitted to defend herself before the commanders of the army. Affectionata is the first of Cavendish's female rhetorical geniuses; a figure of the virginal child Christ who astounds the elders in the temple, she fulfills the feminine imperatives of chastity and obedience, but is freed from silence by her male dress; she is allowed to defend herself with words. Affectionata does not become an author, as some other Cavendish characters do, but this public speaking is preparation for that activity in other plays. Later, in a council of war, her speech transfixes her audience, and Lord Singularity praises her precocious eloquence: "Why, thou didst speak at the Council of War, as if thou hadst been an old experiencd souldier, having had the practice of fourty years, which did so astonish the grave Senators and old Souldiers, that they grew dumb, and for a while did only gaze on thee" (56). Verbal eloquence has transformed the young woman into an old soldier; traditional roles are reversed, and it is the men who are reduced to silence. Men have lost their "prehemency," as Cavendish predicted in the prefatory dialogue to the book.

Affectionata's command of words extends to the battlefield, where she defends her beloved in physical combat: "I think our Generals new made son is a spirit; for when the General was surrounded with the Turks, this adopted Son of his flew about like lightening" (50). We find Affectionata has become a transcendent body: she is a spirit, flying above the enemy, enabled by her disguise and her secret resolve to engage in the glory of battle, to protect her beloved, and to display her wit. Even more importantly, it allows Affectionata to escape her body altogether, to become like those angels in heaven, who neither marry nor are given in marriage. Abandoning her female body allows Affectionata to develop both rhetorical and physical prowess, to beat men at their own games.[35]

Affectionata's fame spreads far and wide: the duke of Venice wishes to adopt her; cardinals dispute with her; the pope desires an audience and wishes to make her a saint, or at least a cardinal. Affectionata's only wish is to remain with Singularity, who has in the meantime resolved to marry her off to herself, to Lady Orphant. Affectionata, in a compliment to the Cavendishes' own May-December marriage, insists she is too young for the lady, and wishes, anyway, to "live unmarried" (68). Singularity's demand for obedience precipitates a crisis for Affectionata. A further complication occurs when her guardians, Foster Trusty and Nurse Fondly, are accused of murder because of her unexplained absence from home. Affectionata frames the conflict in personal terms: "O! How my soul is tormented with love, shame, grief, and fear. . . . I am in love, but ashamed to make it known, Besides, I have given the World cause to censure me, not only in concealing of my Sex, and changing of my habit, but being alwaies in the company of men, acting a masculine part upon the Worlds great Stage, and to the publick view; but could I live thus concealed, I should be happy, and free from censure" (72). Personal choice comes face to face with social and ethical obligation; revelation seems inevitable and necessary for Affectionata. But Affectionata cannot help but lament her loss in abandoning her pretense. Revealing her sex invites censure, while secrecy would guarantee her personal happiness. Living as a man allows her to be close to the man she loves, and also, unexpectedly for her, to enjoy the honors reserved to men. Unlike Shakespeare's transvestite heroines, Affectionata finds a place in the world of men and is willing to forego marriage to stay there. By being most private, she can assume the most public of roles, and live with Singularity, not as a wife, but as an equal.

Her guardians' murder trial becomes the crowning epiphanic moment for Affectionata. Just as the jury pronounces them guilty, Cavendish inserts the stage direction: "Enter Affectionata, drest very fine in her own Sexes habit, and stops the Judges sentence" (74). After the requisite amazement at her beauty and recognition by Lord Singularity, Affectionata apologizes for her subterfuge. This exchange follows:

> *Affectionata.* . . . But since I am discovered, I will otherwise conceal my self, and live as an *Anchoret* from the view of the World.
> *Lord Singularity.* Pray let me live with you.
> *Affectionata.* That may not be, for an *Anchoret* is to live alone.
> *Lord Singularity.* If you will accept of me for your husband, we shall be as one.
> *Affectionata.* You have declared against marriage, my Lord.
> *Lord Singularity.* I am converted, and shall become so pious a devote, as I shall offer at no Alter but *Hymens,* and since I am your Convert, refuse me not. (74–75)

The play ends with a traditional nuptial celebration, but the social order is only superficially restored and confirmed. While some readers may see Affectionata's profession of celibacy as an effective (and socially acceptable) ploy to preserve her virtue and to tame the rakish Singularity, I am suggesting that Cavendish here proposes a new sort of marriage. Cavendish comments on the marriage celebration and illustrates the ideal nature of this marriage through the use of two subplots in the play, each depicting another married couple. The first voices the negative aspects of conventional marriages, while the second demonstrates the need for patriarchal rule when female virtue is absent or weak. Both subplots illumine Cavendish's complex, and apparently contradictory, attitude about the proper role for women in the public and private sphere.

Lady Bashfull is Affectionata's more reserved female counterpart (and another of Cavendish's alter egos).[36] She declines company, spends her time reading, and wishes to avoid marriage. When her woman, Mrs. Reformer, challenges her, she replies: "Because I am now Mistriss of my self, and fortunes, and have a free liberty; and who that is free, if they be wise, will make themselves slaves, subjecting themselves to anothers humour, unless they were fools, or mad, and knew not how to chose [*sic*] the best and happiest life" (28). Bashfull refuses to read, let alone answer, the letter sent by her admirer, Sir Serious Dumb (who communicates only in writing). She gradually permits him to sit in her presence while she reads, and finally succumbs, agreeing to marry him. In her last appearance in the play, Lady Bashfull decides her wedding will be private and that she will not "be drest for a Pageant shew." While Reformer reckons a wedding day as the one triumphant day in a woman's life, Bashfull says: "Do you call that a triumphant day, that inslaves a woman all her life after? no, I will make no triumph on that day" (66). This contrasts with the marriage of Affectionata and Singularity, which is extraordinary, just as Cavendish claimed her own was. For most women, marriage is no solace, but the means by which their individuality is buried and submerged.

The male model for the private and scholarly life in the play is Sir Peaceable Studious, who first enters with book in hand. He reads, he writes—and also has to put up with his gossiping, society-loving wife, Lady Ignorance. She, like other wrong-headed women, "cares not for wide mouthed fame" (14) and regards her husband's closet as "a dull dead statue." As one might expect, Sir Peaceable is the spokesman for a life of study: "You do not wife consider their worth; for books are conversable, yet silent acquaintance, and study, is a wise Counsellor; and kind friends, and poetical thoughts are witty Companions, wherein other Societies and Companies are great inconveniences, and oftimes produces evil effects, as Jealousie, Adulterie, Quarrels, Duels, and Death, besides slanders, backbitings and the like" (14). Lady Ignorance, who frequents a society quite like Jonson's female collegiates in *Epicoene,* is eventually reformed by her husband. The happy couple last appears midway through part 2 of the play, where Sir Peaceable voices Cavendish's praise of solitude:

> How happy is a private life to me;
> Wherein my thoughts ran easily and free;
> And not disturb'd with vanities and toyes,
> On which the senses gazes, as young boys
> On watery bubbles in the aire blown,
> Which when they break, doth vanish and are gone. (54)

Privacy becomes conducive to a properly ruled family life. Sir Peaceable's life is sober, quiet, healthful, and well governed, and thus he is able to govern his foolish wife as well. But neither does the Studious marriage measure up to the Affectionata/Singularity ideal. Sir Peaceable is only a minor character, and is meant to be admired, but he does not appear to be interested in fame or in the publication of the poetry he writes so assiduously. Peaceable fails to follow William Cavendish's advice to the young Charles II: "Too much contemplation spoils action, and virtue consists in that."[37] It will be the female authors in Cavendish's plays who fully transform the solitary life of the imagination into action and the actual publication of their works. Nor is Sir Peaceable and Lady Ignorance's marriage a union of equals, since Lady Ignorance stands so obviously in need of correction.

The last scene of the play, the wedding scene, closes with two celebratory songs (the first of which is attributed to the marquis of Newcastle in the text, the second of which I suggest should be). Affectionata, who is hesitant to leave behind her life in male disguise—a life in which she achieved, not only independence, but confidence—prefers to live alone and be an Anchoret, the closest worldly equivalent to living as a man. Only Singularity's argument for the spiritual and physical oneness of married couples, the promise to worship at her altar, appears to convince her. In their marriage, there will be no unequal division of roles—they will be as one, he says. But here, as in many of Cavendish's plays, the nature of the marriage is unclear: is this a union of minds, or bodies, or both? If only of minds, why should Singularity agree to it? If only of bodies, why should Affectionata, thus losing her independence as well as her mastery over her own body?[38] Affectionata must abandon her virginity *and* her self-containment by accepting Singularity's proposal; in exchange for the abandonment of her male prerogative, she could become the object of Singularity's devotion. But the last song offers another alternative: that this marriage is a conjoining of friends as well as of lovers:

O Love, some says thou art a Boy!
But now turn'd a Girl, thy Masters joy.
Now cease all thy fierce alarms,
In circles of your loving arms.
    Who can express the joys to night,
    'Twil charm your senses with delight,
Nay, all those pleasures you'l controul,
With joyning your each soul to soul.
Thus in Loves raptures live, till you
Melting, dissolve into a dew;
    And then your aery journey take,
    So both one constellation make. (77)

Lord Singularity's eagerness to get on with the ceremony and hasten to the nuptial bed, and the sensual and sexual overtones of the couple's "loving arms," "pleasures," and "melting" "raptures" seem to confirm the physical realities of this marriage. But another dimension is hinted at, and that is the likeness of this marriage to male friendship. The boy (Affectionata) is really a girl, but can fight and talk as well as a man. As such, she is capable of the spiritual joining of "soul to soul" of two equals—melting into one another, not one subsumed by the other. The song ends with the image of the "one constellation" Affectionata and Singularity will form in the sky. It is reminiscent of Ben Jonson's paean to brotherly friendship, "To the Immortal Memory and Friendship of that Noble Pair, Sir Lucius Cary and Sir H. Morison."[39] There, Jonson had compared the friends to the twins Castor and Pollux, who live, "twi-/ Lights," in the heavens as Cary and Morison's fame do on earth: "Two names of friendship, but one star: / Of hearts the union." (ll. 98–99) Cavendish's pair of lovers mirrors (and, in their bodily union, surpasses) Jonson's set of friends. Affectionata's experience as a comrade-at-arms marks her as Singularity's friend as well as his spouse; tellingly, it is a male persona who sings that final song, who confers brotherhood on Affectionata. It would not be surprising if the Lord Newcastle, who was compared to Castor in one of Jonson's epigrams, should recognize his wife in this verse as his Pollux, both his physical and spiritual partner.[40]

Cavendish regarded herself as extraordinarily blessed in actually living such a life; her platonic love for the indulgent husband thirty years older than she enabled her to view herself as both married and virginal: "Though I desire to appear at the best advantage, whilest I live in the view of the public World, yet I could most willingly exclude myself, so as Never to see the face of any creature, but my Lord as long as I live, inclosing myself like an Anchoret, wearing a Frize gown, tied with a cord about my waste."[41] The Cavendish marriage was not a celibate one, because there is evidence that she was treated by doctors for infertility,[42] but clearly this was an area of life that held little interest for her. In her autobiography, Cavendish, speaking of her love for her husband, claims: "For it was not Amorous Love, I never was infected therewith, it is a Disease, or a Passion, or both, I only know by relation, not by experience."[43] Margaret Cavendish's physical, psychological, and feminist impulses coincided and found some resolution in her writing and a metaphorical home in the Catholic tradition of the independent and educated Anchoret.

The Catholic resonances of Cavendish's imagery deserve some discussion here. Both she and her husband expressed a degree of tolerance for Catholics and some disgust with the excesses of the religious radicals; William was even criticized for employing Catholic generals during the Civil

War.[44] Margaret Cavendish's grandfather, Thomas Lucas, may have had Catholic sympathies; St. John's Abbey, her happy childhood home, was a former religious house.[45] She served as a maid of honor to the French-born and Catholic Henrietta Maria and lived in exile in France and Antwerp, headquarters for Catholic propaganda directed against England and a center of the Counter-Reformation.[46] I am not arguing that the Cavendishes were crypto-Catholics—William Cavendish's advice to the restored Charles II inveighs against popery and Catholic "pupett Playes," and his wife would certainly have followed his lead in this matter.[47] But certain aspects of the Catholic imagination may have appealed to Margaret Cavendish. The hidden life required of English Catholics (and perhaps their sense of persecution) coincided nicely with her desire for privacy and solitude, and the language of the cloister provided her with the framework for describing a life for women independent of men. The necessity of having a husband in seventeenth-century society could be resolved imaginatively by taking up the medieval (and very Catholic) notion of spiritual marriage, in which a married couple forgoes a sexual relationship. In her history of this phenomenon in the Middle Ages, Dyan Elliott defines its central aspect: "The move to chastity was most frequently associated with female initiative: very often a woman's struggle for a spiritual marriage appears to be no less than a fight for physical autonomy and self-definition. Release from sexual duties, moreover, is often perceived as potentially altering traditional gender-dictated roles and challenging normative concepts like female submission."[48] Spiritual marriage gave Cavendish the weapon with which to fight for autonomy and against the increasingly sanctified nuclear family advocated by left-leaning Protestants. This doctrine enabled Cavendish to position herself politically, spiritually, and personally against the prevailing winds of her society. In Affectionata, Cavendish offers a female character who enjoys the social advantages of Protestant marriage and the psychological strength of a dedicated and self-sufficient virgin.

Youths Glory and Deaths Banquet

In *Youths Glory and Deaths Banquet,* Cavendish takes up the themes of the life of the mind and the pursuit of fame—the most urgent of problems for women authors in her day. In this play, she merges the characters of Sir Peaceable Studious and Affectionata to create her ideal: a woman who writes and also takes part in the public world of the intelligentsia. Lady Sanspareille, as her name indicates, is of surpassing beauty and intelligence.

Graced with a classical (i.e., male) education by a doting parent, Father Love, Sanspareille is of marriageable age, and the play opens with a dispute between her parents on the method and manner of her upbringing. The argument centers, unsurprisingly, on reading. Mother Love complains that her husband has made the girl "a slave to her book" (123) and has usurped her proper authority to educate her daughter for wifely duties. The dispute over reading poses classical education against practical training, the value of the male imagination against female common sense, the role of men against the place of women in the world. Father Love links literature and all the liberal arts with delight: poetry and science are pleasant companions, toys which help one while away the hours of life. Mother Love, on the other hand, focuses on the dangers of pedantry and escapism; her view is conservative but not quite puritanical, for she homes in on the possible evil effects of a too-active imagination. Mother Love points out that her husband's posterity cannot be "raised from a Poets phantastical brain":

> *Father Love.* I wish my Posterity may last but as long as Homers lines.
>
> *Mother Love.* Truly, it will be a fine airey brood! No no, I will have her bred, as to make a good houswife, as to know how to order her Family, breed her Children, govern her Servants, entertain her Neighbours, and to fashion herself to all companies, times and places. (123)

Father Love desires progeny, but fame even more; the mother wishes her daughter a life founded upon a well-ordered household. Both parents are right, but each sees the issue of their daughter's education from his or her own social (and hence, gender-conditioned) situation. His wants are indeed "airey," as Mother Love charges, but his wife's methods (and all women's) are apt to create another generation of foolish women, as Father Love counters. A male education breeds boys "to swear, swagger, gaming, drinking, Whoring"; besides, her husband's hope for a liberal education for women is illusory: "No, no, let me tell you, a woman will be a woman, do what you can, and you may as soon create a new World, as change a womans nature and disposition" (124). Each character is permitted to cite the strengths and the failings of male and female education; the outcome of Cavendish's plot will indicate which character's views is correct (or even possible in the world).[49]

Lady Sanspareille, predictably, has no wish to marry, "beleiving there is no second" man like her father (125). Even should she marry the noblest and richest of men, her mother could not guarantee her a happy life; marriage is just too fraught with burdens. Instead, Sanspareille, who spends her time "contemplating" and writing verse, wishes to devote her life to the pursuit of fame, not to a life of marital submission. In a long dialogue with her father, Sanspareille distinguishes between "vulgar fame" and fame based on merit: "But know Sir; it is not a vulgar fame I covet, for those that goeth with equal space, and even hights, are soon lost, as in a crowd or multitude; but when fame is inthron'd, all Ages gazes at it; *and being thus supremly plac'd up high; Like as an Idol, gets Idolatry:* Thus singularity as well as merit, advances fame" (130). Cavendish's fictive self, Sanspareille, is not interested in the acclaim of the *vulgus,* the crowd; she wishes to be raised up above the crowd, enthroned as Cavendish is in the frontispiece to her *Philosophical and Physical Opinions* (1655). The problematic words *idolatry* and *singularity* are what we must decipher here, for Cavendish is putting a positive cast on what were quite negative qualities in the seventeenth century. Charges of idolatry were tossed about liberally, especially among the Puritans, and Cavendish herself was lampooned by her contemporaries for her own singularities in dress and thought. Cavendish's Sanspareille yearns to be idolized as was Homer, or one of the saints, for her moral and intellectual virtues. The "singularity" she seeks is not oddity but a quality of wholeness, of oneness, of integrity; this singularity will be derived, not only from her reputation for virtue, but from her separateness and uniqueness. (In Sanspareille and Mistress Odd-Humour, in *The Religious,* Cavendish anticipates the odd, and emancipated, women of George Gissing's 1893 novel.) This is, for Sanspareille and many other of Cavendish's virtuous female characters, at the core of their wish to remain unmarried.

Sanspareille outlines her life's plans for her father in a long speech that is significant because it clarifies in so many ways the supposed contradictions in Cavendish's thought. It also fixes attention upon the questions of privacy and print that are the focus of this study. A virginal life and the cultivation of a unique private self are necessary preconditions for a life of writing and publication. And, without the cover of marriage and a husband, publication becomes, not only the evidence of her genius, but the guarantee of her virtue.

The girl first requests permission of her father to remain single, for her study and work would be "lost in a married condition"; further, her husband might not approve them. The results of her work she will "publish to the world in print" before she makes them "common by discourse." It seems puzzling that Sanspareille/Cavendish should favor publication over discussion in the literary or intellectual coteries traditionally preferred by members of the aristocratic classes.[50] As a publishing woman, she challenges not only expected gender roles but recasts coterie activity as "common." Publication enthrones her work, raises it above the scandalous world of private intrigue and private vice. This is confirmed by Sanspareille's next resolve: she "will not receive, nor give private vissits [*sic*], or entertainments," which are apt to be "senceless, vain, idle, light discourses." Instead, everything she creates will be made public:

> Thirdly, I would never speak but in publick, for if nature, and education, have given me wit, I would not willingly bury it in private discourses; besides, privat hearers are secret Thieves, and boldly steals, having no witnesses, to betray, or reveale the truth, or divuldge their thefts; and so they will adorn their discourses with my wit, which they steal from me. Fourthly, I will never speak of any considerable matter, or subject, or of any new conception but I will have them ready writ to print them, so soon as my discourse of them is past, or else print them before I discourse of them; and afterwards explain them by my tongue, as well as by my pen, least they should mistake the sence of my workes, through Ignorance; for those subjects that are only discourst off, in speach, flyes away in words; which vanisheth as smoak, or shadows, and the memory or remembrance of the Author, or Oratour, melts away as oyle, leaving no sign in present life, or else moulders as dust, leaving no Monument to after-posterity, to be known or remembred by; when writeing, or printing, fixes it to everlasting time, to the publick view of the World. (131–2)

Cavendish, then, sees printing, not as transgressive, nor as an improper encroachment by women into the public sphere, but as essentially moral and edifying. Private discourse encourages lying, conniving, flattery, and gossip; it is for this reason that the heroine of *The Publick Wooing* insists on a public courtship. But clearly Sanspareille's chief concern with holding private discourse has to do with her literary efforts, for private discourse encourages plagiarism, covers over literary theft, and keeps her abilities from being recognized. Print, on the other hand, is permanent and ensures not only everlasting fame but her honesty. Cavendish conflates literary honesty with her physical integrity, capitalizing on the contemporary discourse on women that used honesty and chastity interchangeably. Cavendish wants her readers to see publication as a guarantee of her chastity; she reconciles the conflicting claims of fame and honor.[51]

Books are not only monumental; they form the foundation for the small cottage Cavendish modestly claims to be building in the preface to the *Playes.* Even Cavendish's view of oratory is revolutionary; recall Plato's story warning against the dangers of writing: it would degrade men's memories, because they would begin to rely on the written word, rather than their own thoughts.[52] For Cavendish, the spoken word drifts away like smoke; the only way to imprint the memory of words into people's minds is by placing them on the printed page.

Sanspareille's doubts about the lasting effects of oratory do not, however, prevent her from seeing it as another mode of publication. Her fifth goal is to engage in just such public discourse: "I will select times, for several discourses and subjects, to discourse in publick, to several Audiences; to which, you may, if you please, invite the grave and the wise, to hear me, and being a woman Oratour, the singularity will advance my fame the more" (132). Oratory will give Sanspareille the opportunity to convince the invited few of her wit and wisdom, while the fact of her womanhood will only ensure fame (and not notoriety). Sanspareille will exploit her sex (i.e., it will make her singular, or unusual) but she will also in some sense deny it, for she will remain single, unmarried. Her father agrees to all her proposals, pleased that his daughter's lights will not be buried in a husband's arms; instead, she will become a "Trophy," "thy own fames Tomb."

This rejection of the expected female role frees Sanspareille to belong to all men. It is Cavendish's reworking of the Catholic prescription for celibacy. Rather than succumb to the new Protestant ideal of the nuclear family, the little commonwealth, in which the female was sanctified but still not equal to her husband, the head of the household, Cavendish subscribes to the single state. With a twist on Lord Singularity's desire to hold all women in common, Cavendish's Sanspareille will belong to all men. She overcomes the charge of promiscuity by presenting, ironically, a series of public orations. When her intention of speaking is made public, the philosophers complain of her as a "Monster," a "prodigious thing" who dares to read philosophy to them (134). But after her first discourse (on the dangers of privacy and the right of women to speak in an assembly), the philosophers resolve to burn all their books, so eloquent is she; Sanspareille has escaped the fate of Mary Wroth. After a second speech, her listeners abandon the derogatory language of hermaphroditism and transform Sanspareille into "a generosity of Nature" (145). One gentleman even wishes, contrary to all classical precedent, that he could be a woman such as the Lady Sanspareille. The Ovidian metamorphosis is reversed in this woman, as one of the gentlemen exclaims: "Ovid speaks of a Woman, that wisht her self a Man, and the Gods granted her wish, and she became a man; but I never heard of a Man that was changed into a Woman" (145).[53] This truly is a wonder of nature—that one could be improved by being a woman. "She deserves a Statue for her self, as well as a Library for her Works" (163) (which her father does, indeed, build for her).

In her third lecture, Sanspareille engages in an extended exposition likening young minds to a blank book. The ancient metaphor of the tabula rasa is revamped to encompass Cavendish's peculiar adherence to the individual talent. Chapters 1 through 3 of this book, which are "but short," include knowledge, memory, and understanding. But more than half the book is contained in the fourth and fifth chapters, on the conceptions and the imagination. While the first three chapters are written in plain letters, the later ones are "like Hieroglyphiks," awaiting decipherment.[54] Cavendish compensates for the public nature of print by positing a degree of mystery to writing and the talent for writing. She does not have Sanspareille explain how one is to achieve this understanding, except through education; such discourse seems to get purified into a private language available only to good students and wise readers.

Sanspareille's fifth and last oration (after a relatively brief speech before the Queen of Attention in praise of ceremony and good government) places her before her audience dressed "all in white Satin, like as a Bride," with her father and her audience "all Lovers . . . gazing upon her" (158). Here she again refers to the carelessness and negligence with which private words are spoken; only public speech ensures that words do not become meaningless. But the greater part of this oration is devoted again to marriage, which "is a great hinderance to a speculative life" (159). She has made a vow never to marry, since she has heard "that men are hard to please, and apt to change," and her life would be an unhappy one: "Wherefore if I were marryed instead of discoursing of several arguments, I should be groaning and sighing, and weeping, with several pains and vexations; and instead of a silent solitary contemplation, a clamorous quarrelsome conversation; instead of a peaceable life, I should be alwayes in civil warrs; and instead of being happy, I should be miserable" (161). Nothing can convince her to "break the holy Laws, and pull the Virgin Altars down," to blow out the "Vestal Fire of innocency." In place of marital strife, she will harden her heart like adamant "so hard love cannot enter, nor pity nor compassion wound." Sanspareille vows virginity not only to protect her privacy, to nurture the contemplative life and to sustain her independence—she also wishes to shield herself from emotional harm. By refusing to select one suitor, she frees herself from potentially destructive personal attachments and declares her openness to all men: "But howsoever, I connot [*sic*] be wife to you all; wherefore since I cannot be every mans wife, I will dye every mans Maid." (161) Cavendish rewrites the stereotypes of actual writing women here, for her contemporaries allied female publication with sexual openness.[55] Only Sanspareille's ideas will be held in common, and her power over men will be of the intellectual, not the sexual kind.

After a period of time during which Sanspareille defends the wronged, disputes with scholars, and writes a library of books, she becomes mysteriously afflicted with "a fainting of spirits" (166). A deathbed scene confirms the impossibility of her continued life in the world; she belongs, rather, with the saints and angels: "Let spotless Virgins bear me to my grave, and holy Anthems sing before my Herse, and soft-toucht Instruments to play the while, and keep just time with tears, that trickling fall from the sad eyes of my most sorrowful friends; and on my Coffin spread upon a covering of smooth Sattin, white, to signify here how I lived a virgin, pure I lived and dyed; and let my works which I have wrought, and spun out of my brain, be given to times Library, to keep alive my name" (168). She dies, her mournful father's "she is gone, she is gone," reminiscent of Donne's "Anniversaries," written to commemorate, not an actual woman, but "the idea of a woman."[56] (The Donnean echoes recur in her funeral song, in which six virgins sing "Death be not proud.")[57] The death of this unmarried woman seems a necessity; the single life is an impossible ideal in a world in which comic endings are reserved for nuptial celebrations. Father Love, after a passage of near incestuous longing for his dead daughter, also dies. Sanspareille's statue is to be erected at every college and public place in the city, with the queen building a sumptuous tomb to enshrine her. In a reminder of the engraved frontispiece of Cavendish, Sanspareille will be memorialized, her effigy as ubiquitous as the books that Cavendish distributed so liberally to English university libraries and scholars.[58]

Cavendish's appropriation of Catholic imagery enabled her to canonize her heroine. Rather than enclose her in the domesticity of private life (as society and Mother Love expect), Cavendish frees Lady Sanspareille by making her a secular nun—dedicated, not to God, not to romantic love, but to learning and the life of the mind. The impossibility of such a life in the world (as impossible as open Catholicism in seventeenth-century England) is confirmed by Sanspareille's death and that of her weaker double in the play, the Lady Innocence.[59] The Lady Innocence, betrayed by her lover, becomes a solitary "Votary" (153) and is accused unjustly of theft by a rival. She dies by her own hand, fearing oblivion, and lamenting the absence of "Monumental Fame" or a "famous Monument" to commemorate her (171). Innocence in many ways is Sanspareille's twin: she commits herself to solitude and is thirsty for fame. But Lady Innocence retains her vulnerability and her dependence on a traitorous lover. She cannot achieve the independence of spirit, the hard-heartedness, one might say, of Sanspareille. She generates pathos, but not fame, because her vows and her solitude are not productive but remain hidden and private. Innocence has no recourse to the public life of oratory and publication as lived by Lady Sanspareille.[60] Sanspareille, however, does not exist in the "New World" of freedom for women alluded to by her mother (nor in the one created by Cavendish in her utopian novel, *New Blazing World*). But Cavendish does offer an alternative in another play, *Bell in Campo.* There, the female protagonists succeed where Sanspareille could not and manage to reconcile private life with public expectations, personal autonomy with the social requirement to marry.

Bell in Campo

Bell in Campo, the last of Margaret Cavendish's two-part plays in the 1662 edition, offers partly realistic, partly fantastic, answers to the "problem" of publishing women in the seventeenth century. By building upon the character of Affectionata in *Loves Adventures* and refiguring the role of the vowed celibate Lady Sanspareille in *Youths Glory and Deaths Banquet,* Cavendish permits herself to fantasize outside the framework of socially acceptable behavior for women. Her models in this play are Lady Victoria, the wife of the Lord General of the army, and Madam Jantil, the soon-to-be widow of the officer Seigneur Valoroso. The devoted wife and widow free themselves from men and for publication in different ways, each character representing one facet of Margaret Cavendish's own life situation.

A war between the kingdom of Reformation and the kingdom of Faction ignites the action in this play. The Lord General (whose praises are sung in a thinly veiled homage to William Cavendish in the opening scene) requests that his wife, Victoria, stay at home and wait for his return. Victoria resists the role of a Penelope, who "parled and received Amorous Treaties, and made a Truce untill she and her Lovers could agree and conclude upon conditions, and questionless there were Amorous Glances shot from loving Eyes of either party; and though the Siege of her Chastity held out, yet her Husbands Wealth and Estate were impoverished, and great Riots committed both in his Family and Kingdome, and her Suters had absolute power thereof; thus though she kept the fort of her Chastity, she lost the Kingdome, which was her Husbands Estate and Government" (581). Victoria will go Penelope, the classical emblem of the chaste wife, one better: she will preserve not only her chastity but her husband's estate as well. Victoria regards Penelope's faithfulness to Ulysses as an empty gesture, even doubtful, since she did not guard her husband's property as well as her virtue.

The Lord General permits his wife to accompany him, but not without facing criticism from his men. The lady erases the army dilemma raised by camp followers in a typically Cavendishean way: she becomes a general herself and forms her own regiment of women. Like the younger Affectionata, Victoria calls her fellow "Noble Heroickesses" to arms with passionate eloquence. She urges them to cast aside the erroneous opinion that women are weak and fearful; custom, not nature, is the cause of their inferior status. As Victoria points out to her followers: "Had our education been answerable to theirs, we might have proved as good Souldiers and Privy Counsellers, Rulers and Commanders, Navigators and Architectors, and as learned Sholars both in Arts and Sciences, as men are; for Time and Custome is the Father and Mother of Strength and Knowledge, they make all things easy and facil, clear and propitious" (588). It is not women's nature but time and custom that keep women out of the public sphere. A change in custom, participation in the world of men, will make women fit to be "Copartners in their governments" (588) and justify Cavendish's own forays into the male-dominated world of print.

Victoria's company of women is governed, not only by her charisma, but by a table of rules and laws. There is a ritual reading of these fifteen laws, most of which deal with military discipline. But two of the regulations have a social, rather than a military, object. When the army marches, the female soldiers are to sing of "the heroical actions done in former times by heroical women" (592). As she did with the mythical Penelope, Cavendish repeats with a difference Virgil's "Arma virumque cano." The epic poet becomes a poetess, and the subject henceforth will be the glorious deeds of women; she will write "like a man" but choose subjects that enhance the fame and honor of women.

Their rules also require "that none of this Effeminate Army admits of the Company of man, whilst they are in Arms or Warlike actions, not so much as to exchange words, without the Generalless her leave or privilege" (593). Victoria's army, though "Effeminate," is masculine in its action, and must maintain its independence from men. Victoria enforces this rule to protect her women from men, who exercise their authority with language, either seducing with "flattering words, and pleasing and subtil insinuations," or frightening women into a "slavish obedience." While the female army appropriates the glorious diction and the heroic activity of male singer/poets, it must also guard against men's words, which conjure women to obey. The women's physical separation from men serves to reinforce this spiritual and psychological independence (and not incidentally, their reliance on their leader, the Generalless Victoria).[61]

Women join Victoria's regiment for a variety of reasons: "either out of private and home discontents, for honour and fame, or for love of change, and as it were a new course of life" (594). In a blunt attack on bourgeois women, Cavendish places these rumors in the mouths of the citizens' wives who hear of Lady Victoria's exploits and willfully misconstrue her mission: "They say she hath brought Articles for all women to have as many Husbands as they will, and all Trades-mens Wives shall have as many Apprentices as they will" (630). Cavendish makes clear that women who join armies (or, by extension, write and publish books) are not made free for sexual license but for personal autonomy and virtue. Every example of a "public woman" in Cavendish's dramas is a wise and virtuous woman, and every case reinforces her notion that writing women can do just as well or better than men in the literary world. Like virtuous men, Cavendish's women enter public life in order to participate in good government, either in the Commonwealth or in their little commonwealth, the household.

Victoria issues a series of pronouncements making women mistresses of their own households and giving them the right to wear what they will and to go where they will, and especially, to "be of their Husbands Counsel" (631). The kind of joint governance depicted by Victoria is something of an anomaly, even in the ideal world of Cavendish's play. Cavendish's frequent satirical comments on married women and the fulsome praises of her husband in her prefaces and biography have puzzled critics who view Cavendish as a protofeminist. But Cavendish believed Victoria's case (like her own) was unusual: both were superwomen. In compensation, Cavendish offers another model of the moral life for ordinary women, in the character of the Lady Jantil.

Jantil, like Penelope, stays at home during the wars. Even though she does not aspire to Victoria's ambitions, Cavendish permits her to share in Victoria's fame after her husband is killed. She lets go all her servants, sells her earthly goods, and orders the construction of a marble tomb in honor of her husband. Her instructions are extremely detailed; they are a verbal construction of a monument—the one so carefully disclaimed (yet embraced) by Cavendish in the general prologue to the book. Jantil, if she does not build herself, at least offers herself as a patron of those who do build and write. She resolves to live in this newly constructed tomb, which will become her cloister: "From this House which shall be my living Tomb, to the Tomb of my dead Husband, I would have a Cloyster built . . . and this Cloyster I would have all the sides thereof hung with my Husbands Pictures drawn to the life by the best Painters, and all the several accidents, studies and exercise of his life; thus will I have the story of his life drawn to the life" (600). To supplement the visual picture, she commissions a life of her husband, to serve as "Registers of memory" (601) during her future life of contemplation and seclusion. Jantil's actions anticipate Cavendish's own, from the publication of *Nature's Pictures* (1656) to the composition of her life of William Cavendish (1667). Jantil's hidden life is for Cavendish the proper response to a husband's death. Having fulfilled the social imperative that women marry, Jantil can now aspire to a kind of sanctity and spiritual integrity in her secular cloister. Cavendish makes Jantil the chaste widow, devoted to her husband's memory, and yet permits her to share in Victoria's public activities in quite a different manner. Jantil becomes associated with writing, reading, and contemplation (as does Lady Contemplation in the play of the same title):

> My Tongue like as a pen shall write his name,
> My words as letters to divulge his fame;
> My life like to an Arch over his Ashes bend,
> And my desires to his grave descend; (602)

In a quasi-religious ceremony, Jantil cuts her hair, exchanges her rich garments for a white silk dress and black veil, and vows herself to a life of contemplation. Her time is spent reading and praying until she begins to sicken and die. Her will bequeaths her husband's library to his old college and provides for the foundation of a religious order to maintain his tomb. Moreover, she wills her maid a thousand pounds to live a single life. Cavendish's overt use of Catholic imagery might have been troublesome for her in an era in which the suspicion of papist leanings continued to be strong, but it accomplishes several things: it reaffirms the connection of Catholicism with the works of the imagination (as we saw in Southwell's *Short Rules of a Good Life* [1595]); it flouts conventional religious and political wisdom, as both the Cavendishes did in their personal lives; and it capitalizes on the Catholic emphasis on bodily virginity to rewrite the role of chastity in women's lives. Chastity becomes reservation of the self, not just for a husband, but for oneself.

Jantil can only be a patroness, building tombs and libraries and convents, but Victoria will play no secondary role. Victoria's temporary virginity frees her to lead her troops, win the war, and inspire great poetry. The end result of Victoria's virginity is not death, as it was for Sanspareille, but everlasting fame. The Lord General does not appear in part 2 of the play, and though the play ends with a comment by one of the gentlemen on how proud the general is of his wife, the glory is hers alone. Victoria, the woman who leads armies, is also honored for her writing, as the king himself licenses the publication of her literary works:

> First, All Poets shall strive to set forth your praise.
>
> Secondly, That all your gallant acts shall be recorded in story, and put in the chief Library of the Kingdome.
>
> Thirdly, That your Arms you fought in, shall be set in the Kings Armory.
>
> Fourthly, That you shall alwayes wear a Laurel Garland.
>
> . . .
>
> Seventhly and lastly, Your figure shall be cast in Brass, and then set in the midst of the City armed as it was in the day of Battel. (632)

Victoria not only becomes the object of poetic praise but wears the laurel garland (the symbol both of victors and of poets) herself. Better than Lady Jantil's monument to her husband, Victoria's statue stands in memory of her own accomplishments. Victoria, the woman who succeeds in the public sphere, is Cavendish's ideal; Jantil, the virtuous and faithful wife who lives in secret, is the model for most real women.

In the plays of 1662, Margaret Cavendish offers a range of female characters who attempt to reconcile virtue, chastity, and the ideals of the private, contemplative life with her personal desire for fame and the recognition of her literary efforts. Cavendish challenges the reader to create her own vision of the successful writing woman from among the multitude of characters she creates. Royalist and conservative though her sensibilities were, she recognized that her contemporaries held a very narrow view of women's roles. Since Cavendish felt graced by her own talent and the attentions of an indulgent husband, she offered her readers utopian as well as more realistic pictures of women's lives. Cavendish structured her apology for her own writing by focusing on two complementary contemporary issues: the development of the private self, with its dangerous potential for anarchy and the destruction of societal norms, and the proper function of publication, especially by women.

Cavendish isolates two aspects of privacy, and her ability to distinguish the two is what also gives her the wherewithal to detach the private self from its gendered constructions. Privacy, in its most positive form, permits the development of an independent self, nourishes creativity, provides the ground and the philosophical underpinning for actions in the public interest. The public acts that follow from the properly lived private life advertise its goodness. In Cavendish's time, access to privacy of this sort was restricted to men, as was the opportunity to present its results to the world; publication of any sort was a male prerogative. The second type of privacy is associated for Cavendish with self-interest, unhealthy ambition, treason, and deceit. Both men and women are all too prone to these qualities, and so the avoidance of selfish private interests is what leads Cavendish to propound the necessity of publication, of revelation for both men and women.

However, constrained by social expectations, Cavendish's female characters are not always permitted to cultivate a private self. The marital imperative destroys the autonomy of women; the challenge for women, then, is to maintain an intellectual and spiritual integrity that Cavendish figures as bodily virginity or, possibly, as chastity within marriage. The choice for the single life by the Lady Orphant and Lady Sanspareille and the decision not to remarry by Lady Jantil are actually expressions of independence, of the need to cultivate an inner self independent of men in order to act as freely as men. As if recognizing the impossibilities of an academic and public life for women, Lady Sanspareille has to die; Cavendish knows she is only the "idea of a woman." In the comic mode of *Loves Adventures,* Lady Orphant accedes to marriage, giving up the glories of military life. But she retains at least one of Cavendish's desiderata: she is blessed with a husband who both worships her and is also a brother-at-arms. Cavendish seems to reward the widowed Lady Jantil both for her virtue and for having fulfilled society's expectations. Faithful wife that she is, she is freed for the pleasures of the cloister, where she can read, write, pray, and patronize other authors. Her proven virtue is bedrock for the monument she builds to her husband, whose memorial she builds and writes. The Lady Generalless Victoria, impossible a model as she is, appears to have everything that Cavendish desires for women: an understanding and noble husband, a self-directed life, success in a man's world, and recognition for her exploits in battle and her skill with the pen.

The only one of Cavendish's characters who manages to stay alive without making the "sacrifice" of marriage is the larger-than-life Grand Esprit, in *Natures Three Daughters.* As her name indicates, she is a nearly mythical figure, the patron saint of aspiring women writers. While most women become "Martyrs for the good cause of the Common-wealth," Grand Esprit, rather, is "resolved for my part to live a single life, associating my self with my own Thoughts, marrying my self to my own Contemplations, which I hope to conceive and bring forth a Child of Fame, that may live to posterity, and to keep a-live my Memory" (525).

Denied an entrée into the elite and private world of male intellectual life, Cavendish cultivates her own spiritual privacy—and offers her female characters as visionary examples of women speaking out, writing, leading armies. A privacy that remains centered on the self, Cavendish seems to say, is both deadening and dangerous to men and women and destructive of the society in which they live. The salutary effects of privacy, with its modern emphasis on the cultivation of an independent and integrated self and the mental world of the imagination, can only be verified by public display. For Cavendish, publication is the only true sign of virtue. The writer's cloistered existence, her private life, can only be justified by the printed book, the verbal monument to the author's fame.

5

Discovery, Pornography, and the Novel: Aphra Behn's *Love-Letters Between a Nobleman and His Sister*

BY THE TIME Aphra Behn published her *Love-Letters Between a Nobleman and His Sister* (1684–87), seventeenth-century authors, publishers, and readers were well aware of the power of the printed word to reveal the truth, to discover new facts and whole new lands.[1] The Bible and the flood of other religious writings published during this period were regarded not only as tools for personal self-examination and self-discovery but also a way for the righteous to overcome their political and religious enemies. Printed pamphlets could reveal the weaknesses of kings, as we have seen in the publication of the letters of Charles I, or they could awaken the reader to a spiritual renewal, as in the conversion narratives published in the last two-thirds of the century. From Samuel Harsnett's *Declaration of Egregious Popish Impostures* (1603) to *The Triall of the Protestant Private Spirit* (1630) to the *Eikon Basilike* (1649) and Milton's response, *Eikonoklastes* (1649), authors' and readers' roles were established and clear-cut, and books had a decidedly moral mission: authors were to uncover the truth, readers were to decipher it. In seeking to overcome the "stigma of print," authors insisted on the honorableness, truthfulness, and worthiness of their work. This was important at first only for the literary amateur, who hesitated to write for monetary gain, but it became an even more urgent need for women authors, as is evident with Margaret Cavendish. We have also seen that increased opportunities for literacy and the emphasis by religious leaders on the development of a personal spirituality created, quite unexpectedly, a greater sense of personal autonomy and a greater acceptance of individual, rather than official, interpretations of texts.

The popular conversion narrative showed the book's moral and reforming functions keeping uneasy company with what it sought to erase as the book became both seductive and entertaining.

Aphra Behn's book is a novel, new in form and function, because it invites reading as sheer entertainment. At the same time it participates in the older tradition of the conversion narrative, with all the weight of teaching authority which that genre implies. Behn herself is a new type of author—a woman who writes for pay—but she writes anonymously, and the narrator of her story is strangely nonintrusive. Her novel is a particularly good example of a text that has been bypassed as seminal, or originary, or original; until recently, the supposedly more moral fictions of Fielding, Richardson, and Defoe have been the prime candidates for the first English novel, as Watt's influential study reminds us. *Love-Letters,* which participates in both older didactic forms and in the newly emerging genres of the novel and pornographic and erotic fiction, challenges the reader to read it and its author's intentions correctly. My own first reading of the book illustrates that readers can read it superficially: I saw it as a precocious example of the modern erotic novel, and little else. One may judge a literary work on its outward apparatus, just as one may judge a person on the basis of dress, or family, or educational attainment. Behn shows that authors, rather than being standard-bearers for truth and virtue, can tease and titillate the reader, offer facts or withdraw them, dissemble despite the seemingly sincere revelations of a first-person narrator. In short, books and authors can act quite like people; they may clarify or obfuscate, reveal or conceal. *Love-Letters* is important because it describes in fictional form the implications of a divided public and private self. It demonstrates the essential unknowability of the person.

Behn demonstrates the actuality of this split between the public and private self in two ways: first of all, through thematic adaptations of the traditional conversion narrative, but especially those narratives that focus on the fallen female; and secondly, through her use of the female voice to trade upon and question the authority of the typically male narrator/author of the earlier forms of these narratives. In Behn's rewriting of the prototypical fallen woman, Mary Magdalen, she opens herself up to the charge of writing pornography, of writing to excite the reader. As I hope to demonstrate, however, earlier treatments of the Magdalen story, as well as an early epistolary work, Thomas Cranley's *Amanda: Or, The Reformed Whore* (1635), establish a context for Behn's *Love-Letters* and are not entirely innocent of these same charges. The two earlier works focus on the female sinner; their male authors or narrators traffic in female virtue; they portray the female as reading or written upon, the male as active author or agent of conversion. In Cranley's work, the author's voyeurism is apparent despite his professions of concern for the woman's virtue; the author relishes his words as he does the sight and thought of his Amanda. Behn's work manages to question the sincerity and moral purity of the earlier works by replacing the male narrator with a female one, by putting the pen in the hand of the female sinner. By making the new voyeur a woman rather than a man, Behn forces the reader to examine his or her own reading of those earlier texts in light of her own; the precariousness of her own role as a woman author,[2] one who sells her work (and thus, in a sense, herself) to the public, asks the reader to reconsider the ostensibly moral aims of those earlier works of "pornography," a term I shall use most literally (and ambiguously and without quotation marks) to mean "writing of harlots."[3] Behn's narrative is complicated by layers of secrecy, by the invisibility of the author and the hiddenness of the narrator/editor. Discovering what lies underneath these literary layers of clothing should help us determine the purpose of Behn's novel, help us decide whether it is pornography just because it tells the story of a "fallen woman" or whether it is instead more moral than its predecessors in the conversion tale and its successors in the canonical, male-authored novel.

Since secrecy and sex are implicated in the reading and writing of pornography, I would like to revisit two notions about privacy I proposed for the reader's consideration in the introduction to this study, for they are central concerns in Behn's novel. Of particular importance here is the idea that private places are conducive to a sense of privacy, that reading (and writing) in private help create a sense of the self that may differ from the individual's public presentation of himself or herself. I have also suggested that secrecy, concealment, and authorial self-disclosure modify both the nature of the author's revelations and the reader's judgment of the author and narrator. In the following discussion, I will focus on the way in which Behn's use of the trope of reading and writing presumes a new sophistication on the part of both author and reader, as she plays with the characters' self-revelations to highlight their (and the reader's) essential hypocrisy. The difficulty with discerning Behn's true intent is that she, more than her literary ancestors, shifts the burden of moral choice to the reader. Rather than assume the role of moral teacher, Behn leaves her readers free to form their own judgments, to read *Love-Letters* either as entertainment or as a cautionary tale, a vehicle for enjoyment or for moral reckoning. The reader, not the author, must derive the lesson from the story, if indeed there is one. Like the believer freed from the ministrations of a priest by her devotional reading, Behn's readers are freed from the guidance of the all-knowing, dogmatic author.[4]

The Pornographic Tradition

The novel began to reach maturity at about the same time as modern pornography became easily accessible in print.[5] Both genres had to be read in secret; both were regarded as especially harmful to the sensitive or naive reader.[6] Silvia, the central female character in *Love-Letters,* violates social, moral, and literary norms: she is not only the traditional object of erotic discourse but also a pornographer herself, a recorder of her own sexual activity.[7] Silvia acts very like the female heroines of early pornographic books: their bodies and their narratives both have the ability to arouse; they empower themselves (and the newly emerging genre of the novel) even as they manipulate the literary marketplace.[8] It may be that, just as the erotic works of the French philosophes were both pornography and philosophy-political science,[9] Behn's novel can arouse both mind and body, can be both moral and sensual at the same time. Jean Marie Goulemot has said that erotic literature is "univocal, produces one meaning and is hostile to any attempt at interference or blurring."[10] Readers of didactic fiction and pornography have this in common: they insist that all literature reflect such clarity of purpose. *Love-Letters* resists easy assignment to one category; the remainder of this chapter will attempt to disentangle Behn's presentation of herself from her presentation of her narrator and her central female character.

Erotic fiction, and *Love-Letters* in particular, can trace its roots to religious narratives of fallen women. By reversing the trajectory of sin and repentance, Behn has created an inverted conversion narrative, one in which the heroine chooses sin rather than grace. Rather than electing the certainty of the virtuous life, with its clearly defined moral prescriptions, Behn's female protagonist prefers to rely on her own wit and charm. While the profit for the conversion narrative's heroine is spiritual, Behn's central character, Silvia, comes to see her body as her chief capital.[11] She is an example of what Kathryn Norberg calls the "libertine whore," the opposite of the "virtuous courtesan" who forms the ideal convert in the male-authored narratives I shall discuss. Though Silvia comes from a well-born family, she comes to fit the mold of the libertine whore, who "is independent, sensual, sensible and skilled. She is healthy and possessed of a very healthy—that is, normal—sexual appetite. She is a businesswoman and an artist who provides 'varied' sex for men who can afford it. She is a courtesan who lives in luxury and abides by 'philosophy,' usually materialist philosophy. Intelligent, independent, proud and reasonable, she is *not* diseased or monstrous; she is not humiliated or victimized either by life or by her clients."[12] Silvia suffers neither emotionally nor socially for her moral trespasses; by the end of the novel, it is clear that she has quite successfully established herself as a demimondaine of the English upper classes.

Even as the erotic narrative rejects the traditional outcomes of the conversion narrative, it shares a common characteristic of that genre, for both portray female protagonists enmeshed in books and reading, which reading creates and fortifies an inner, independent self. Whether these narratives are instruments of conversion or of sin, the female subject is central to the plot. Indeed, claims Debora Shuger, early modern eroticism and spirituality are closely linked and are implicated in the "discursive formation of inwardness as erotic, abandoned, and female."[13] Both types of story privilege private matters, the affairs of the soul or the heart. While the conversion narrative and the erotic novel appear to veer off into two different directions, they have common roots, in the story of the reformed sinner Mary Magdalen. I begin my discussion of the history of pornography with a familiar story from the Gospel of John, that of the woman taken in adultery:

> And the scribes and Pharisees brought unto him a woman taken in adultery; and when they had set her in the midst, They say unto him, Master, this woman was taken in adultery, in the very act. Now Moses in the law commanded us, that such should be stoned: but what sayest thou? This they said, tempting him, that they might have to accuse him. But Jesus stooped down, and with *his* finger wrote on the ground, *as though he heard them not.* So when they continued asking him, he lifted up himself, and said unto them, He that is without sin among you, let him first cast a stone at her. And again he stooped down, and wrote on the ground. And when they which heard *it,* being convicted by *their own* conscience, went out one by one, beginning at the eldest, *even* unto the last: and Jesus was left alone, and the woman standing in the midst. When Jesus had lifted up himself, and saw none but the woman, he said unto her, Woman, where are those thine accusers? hath no man condemned thee? She said, No man, Lord. And Jesus said unto her, Neither do I condemn thee: go, and sin no more. (John 8:3–11)

This is the forerunner of and pattern for all woman-centered conversion narratives. The Gospel passage is traditionally interpreted as a caution against falling into the trap of hypocrisy, as the Pharisees had done, or as Christ's abandonment of the old law of punishment and retribution for the new dispensation of love and forgiveness.[14] But there are other aspects of the story I would like to highlight because they determine the nature of most fictional treatments of women for the next nineteen centuries and because Behn is one of the few authors to depart from this tradition. Note that the readers and writers in this narrative are all men: from the Pharisees reading the law, attempting to engage Jesus in a mock debate, to Jesus writing in the dirt, to the evangelist John narrating the whole. The men's private sins are never revealed or written out; they are not publicly humiliated—they need deal only with the prickings of their own consciences.[15] The woman (often, quite wrongly, conflated with the sinner Mary Magdalen) is forgiven for her now quite unsecret sin.[16] The public nature of the woman's adultery earns her public forgiveness, and she, rather than the equally sinning men, becomes the heroine of the story. Public exposure of her private guilt and a rather submissive, self-effacing attitude won her the approval of generations of readers and preachers. (The woman's only words are, perhaps tellingly, "No man, Lord.") Though she has sinned, she is drawn back into the fold; she (unlike her absent male partner in sin) has satisfied the prurient curiosity of the elders and has provided a model for proper female repentance.[17]

Despite her salvation by the written words of Christ, this Magdalen was almost certainly illiterate. The Renaissance hagiographical tradition on Mary Magdalen, however, eventually remedied that defect, thus providing even more opportunities to exploit the image of the penitent prostitute in the age of print. Lancelot Andrewes, in an Easter sermon delivered in 1620, takes as his text the meeting of Mary and Jesus in the garden after the Resurrection.[18] He identifies Mary first of all as "the name of a woman," "*Mary Magdalen,* of a sinfull woman," and links her with Eve, another woman in another garden. The fate of these two women proves that "no infirmity of sex" and "no enormitie of sin" can prevent his listeners from sharing in the resurrection.[19] Andrewes concludes his sermon by contrasting Christ's appearance to Mary and to the disciples at Emmaus. He "Came to be knowen to her by His voice, by the word of His mouth." Her vision is a promise to his congregation that Christ will "vouchsafe every one of us as Hee did *Marie Magdalen* in the Text, to *know him and the vertue of His Resurrection;* and make us partakers of both" (216). In Andrewes's interpretation of the events on Easter morn, Mary is not only a hearer of the word but becomes associated with the "Text," while the "breaking of the bread" at Emmaus becomes an emblem for the Eucharist, the sacramental liturgy. The Catholic saint is rehabilitated for the Protestant reader of Scripture by being connected with word rather than sacrament. And, as in the passage from John, the fallen woman is the guarantee of everyone's salvation. The story of the Magdalen's conversion is security for the rest of the world's sinners, for those whose sins remain secret. Wendy Wall, in her analysis of male authorship of female complaint poetry, relates this concern about private falls to the fact of publication:

> When poets become preoccupied with telling, rumor, slander, and fame in these complaint texts, they give voice to the anxieties surrounding public writing. The complaining woman's status as a tainted and sexually polluted *woman* is crucial for this displacement. For these figures absorb and re-present the shame of publication by translating it into terms to which the male writers could not be equally vulnerable. The woman acts as the "other" from which the author promotes his own fame by publicly reporting her private shame, a peculiar type of violation that a man could not suffer in the same way: the loss of chastity.[20]

The body and psyche of the fallen, abandoned woman are not only connected with texts; they are the site to which authorial anxiety and guilt are transferred. Part of readers' uneasiness with Behn's *Love-Letters* may stem from the fact that the central female character prefers the role of antiheroine rather than submissive and sorrowing heroine. Silvia is not converted, hardly even seems cognizant of her own guilt, and would surely reject the burden of anyone else's sin. Just as Behn tests traditional conceptions of the public woman in her role as author, Silvia, her Mary Magdalen figure, declines the role of conventional penitent.

An examination of the iconography of Mary Magdalen also reveals some interesting details about Renaissance views of her role and symbolism. Early writers on Magdalen had merged several different Mary figures: the adulterous woman (John 8:3–11); the woman who wept and anointed the feet of Jesus (Luke 7:37–50; John 12:1–8); Mary, the sister of Martha (Luke 10:38–42); the Mary at the foot of the cross; and even the early Christian saint, Mary of Egypt. An elaborate set of stories arose concerning her exploits after the death of Christ, including missionary work and sermonizing in France and life as an anchorite in the desert. Her iconographical traits were most usually long (red) hair and the pot of holy oils with which she had anointed Christ.[21] During the sixteenth and seventeenth centuries, however, Mary Magdalen began to be depicted with books—either as a devout and attentive reader or as a voluptuous penitent in ecstasy over a book. Examples of the former include *Mary Magdalen reading* (c. 1520–40) by the Master of the Female Half-Lengths; *The Magdalen* (15th cent.) and *Mary Magdalen reading in a Landscape* (c. 1522), both by Correggio; and, in a late example, *Miss Catherine Voss as Mary Magdalen* (1705). A less restrained saint is to be found in works such as Marcantonio Bellavia's engraving *Mary Magdalen contemplating a crucifix* (17th cent.), Orazio Gentileschi's *The Penitent Magdalen* (c. 1625–28) (painted for Charles I), and Elisabetta Sirani's *Mary Magdalen scourging herself* (1663).[22] The paintings and etchings reveal two models for reading, each linked to the literary genres I have been discussing. The first type of Magdalen is self-contained, eyes on the book, apparently unaware of the observer, and almost always fully clothed. Her reading is inner-directed, involving a proper self-contemplation. The other Magdalens, however, look keenly aware of bodies—theirs or someone else's. Bellavia's is bent over a crucifix; Sirani's is flagellating herself; Gentileschi's is leaning on an elephant folio and gazing up into what might be the heavens or simply her own personal visions. The first Magdalen is nothing but a demure seventeenth-century girl; the second is dangerous, masochistic, erotic. Despite the different portrayals of the reading Magdalen, the shift in iconographic depiction marks a new sort of fallen woman. Magdalen becomes associated, not with overt acts of piety, but with reading and writing, with the inner actions of the soul.

Amanda: Or, The Reformed Whore

One example of the transfer of the myth of the Magdalen to seventeenth-century fiction is Thomas Cranley's *Amanda: Or, The Reformed Whore.* I offer it as a counterpoint to Behn's *Love-Letters* and as a transitional work between the Gospel narrative and Behn's own more honest appraisal of the sincerity of the author/narrator. Cranley's voice is the moral center of the narrative; he relies on the reader's willingness to accept the author's pronouncements on Amanda at face value and to disregard his own possibly base motives, which are hinted at throughout the narrative. *Amanda* is an old-fashioned story, not just because it derives from the earlier traditions of female fallenness, but because it carefully controls the reader's access to both the female subject's and male agent's inner selves. It depends on an old-fashioned kind of reading, in which the reader can depend upon characters and authors to act in the same way as they speak, to speak as they presumably would think. The story is not only a statement on sexual morality but a proclamation of authorial rectitude and authorial control. Even the reading that occurs within the text attempts to serve public ends, not private desires.

Thomas Cranley's little work participates in several generic categories. It is prison literature, composed, as its title page proclaims, "in the Kingsbench"; its form is epistolary and poetic, consisting primarily of verse letters between the prisoner and Amanda; and it persuades toward conversion, both in the narrator's long diatribe against whores and prostitution and in Amanda's final repentant response. *Amanda* might even be termed hagiography, since Amanda, the one who must be loved, is herself saved (and safely dead) by the end of the story.

Amanda insists upon the force of the printed word, from its perplexed dedication through its closing verses. Cranley is sharply aware of his readers—of their tastes in literature, of their social and financial status, and even of the potential effects of reading upon them. In his dedication to "his worthy friends, and Brother in law, Thomas Gildovene,"[23] Cranley explains that he had originally intended to dedicate his book to a gentleman who was "an especiall favourer of the *Muses.*" But, having no acquaintance with the man, and keenly aware that his writing might be misunderstood by a stranger, he has decided to dedicate it to a man whom he knows and to whom he has "a conjugall affinity." In imitation of classical practice,[24] Cranley addresses his book in "The Author to his Booke":

> Goe little Booke, the issue of my braine.
> Begot in bondage, now at last made free:
> To keepe thee still in prison, 'twere in vain.
> Make triall how the world will favour thee,
> If none receive thee turne againe to me. (sig. A3r)

The author contrasts the freedom of his text (able to go and return if it wishes) with his own confinement. From the imaginative space that is his "braine," the book has the potential to travel the world, to many different readers. (Given Cranley's situation, he may be as envious of Amanda as of his book for their shared ability to go about at will.) Cranley considers his possible audience: the "Criticke," Momus, and Zoilus,[25] and rejects all these for readers who will respect the book's "unlearned plainesse":

> Chiefly, I send thee to the female sexe,
> Whom I doe truely honour, and regard:
> Thy ready service shall attend their becks,
> Without expecting profit, or reward:
> Oh that some one, would take thee to their guard. (sig. A3r)

Though Cranley claims his "lines are not didacticall," his directives to the book tell otherwise:

> In thy first interprize, thou conquered'st one,
> And drag'd her by force out of the mire.
> Let that encourage thee, and suffer none
> To shun thy strong encounter, till thou try her,
> Boldly goe on, and neither faint nor tyre.
> God knowes, so happy the successe may be,
> To one resisting, thou mayst conquer three. (sig. A3v)

There are several rather disturbing aspects to Cranley's address, and they will reappear in the text proper. The "Criticke," Momus, and Zoilus are unsuitable readers—they will "carpe" at his work; the book will have a safer journey if it avoids their wrangling in its travels and if it needn't compete for literary profit or reward, for Cranley is simply not up to the literary battle. Female readers, on the other hand, are suited to submission to the text, not critical reading; they will succumb to his words' "masculine perswasive force."[26] Note the license Cranley gives his book to conquer, to "force," to "try" its female readers. Cranley's book has already proved its effectiveness with one reader, the Amanda whose name graces the title page. While Cranley will describe himself as the savior of the lost Amanda, spying, coercion, and emotional browbeating, rather than the gentle force of words, are his tools.

The text proper opens with a declaration of property, the title *Cranleys Amanda. Or, The Reformed Whore.* The author explains that, to while away the time in Fleet prison, he spent his time walking.[27] One day, he "espied" a "young Gentlewoman" in one of the houses nearby and could "easily discerne her, without being seene my selfe" (sig. B1r–B1v). On a later walk, he "darkly perceive[s] through the Glasse" the same woman but cannot tell what she is so busy about. At first, he wonders that such a lady should dwell in a neighborhood filled with prisoners, but eventually learns that "she was a woman apt to give entertainement to any that desired her company, by reason whereof her honesty was much suspected, and the generall report about the street was, that she was no better then a whore" (sig. B1v–B2r). In order to prove or disprove this rumor, he continues to observe her and finally decides to write to her. The motives for Cranley's interest are ambiguous, though his scrutiny of her activities is troubling, and there is a hint of jealousy when he mentions the gentlemen who "had free accesse to her chamber" (sig. B2r). While prisoners in the Fleet were relatively free to come and go during this period, the contrast between Cranley's own condition and the free lifestyle of the young woman is apparent.

In order to make her acquaintance without giving her to understand that he was "one of the assaylants of her love" (sig. B2v), the narrator Cranley (there is no clear division between author and narrator) writes a letter of introduction in verse. He tries to assure her that his writing will do no harm to her:

> Let it vanish as a vapor,
> Tis but naked Inke, and Paper . . .
> When I first did write, my pen
> Fearing your displeasure fainted, (sig. B2v)

He presents his writing implements as powerless, naked, and fainting, even impotent—no threat of masculine force here, he seems to be saying. He hopes to become her acquaintance and, in a most telling phrase, her "debter" (sig. B3r) (perhaps a paying customer, whose "fainting pen" will be restored by her?). If they should meet, he promises "Riddles to content yee, / Purposes, and Sonnets plenty," "tales of Kings / And of Noble Princes loves" (sig. B3v). He urges her to write back, to make him "reader of [her] writing" (sig. B4r). The metaphors of reading and writing, of storytelling and listening, are fraught with the idea of amorous and financial exchange and an unequal distribution of resources. Though he has his pen, he is nonetheless a prisoner; the woman Amanda has the power to accept or reject his suit, whose thrust the narrator (though not Amanda) seems quite vague about. And she does reject it, in anger, when a friend of Cranley's delivers the letter to her. Cranley, convinced that "women are not alwayes angry when they seeme so to be" (sig. C1v), writes her another, which he delivers secretly "with the helpe of a long Pole" which he has in his chamber. Receiving no immediate reply, he continues to watch her in her rooms, where she spends much of her time embroidering. Determined to know "of what coyne she was stamped, whether Gold or Copper," he resolves to "use the best art, and skill I could, to have her cast in a new mould, and to purge the drosse out of her, that she might be refyned to purer mettall" (sig. C3v–C4r). The economic resonances are obvious, as are the scriptural echoes,[28] but the reference to the stamping of coins also connects Amanda with the press. The first printers and typefounders were also goldsmiths;[29] Amanda is the metal or paper awaiting impression, not only the reader of the texts issuing from Cranley's pen, but also a potential text herself, matter for publication.

Cranley is finally bold enough to speak to her through the casement window; she accepts his advances, and invites him to her room. She is convinced she will "take great delight" in reading his work, and he is overjoyed at the "opportunity to conferre privately with her at her chamber" (sig. C4v–D1r). They begin a series of regular visits, during which they read "idle pamphlets" and have "conference together." Cranley perceives that "a little siege would batter the fortresse of her honesty" (sig. D1r) and notes that she is poor and without friends or family; even a few words will have the power to seduce her. When Amanda moves away, she makes him promise to visit her at her new lodgings. When Cranley fulfills his promise, he discovers she is at dinner with some other men, and arranges to spy on her from a secret place in her lodgings. Despite his dismay at her conduct, he stays to "see the conclusion" and follows them out of the tavern until she returns home with one of the men. Cranley, in his supposed efforts to reform Amanda, has instead become a kind of secret policeman, a voyeur—an author. A man who is imprisoned, who writes veiled love letters and delivers them secretly, who holds private conference with a woman commonly known to be a whore, objects to the public behavior of this woman he obviously desires. The writer links his own virtue with privacy and secrecy, and her self-presentation in the public tavern with immorality. Further, he sees no incongruity between his judgments of this woman's virtue and his surveillance activities. It is just this sort of hypocrisy that Behn's work will do away with.

Deciding to take "some paines for her conversion," the narrator composes a poem of 190 stanzas and makes them up in "a little booke." This variation on the commonplace book, in which one could record private prayers and meditations on one's spiritual reading, will become the agent of Amanda's reformation. As in the conversion narratives examined in a previous chapter, the written word will lead to the conversion. Writing in rime royal, the form used frequently for the complaint poetry of abandoned women,[30] Cranley admits he has invaded Amanda's life:

For know (Amanda) to thy griefe, even I
Have pri'd into thy secret passages,
And I have observed with a watchfull eye
Such as to thee come with Embassages,
And understood their private messages. (sig. D3v)

Cranley's admission combines the tropes of seeing and watching, reading and writing, and confirms the sexual force of his acts of writing. His political helplessness is confirmed as well, as he conscripts his eyes to spy on the powerful woman who welcomes other "ambassadors" to her "court." Cranley intends to use the verse letter to vanquish this woman. He claims that all his earlier invitations were a trap, a test of her virtue, but inadvertently lets the reader know that they were really sexual propositions:

Did not I tempt thee minding for to try,
And found the depth of thy too loose condition?
Remember well, didst thou not answer I?
When as that answer strooke in me contrition,
Sorry to see so ready a submission;
 And no repulse at all, but giving fire
 Vnto the fuell of a hot desire. (sig. E1r)

The seat of this "hot desire" is still ambiguous—is it his or hers? But Cranley goes on to warn Amanda of the unhappy fate that awaits her should she continue down this path. (Throughout, Cranley's writing blurs the distinction between seduction and conversion, but he clearly expects the common reader to trust in his implied professions of virtue.) He first catalogs the difference between her outward appearance and her soul by invading her bedroom. He describes her jewels, the bedroom with its fair hangings, the cosmetics locked in a cabinet, and the clothes and wigs with which she disguises her real self (sig. E3v–E4v). Part of her faults derive from her reading, which is strikingly similar to Cranley's own taste for pamphlets and romances:

And then a heape of bookes of thy devotion
Lying upon a shelfe close underneath,
Which thou more think'st upon then on thy death,
 They are not prayers of a grieved soule,
 That with repentance doth his sinnes condole.

> But amorous Pamphlets, that best likes thine eyes,
> And Songs of love, and Sonets exquisit.
> Among these Venus, and Adonis lies,
> With Salmacis, and her Hermaphrodite:
> Pigmalion's there, with his transform'd delight. (sig. E4v)

Cranley, too, offered Amanda sonnets and tales of love, but hers seem reprehensible because they have replaced devotional reading with stories of uncontrolled lust, classical perversion, and transformation. He associates Amanda with those Ovidian metamorphoses: she moves frequently to avoid detection and changes her name, "Forgetting that which thou hadst from thy mother" (sig. G3v). Amanda does not keep Sundays holy and knows nothing of private or public prayer (sig. F3v). Instead of plumbing her secret soul in prayer, Amanda plays roles. In several verses on her theatergoing, Cranley engages Amanda as the actress, at center stage in the audience of the "amorous spectators" (sig. F2r) who frequent the theater. She has an actress's or sorceress's command over words, as well. She is "A Magicke spell within a golden booke" (sig. G2r), or like a "blacke Crosse, before the row of Letters" (sig. G2v).

Cranley lists famous courtesans of history and then recounts stories of miraculous cures and the ability to carry water in a sieve, feats conventionally attributed to chaste and virginal women. To urge her to emulate their example, he mentions prostitutes who turned from their lives of sin, including Aphra, a "famous Bawd" who suffered martyrdom (sig. I1r–I1v). He envisions Amanda's judgment by the "grave, and solid men" of Bridewell, and her punishment:

> A beedle comes, and takes thee by the hand
> To bring thee forth, and lets thee understand,
> That thou for all thy bravery, and cost,
> Must walke with him unto the whipping post.
> Whither he brings thee, straightwaies without staying,
> Puls off thy robes, and lockes thy hands up fast.
> Then to his office, without long delaying,
> Thy clothes pul'd downe, starke naked to thy waste,
> He thereby lets thee understand the taste,
> Of his smart Whipcord, where there doth imprint
> Each lash a seame, and every knot a dint.
> For flourishing with hand above his head,

And shaking of his foure limb'd instrument,
In the descent, so learnedly they spread
About thy shoulders, that incontinent
Thy dainty skin, is all sanguinolent,
    And so he deales his lashes one by one,
    Till the set number of his stripes are done,
Thus being of thy silkes, and Sattins stript,
Exposde to publique shame, and so disgrac'd.
And for thy impudent abuses whipt
A poore blew gowne upon thy backe is plac'd,
And Canvas coyfe upon thy head unlac'd. (sig. I2r–I2v)

Cranley's language is deeply disturbing and threatening, with its obsessive focus on her naked body; he devotes nearly a whole page to the imagined punishment. Her conversion is predicated upon stripping and shaming her, upon imprinting her with the lash. The learned cords of the whip will reeducate her; her "sanguinolent" skin will remind her of her previous unlawful openness, of her too-eloquent body.[31] Cranley's view of Amanda is pornographic, invasive, brutal; he overgoes the beedle by exposing her publicly and in print. Cranley's crime had merited him prison, an enclosure that nevertheless still allowed him a measure of freedom. Amanda's, however, demands public punishment, like that almost meted out to the woman taken in adultery in John's Gospel. Even if Amanda never suffers this punishment, the words of this letter are sure to lacerate. Indeed, Cranley is counting on the effectiveness of his pen to convert her:

And when thou hast this little Pamphlet read,
And seene the scope whereto these lines doe tend,
Let them not passe an hower out of thy head,
Vntill thy sorrow make thy life amend,
And worke a reformation in the end. (sig. I3v)

Cranley's letter does its work; Amanda reads it, falls deathly ill, and invites Cranley to visit her. (His exhortations to conversion are apparently powerful enough not only to reform but to kill her.) The next section of the book, "The penitentiall answer of the reformed Amanda" (sig. K1r), is his report of her words; she is now too weak to write on her own. Overwhelmed by his kindness (and his attentions), she is pleased that he has revealed her sins to her: "Thou plainly hast discover'd unto me, / And made me see what erst

I could not see" (sig. K2r). Amanda characterizes her previous life as a perverted religion: her cloister was a "stewes" (sig. K3r); she was "fuller of fiends then Mary Magdalene" (sig. K4r). Like the Magdalen, Amanda wishes to reform her life and her reading:

> Helpe me oh helpe me to some holy booke,
> To stirre my heart up to devotion.
> Get me a Bible I therein may looke,
> That Gods good Spirit in me may have motion,
> And of his holy Word I may have notion. (sig. L3r)

She wants a room "in some private place," "in a lonely private habitation" (sig. L3v) in order to live out her new existence.

Cranley responds to Amanda's confession with something like a marriage proposal—a reward for her change of heart, for her willingness to abandon the public life of taverns and theaters. "Here take my hand, and with my hand my heart" (sig. M1r), he says. The sign that his earlier proposition has been transformed into a proposal is their new reading matter and spiritual regimen. She will pray set forms of prayer (as befitting a beginner and one who adheres to the official doctrines of the Church of England), and he will read to her daily from the Bible and other "holy bookes." Amanda spends the rest of her life battling "blacke despaire" (sig. M3r), reading, and praying. On her deathbed, her total self-abnegation is apparent, as she thanks Cranley again for writing that little book and ponders her own worthlessness:

> The booke thou sent'st, that little Paper booke,
> Wherein thou did'st unmask my foule offense;
> Behold, and see what true effect it tooke,
> That booke, I say did worke in me the sence
> Of my owne follie, and my impudence.
>   I bless the time, for this thy blessed favour,
>   And blesse the Lord, that blest thy good endeavour.
> And here my latest thankes to thee I give.
> And with these thankes of mine, this little Ring.
> My houre is come, I can no longer live,
> Wear't for my sake, although a worthlesse thing,
> I cannot recompence thy meriting. (sig. M4r–M4v)

Amanda is a seventeenth-century Magdalen, fulfilling all the traditional expectations for the fallen woman. As in John's Gospel, men's sins remain hidden, while women's are marked for exposure, imprinted into a text. Writing is the man's role; reading the woman's, the method by which her transgressions are revealed to herself and to the world. The person who educates this female sinner is a male author—the pornographer, one who writes about whores.[32] Female sexual power is subverted by the power of the pen, and the reformed sinner comes to believe that powerlessness and seclusion are more appropriate to her station in life. She is converted into believing that the ability to cover over sin, to wield the pen, is a male privilege and gift, and she can only be a submissive, sacrificial, and eroticized subject.

Love-Letters Between a Nobleman and His Sister

Such conventions are overturned in Aphra Behn's *Love-Letters Between a Nobleman and His Sister,* in which the site of power moves to women: to the female author, a female narrator, and a female protagonist. Behn was accused of writing lascivious matter in her lifetime, of writing in a style appropriate only to men.[33] In *Love-Letters,* she arrogated to women the privileges of the male narrator of *Amanda* and transformed the religious idiom of the earlier fallen-women narratives into the passionate language of lovers. The distance between the asceticism of Mary Magdalen, the repentant mood of *Amanda,* and the libertinism of a Silvia is not so great as one might imagine, however. As Octavio Paz has stated: "Eroticism is embodied also in two emblematic figures: the ascetic and the libertine. Emblems that are opposed yet move in the same direction: both, rejecting reproduction, are attempts at salvation or personal liberation from a fallen, depraved, incoherent, or unreal world. The same goal impels sects and communities, except that for them salvation is a collective undertaking—they are a society within a society—whereas the ascetic and the libertine are asocial, individuals confronting society or rebelling against it."[34] The connections between the erotic and the religious obtain also in the acts of reading and writing. Susan Sontag calls pornography "a species of proselytizing," writing that aims to excite in the same way religious experience excites conversion.[35] Marshall McLuhan suggests that the mass production of books, with its ability to pour forth "private news and views" made print a substitute for auricular confession;[36] Roger Ascham saw the printing of bawdy Italian books in England as a plot to entice young people with their cunning ways and pave the road for Roman Catholic control;[37] critics of Charles II linked his sexual excesses with both Catholicism and potential tyranny.[38] In *Love-Letters,* Aphra Behn gives us a nonconvert, one of the women who got away from the authors of conversion narratives. Behn's protagonist eschews religious conversion and submission to authority for amorous conquests and the pursuit of personal pleasure; she slips out from under the gaze of the male author who wishes to convert her and writes her story herself.

If Thomas Cranley's *Amanda* tells the story of a woman who finds that her place in the world is in private lodgings, at the receiving end of male-authored texts, Aphra Behn's central character is about a woman who turns privacy, the private self, and authorship into her own instruments for control over men and over her life. She is a letter-writer whose desires will eventually be purified and sanitized in Samuel Richardson's revolutionary epistolary novels *Pamela* (1740–42) and *Clarissa* (1747–48). Not passive, and certainly not powerless, Silvia is a woman who usurps the conventionally male roles of lover, aggressor, and author.[39] She is a reader as well, but her reading feeds her imagination and her authorial activities, rather than suppressing or sublimating them, as it does for Mary Magdalen and Amanda. Silvia is so remarkably strong a writer that she even overshadows her creator, (whose name did not appear on the title page of any edition of the work during her lifetime), and the editor/narrator, the unnamed collector of the letters and infrequent commentator on the story.[40] Silvia, as one of her lovers carelessly remarks, is a whore, and, as such, her writing is true pornography: she uses her pen to advertise herself, to create herself as an object of desire. With her literary confessions, Silvia, as Michel Foucault has suggested, transforms her "every desire into discourse." Foucault's connection of the confessional with the production of sexual discourse is important, because the image of the dark confessional box signals the hiddenness of the narrator and author; the confessor (or author) becomes unnecessary in the face of Silvia's own discourse on her self.[41]

Love-Letters was based upon a series of historical incidents that began in 1682. Ford Lord Grey, a prominent Whig who supported the Duke of Monmouth's challenge to the throne of James II, eloped with his sister-in-law, eighteen-year-old Henrietta Berkeley. Grey's trial before the King's Bench for the young woman's abduction provoked a good deal of public outcry and curiosity and revealed that the lovers' escape had been preceded by a surreptitious exchange of letters. Behn's novel consists of three books, published in 1684, 1685, and 1687, the last part issued under the title *The Amours of Philander and Silvia.* The first part of the trilogy was written in epistolary form, while the second and third parts are in the third person and make only sporadic use of the letter form to move the story along. The editor of the most recent edition of *Love-Letters,* Janet Todd, surmises that Behn must have been writing at great speed in order to incorporate references to the political events of the time, which form a major subplot in books 2 and 3.[42] When the fictionalized account was published, some readers took the letters to be genuine, thus marking the first disruption of the security of this novel's readers.[43] The certainty of fictionality is absent. As Linda Kauffman has said of other epistolary fictions scripted by females: "Each subsequent heroine sustains the fiction of a conversation with the beloved in her letters, while simultaneously revealing her awareness of the fictiveness of the endeavor. The inscription of desire is alternately rhetorical, erotic, spontaneous, calculated. It is a consciously staged utterance."[44] In keeping with Behn's theatrical background, Silvia becomes a character who creates the role of femme fatale for herself, a role she puts on and off as easily as a stage costume. Unlike the reformed Amanda, who abandoned the theater and her "role" as a prostitute, Silvia embraces deception. Silvia shocks and surprises because unlike some other epistolary heroines, she seems to lack the traditional feminine traits a seventeenth-century audience might have expected: modesty and sorrow for her transgressions. Although Silvia bears a superficial resemblance to the impressionable Amanda in her receipt of letters from her brother-in-law, two aspects of her character illustrate that Behn is departing from the tradition of the receptive, repentant fallen woman. Silvia defines herself as an author-reader, and she uses her writing and her body as modes of self-presentation. She is more author than reader, more powerful and politically astute than the men whom she eventually seduces. Like a pornographer, she titillates, challenges the reader and the men who observe her with her studied and calculated self-disclosures. Silvia's "discoveries" of herself, moreover, revoke any certainties we might have that what appears in print is "true," that what individuals present to the world truly has some correspondence with their inner lives. Behn offers Silvia as the mouthpiece for the author: she gives her the male role of discoverer, and at the same time Behn resists identification with Silvia by her authorial and narrative silences. Silvia's deceptions of the world are a sign to the reader that authors, like their characters, ought not to be judged hastily or superficially.

Though some critics have described Silvia's progress as a move from innocence to experience,[45] I would argue that Silvia is guilty (as guilty as the male characters in the novel) from the minute she picks up the pen to write her first letter to Philander; she opens herself up to possible seduction, to the potential power of Philander's written words. By associating Silvia with male authorship, Behn not only confirms Silvia's openness but turns men into readers, and it is readers, as we have seen, who are in most need of conversion. If Silvia is a whore because she writes, are not men who write whores as well? Behn exposes this contradiction; her Silvia is a challenge to arbitrary attitudes about reading and writing and about men and women.

Silvia challenges authority the moment she decides to engage in an illicit correspondence with her brother-in-law, Philander. The transgression is threefold: it implies a disregard of moral, social, and familial bonds. Though the whole book focuses on Silvia's (and Philander's) various sexual escapades, sex stands in here for the exercise of personal choice, a privileging of the private individual over society at large. An excerpt from the original trial (an event that occurs nowhere in the novel) pinpoints some of the issues. The indictment charges Grey and his accomplices with having caused

> the said lady Henrietta Berkeley, to desert the aforesaid right honourable George earl of Berkeley, father of the aforesaid lady Henrietta; and to commit whoredom, fornication, and adultery, to live with the aforesaid Ford lord Grey (the said Ford lord Grey, then and long before, and yet, being the husband of the lady Mary, another daughter of the said right honourable George earl of Berkeley, and sister of the said lady Henrietta) against all laws, as well divine as human, impiously, wickedly, impurely, and scandalously, to live and cohabit, did tempt, invite, and solicit, and every of them, then and there, did tempt, invite, and solicit. (444)

The charges, then, encompass moral and civil wrongs, "laws, as well divine as human." Grey has caused Henrietta to "desert" her father, has committed incest by fornicating with his wife's sister, and is guilty of soliciting for prostitution. He has encroached upon a father's authority, disregarded the religious and social obligations imposed by marriage, and introduced monetary factors into a relationship in which economics should not rightfully be a consideration. That Henrietta was considered property was apparent, for part of the restitution her father sought was that she "be restored" to him. Henrietta was seen as equally culpable, and though she was called upon to testify, she was not permitted to explain why she had left her father's house. The Lord Chief Justice blames her for the loss of her reputation: "You have injured your own reputation, and prostituted both your body and your honour, and are not to be believed" (459). He has linked the loss of the lady's chastity, her "honour," with the loss of her credibility. The insinuation of prostitution, of whoredom, cost Henrietta her day in court.

Aphra Behn responds to this injustice, not by creating a conventionally sympathetic fictional heroine (the real Henrietta appears to have been a more sensitive and scrupulous person than is Silvia), but by creating a new fictional heroine who has a voice. It is perhaps no accident that the writing and self-creating Silvia, like the men, escapes punishment for all her sins.

Marriage and the ties of kinship—the issues at stake in Grey's trial—are the subjects of the Philander's first letter to Silvia. Philander, a supporter of a rebellion against the king, aims to acquire Silvia by proving the special nature of their relationship. They are no ordinary lovers, bound by customary laws; their private desires elevate them above all such concerns:

> You my lovely Maid, were not born to be obtain'd by the dull methods of ordinary loving; and 'tis in vain to prescribe me measures; and oh much more in vain to urge the nearness of our Relation. What Kin my charming *Silvia* are you to me? No tyes of blood forbid my Passion; and what's a Ceremony impos'd on man by custome? what is it to my Divine *Silvia,* that the Priest took my hand and gave it to your Sister? what Alliance can that create? why should a trick devis'd by the wary old, only to make provision for posterity, tye me to an eternal slavery. No, no my charming Maid, tis nonsense all; let us (born for mightier joys) scorn the dull *beaten road,* but let us love like the first race of men, nearest allied to God, promiscuously they lov'd, and posses'st, Father and Daughter, Brother and Sister met, and reap'd the joys of Love without controul, and counted it Religious coupling. (11–12)

Philander and Silvia, the new Adam and Eve, cannot be constrained by men's arbitrary laws but follow a natural, more truly religious law. They are a singular couple who may disregard both the older generation, with their ceremonies and alliances, and the yet unborn, their own descendants. Neither parents nor children should interfere with their love. The "careless forc'd insipid duty's" of conjugal life will be replaced by the private vows conveyed in their letters. Philander denies that he was ever truly married to Silvia's sister, claiming his soul "was Married to yours in its first Creation; and only *Silvia* is the Wife of my sacred, my everlasting Vows" (16). In this through-the-looking-glass version of a conversion story, love becomes a religion, and the sinners are those who obstruct the pursuit of passion.

Silvia, after surrendering her virginity to Philander (and continuing their correspondence for another hundred pages), also becomes convinced that their love was no crime "till man made laws" (110). Marriage, she insists, is

> a trick, a wise device of Priests, no more—to make the nauseated, tir'd out pair drag on the carefull busines of life, drudg for the dull got family with greater satisfaction, because they're taught to think marriage was made in Heaven; . . . No, *Philander,* that's a heavenly match when two Souls toucht with equal passion meet (which is but rarely seen)—when willing vows, with serious consideration, are weigh'd and made; when a true view is taken of the Soul, when no base interest makes the hasty bargain, when no conveniency or design of drudge, or slave, shall find it necessary when equal judgments meet that can esteem the blessings they possess, and distinguish the good of eithers love, and set a value on each other merits, and where both understand to take and pay; who find the beauty of each others minds, and rate 'em as they ought, whom not a formal ceremony binds (with which I've nought to do; but dully give a cold consenting affirmative) but well considered vows from soft inclining hearts, utter'd with love, with joy, with dear delight when Heaven is call'd to witness. (111–12)

Silvia argues that personal commitment, rather than social or economic ties, should form the basis for marital union; marriage should be a union of hearts, not a contract. Passages of this sort are what lead critics to claim that Behn views love as heroic and passion as inherently unselfish.[46] Perhaps that is the case in Behn's stage-plays, but I think the issue is more complicated here (and that those critics are operating under a postromantic sensibility about the nature of passion). Silvia is quite right in condemning hollow ceremony, in viewing marriage as a simple economic bargain. Later, she will prove her own point about the emptiness of ceremony by agreeing to marry Philander's servant, Brilliard, rather than marry a man of her parents' choosing. Behn does not make it easy for us to judge Silvia—the reader, along with her suitors, can be overcome by her charm, her wit, her writing ability. Silvia is an example of the way in which self-determination and the privileging of personal autonomy can devolve into venality and self-centeredness. We value power, and in more recent times, we have especially come to value power in women. Since Silvia is a woman who knows how to exercise power, it is tempting to valorize her beliefs and behavior. If I read Behn correctly, however, I think she wishes us to see Silvia in the context of all those earlier male authors and commentators on women's virtue. She is not suggesting that the female exercise of authority is somehow more virtuous or more preferable to that of men—she simply wants to remind us of the equal possibility for good and evil in either sex. While, at this point in the story, she rejects the sexual double standard and the idea of marriage solely as an economic contract, the rest of the novel offers the reader a more ambiguous picture of emotional self-determination, of self-creation, and of authorship itself.

Silvia's first exercise of personal power, her authorial training, begins in secret, in the confines of her own room. The absurdly long letters that comprise the entire first part of the novel detail the lovers' actions. The presence of household spies, the sense that Silvia never leaves her home, the enclosed space—all serve as the incubator for Silvia's authorial efforts and for Silvia's developing public persona. Very early on, Behn makes the pen Silvia's emblem and links her, not only with letter-writing, but with the metaphors of press and print. Reading and writing, especially in book 1, are the only connections between the lovers, between the lovers and their pasts, and of course between the narrator and implied reader of the text. We do not witness an early meeting between Silvia and Philander in the woods; we read about Silvia writing about it. Even Silvia finds the recollection unreal; letters distance her from her own experience, from a lived connection with her lover. Silvia recalls walking in the grove that was the site of their meeting: "I threw my self down on that bank of grass where we last disputed the dear but fatal business of our souls: Where our prints (that invited me) still remain on the prest greens: There with Ten Thousand sighs, with remembrance of the tender minutes we past then, I drew your last Letter from my Bosome; and often kist and often read it over" (13–14). Silvia's life is already literary, rather than real. The classically remote setting in a grove, the substitution of a letter for the lover as the object of affection, even the "prints" in the grass point to a reliance on literary self-fashioning, to a possible separation between written and lived experience. Silvia already begins to enact a role, this time as the tearful shepherdess unhappy in love.[47] Her literary excess is already apparent, and one wonders whether Behn meant us to laugh at or sympathize with Silvia at this point. The reader's tendency to do both is the sign of Behn's own ability to present all action as uncertain and indeterminate, all motive as secret and hidden: "I found my soul agitated with a Thousand different passions, but all insupportable, all mad, and raving;

sometimes I threw my self with fury on the ground, and prest my panting heart to the cold earth, then rise in rage and tear my hair, and hardly spare that face that taught you first to love: then fold my wretched Arms to keep down rising Sighs that almost rend my breast, I traverse swiftly the conscious Grove; with my distracted show'ring eyes directed in vain to pitiless Heaven, the lovely silent shade favouring my complaints, I cry alowd" (14). The grove, "pitiless Heaven," the "silent shade," and of course the multiple-layered readers of Silvia's letters are witness to her displays of passion; even in private, it is already difficult to know whether Silvia is acting sincerely or acting for an audience. I would like to suggest that Behn does not want the reader to know who Silvia is, that she wants her readers to experience the same uncertainties about Silvia's character that Silvia's acquaintances do. Silvia's physical charms and her literary abilities are talents that make her a twin of the author and narrator, who also have the power to speak or remain silent, to reveal, or to retain an authorial discretion about themselves.

Silvia herself begins as the thing written upon, as one of Philander's early letters to her tells us: "Ten Thousand times a day I breath that name my busie fingers are eternally tracing out those Six mystick Letters, a Thousand ways on every thing I touch, form words, and make 'em speak a Thousand things, and all are *Silvia* still" (20). Two things emerge here for our consideration: Philander's manipulation of the six letters that form Silvia's name and Silvia's apparently infinite changeability into still other words. Philander is doing the tracing, the writing, the speaking, the word formation; Silvia, like any Petrarchan heroine, merely forms the body of Philander's praise.[48] But Silvia's mutability and mystic qualities promise that Philander will lose control of his creation, that the meaning of Silvia will become obscure even to him.

Philander, of course, as the male and the initiator of the lovers' correspondence, expects to be the hero of the story. He imagines people reading their tale, and as his poetic craft displaces the beloved, he becomes the center of the love story: "I am sensible that when my story's told (and this happy one of my Love shall make up the greatest part of my History) that those that Love not like me, will be apt to blame me, and charge me with weakness for revealing so great a trust to a Woman; and almost all that I shall do to arrive at Glory, that will brand me with feabless, but *Silvia* when Lovers shall read it, the men will excuse me, and the Maids bless me! I shall be a fond admir'd president, for them to point out to their remiss reserving Lovers, who will be reproached for not persuing my example" (44). Philander, like the speaker in Donne's "Valediction to His Book," and echoing that poem's ambiguities about the role of the male lover, valorizes his part in the love affair. But Philander's weaknesses are apparent early on. He is not only unsuccessful in the bedroom during his first night with Silvia; he is a traitor to his king, despite Silvia's exhortations to loyalty (40–43).[49] His sexual impotence foreshadows the eventual exchange of roles with Silvia, who, wearing men's clothes, assumes the power of the pen and becomes the sexual aggressor and author of events.[50] Not only is Philander rendered impotent, but, startled by a noise, he is forced to flee Silvia's chamber dressed in her maid's clothes. Philander is chagrined to realize that he will become a laughingstock, rather than the heroic lover: "Where shall I hide my head, when this lewd Story's told?" (57).

Silvia's liaison with Philander presents her with an unpleasant choice: abandoning Philander and returning to a socially acceptable life with the husband her parents have selected; or a self-directed life, that, to the outside world looks like prostitution, incest, and deception. She never seriously considers the first—the lovers' belief in their own specialness, in the literary value of their experience, precludes adherence to any conventional moral standard. Silvia's choice is for prostitution—and that means she must become more adept at acting and at writing. That I define one of Silvia's options as prostitution may seem excessive, but the identification of Silvia with harlotry occurs very early in the book. She herself asks whether "base poor prostitution" is the price of Philander's heart (25); she finally agrees that it is. Her sister (who has somehow been made aware of the affair) puts it to her quite bluntly:

> Consider, oh young noble Maid, the infamy of being a Prostitute! and yet the act it self in this fatal Amour is not the greatest sin, but the manner which carries an unusual horrour with it; for 'tis a Brother too, my Child, as well as a lover, one that has lain by thy unhappy Sister's side . . . Alas, consider an action so shamefull, thou must obscure thy self in some remote corner of the world, where honesty and honour are never heard of: No thou canst not shew thy face, but 'twill be pointed at for something monstrous: for a hundred ages may not produce a story so lewdly infamous and loose as thine. (74)

Silvia is doubly a prostitute: because she has infringed on her sister's marital rights and because she has caused scandal, made her sin public. But there is some question about whether Silvia's sister occupies the moral high ground here. Though Silvia has usurped the position of wife and is on her way toward becoming a "Whig capitalist, going to market with herself,"[51] Behn silently implies that her sister's marriage has its basis in her secure financial position as a wife.

Silvia chooses to deal with the prospect of public infamy by developing both her writing and her acting skills.[52] As Catherine Gallagher has noted in a discussion of Behn's plays and their largely male audiences, women writers, acting, and prostitution were thought to be all of a piece: for both the actress and the prostitute, sexual desire is the primary motivator, and "professions of amorousness and theatrical inauthenticity" amount to the same thing.[53] As James Grantham Turner has noted in his discussion of *The Whores Rhetorick* (published in 1683, the year before *Love-Letters*), the prostitute creates the impression that she acts from love; she uses her body and the rhetorical arts of persuasion to arouse and at the same time to protect the identity beneath the mask.[54] Silvia's convincing acting obscures her real self but, more perplexingly, also obscures the moral stance of the author.

The first instance of Silvia's acting occurs when Silvia's mother finds her writing a love letter to Philander. Pretending that she is writing on behalf of her maid Melinda to her lover Alexis, Silvia reads the letter aloud, turning it "so prettily into Burlesque Love by her manner of reading it, that made Madam the Dutchess laugh extreamly" (53). The duchess accepts the premise that "Silvia and Philander" are really "Melinda' and Alexis." Silvia, the realist, takes advantage of the conventions of romantic intrigue to mask her illicit love affair with the amours of the pastorally named Melinda and Alexis.

Behn's insistence on the public revelation of the letter is significant. Though Silvia, to all appearances, convinces her mother of her innocence, the narrator, Melinda, Philander's servant Dorillus, and, later, her own sister are aware of the correspondence. The success of Silvia's performance is precarious, for though it protects Silvia's public reputation, and is recognized as a noble piece of acting, everyone surrounding Silvia eventually learns that she is acting—and accepts it as the hallmark of her character. Silvia writes secret love letters, pretends to an innocence she can no longer claim, sleeps with her sister's husband—and seems to get away with it, both with the reader, and in her social circle. Her assumption of the male prerogative to write and act, to fashion a public self, also seems to grant her the impunity of the male rake. Silvia is viewed as a charmer, not a sinner: no penitent Magdalen, she.

A "tale-bearing flatterer" (90) informs Silvia's father of Philander's second (and successful) nocturnal visit. Intercepting Philander's letter describing his blissful night with Silvia, the father confiscates her stationery and plans to marry her off to someone else. Silvia is forced to write in leaves of a table-book, a memorandum book, almost as though her love letters had already become business correspondence. Writing to Philander to plot her escape from home, she acknowledges to Philander that she is the subject of public scandal: "I am arm'd for the worst that can befall me, and that is my being rendred a publick shame, who have been so in the private whispers of all the Court for near these three happy months, in which I have had the wondrous satisfaction of being retir'd from the World with the charming Philander" (107–8).

There are no easy oppositions here between public and private, between what is secret and what is known. When Aphra Behn describes what Silvia is, and what she pretends to be, what her family and society know, and what they gossip about behind closed doors, she is describing the roles of author and reader, and, more particularly, the roles of a female author and her audience. As readers do with authors, observers could only guess at, but never confirm, what constituted the person. Silvia and Philander have reversed roles, and Silvia, the self-creating author, is at the epicenter of power. Behn's presentation of Silvia, of course, verifies the existence of the double standard for women, both sexually and as authors. The fact of Silvia's womanhood restricts her to private life and is in conflict with her role as an author and whore, in which she becomes a public woman. Behn is silently pointing out that women can only remain respectable if they keep silent, if they sin only in secret, or write anonymously or pseudonymously. Behn is mocking and teasing her readers, who are willing to accept Silvia's hypocrisy, her private writing and fornication, provided they do not intrude upon public decorum.

In book 2 of *Love-Letters,* Silvia begins her career as actress, prostitute, and author in earnest; she becomes, as it were, a professional working for her keep. Dressed as a cavalier during her escape from her father's house, she begins to enjoy the privileges which "wou'd have been deny'd to Women" (126) and discovers that male dress enhances her attractiveness to both men and women.[55] Dress, like writing, becomes the instrument for both concealment and self-revelation (or pretended self-revelation).[56] Putting on and taking off clothes become another way, Silvia finds, of exercising power.[57]

Still dressed as a man, Silvia attracts the attention of Octavio, a handsome young man who is confused and distressed by his attraction to her. Sharing a room with him, Silvia plays with her identity, disguising and yet revealing her female sexual power in her demeanor and dress: "Every motion, every Limb as carelessly she lay, discover'd a thousand Graces and more and more inflam'd the now beginning Lover; she cou'd not move, nor smile, nor speak, nor order any charm about her, but had some peculiar Grace that begun to make him uneasie; and from a thousand little Modesties both in her blushes and motions he had a secret hope she was not what she seem'd, but of that Sex whereof she discovered so many softnesses and beauties" (123). After Silvia's sex is revealed, she repeatedly presents herself in a state of deshabille to Octavio: her gown "open and discover'd a World of unguarded Beauty" (149); "her Night Gown thrown loosely about her lovely body and which left a thousand Charms to view" (156). Silvia's physical "discoveries" incite Octavio to love, and she declares him "a young *Columbus,* that have found the direct, unpractic'd way to that little and so much desir'd World" (161). Writing to Octavio arouses Silvia to dress herself "to advantage" (162); dress from then on becomes her mode for both seduction and concealment. (Philander has already lost interest in her and has found another lover, and Silvia is bent on retaliation.) Silvia appears before Brilliard, Octavio, her page, her last lover (Alonzo), and even Calista (Philander's new lover) in either male dress or in various states of feminine undress. Each situation is an occasion for duplicity or manipulation, even between the two women, each of whom finds the other attractive. Like the erotic language of her letters, her dress promises intimacies, access to her self and her body.

Silvia's reading and writing by this time in the novel reveals a new sophistication, a new realization of the seductive power she wields with her pen. Her pen is unlike that of the would-be conqueror, Cranley, who intimidates and expresses desire under cover of morality. Silvia uses her writing and her body to attract men or to defend herself from them: inviting, then withdrawing; teasing, then denying. Perhaps Silvia pleases more than does Cranley because she is wittier, less heavy-handed, craftier in her seductions of men, other women, and the reader.

Silvia's power is proved in her relations with Brilliard and Octavio. The fake marriage to Brilliard leads to a power struggle as Brilliard (who had been witness to the nightly lovemaking of the fleeing lovers), begins to "fancy fine injoyment, to fancy Authority which he durst not assume" (125). Brilliard wants sensual enjoyment, as well as a husband's authority over Silvia, but he is thwarted at every turn. When she learns of his desires, she threatens him with her penknife, the sign of her power (158).[58] Brilliard's attempt at rape is prevented by the timely intervention of Octavio. However, the real test comes for Silvia when Brilliard forges a letter from Octavio and demands a night in Silvia's bed. She is enraged at Octavio, resents being treated "like a common mistris of the Town" (207). (The narrator notes, ironically, that Silvia still possessed "a certain Honour" [207].) In a note to Octavio, Silvia promises a tryst but privately plans to substitute her maid for herself. Brilliard intercepts the note, overindulges in an aphrodisiac and fails to perform, leaving both Silvia and her maid physically untouched. The bed trick, like Silvia's writing and dressing, at the same time obscures and reveals her identity. Bed tricks, in some sense, presume that one partner is much like another, that one cannot know the real identity of the other person in the dark. Silvia guesses that Octavio/Brilliard, who can be fooled in broad daylight, will also be tricked in the dark; she can preserve her public claims to chastity, not only because she wields authorial power, but because men (and readers) are so susceptibile to trickery. Even after Octavio has seen Brilliard skulking into Silvia's apartments and angrily offers to pay for her services, Silvia is able to convince him of her innocence. Finding Silvia preparing to leave town disguised as a boy, Octavio ignores the implications of her dress and the evidence of her pregnancy by Philander and proposes marriage, rather chivalrously resolving not to touch her till they are married. This is both a tribute to Silvia's acting and an indictment of his own reading skills. A reader of French novels (293), Octavio idealizes Silvia as "the Star that Guides the Traveller, or wandring Seaman, or the Lamp at *Sestos,* that Guided the Ravish'd Lover o'er the *Hellespont*" (293). In a case of gender reversal, she is the powerful author and seducer, he the receptive lover who will inevitably be betrayed. It is Silvia who "rifles him with extravagency" (280), both sexually and financially. She betrays him with his uncle Sebastian and with Philander, whom she sees again out of boredom and jealousy. Octavio, disappointed in love, joins a monastery, praying that he "could convert her from the World" (378). Bad readers all, Philander, Octavio, Brilliard, and Sebastian all attempt to seduce Silvia, but it is Silvia, the astute author of her fate, who finally determines their place in her life and the role men should serve for her.

Finally, the adaptable Silvia "resolv'd upon a Design, in which she could trust no body but her Page, who lov'd his Lady to the last Degree of Passion" (385). Her aim is adventure—sexual adventure, to be precise. She is apparently unburdened by the child she has borne; her ability to expunge the child from her life marks her skill in transcending the limitations of her maternal, weak, female self. Dressed again as a man, Silvia ensnares the young Spaniard Alonzo and shares in his male confidences. Alonzo has become infatuated with the female Silvia, whom he has seen about town: *"I knew assuredly she was a Whore—and how fine a one I had mist:* This call'd all the blood to *Silvia*'s Face, and so confounded her, she could not answer; she knew it was her self, of whom he spoke; and that course word tho' innocently spoken, or rather gayly express'd, put her quite out of Countenance; however, she recover'd again, when she considered they were not meant as rudenesses to her" (393). Though she recognizes herself in Alonzo's description, Silvia no longer takes offense at being called a whore; rather, she excuses his comment as unintended rudeness. Politesse, rather than virtue, is the order of the day. After a series of encounters with Alonzo in which she alternately plays man or woman, Silvia finally "confesses" that the two "Silvias" are brother and sister. In her role as the commanding brother, she can exercise her male prerogatives fully and give her "sister" over to another man. In her role as desirable and available female, "all undrest and in her Night-clothes" (421), she can wield her sexual power over men.

With the realization that she herself is aging, Silvia jettisons all feminine reserve: "But now, that she had lost all for *Philander* and *Octavio,* and had a Heart to cast away, or give to a new Lover; it was like her Money, she hated to keep to it, and lavish'd it on any trifle, rather than hoard it, or let it lie by: 'Twas a loss of time her Youth could not spare" (395). Female containment is no longer possible for her; like money, her virtue, youth, and beauty must be spent while she still has them in hand.

Silvia benefits in two ways from her newly assumed lifestyle. As a man, she participates in the freedom and libertinism of the world of men, even to sharing their man-to-man vulgarities. As a woman, she has the luxury of knowing that, whatever her behavior, polite society will welcome her provided she remains young and charming. With Brilliard, she establishes a partnership of rogues, becoming "the Talk of the Town" (439). She has moved from the seclusion of her father's house into a world in which she can act either male or female. The sexual connotations of Silvia's earlier "correspondence" with Philander become obvious; her writing and her sexual behavior have made her into a "public woman." And as a public woman, Silvia can exercise men's freedom of movement, even escape the confining roles of women by sharing in the cheats and deceptions of men. Behn is not, however, suggesting that private life is necessarily the setting for virtue; instead, Silvia's role is rather like that of the novelist. D. A. Miller suggests that authors act as keepers and revealers of secrets, while readers agree to "forget" their knowledge in return for "the pleasures of suspense and surprise." There is mutual collusion between writer and reader: "The fact the secret is always known—and, in some obscure sense, known to be known—never interferes with the incessant activity of keeping it. The contradiction does not merely affect characters. We too inevitably surrender our privileged position as readers to whom all secrets are open by 'forgetting' our knowledge for the pleasures of suspense and surprise."[59] It is interesting that Miller conceives of this secret-keeping as a "spiritual exercise," for what Behn's novel reveals is the extent to which literary, even erotic language, replaces religious language, the extent to which spiritual reading has been replaced by reading for pleasure. In *Love-Letters Between a Nobleman and His Sister,* the guilty reader is trapped into identifying with Silvia, the heroine of a story that has all the marks of a didactic conversion narrative. But Silvia departs from the tradition of repentant whores, and as Behn gradually discloses Silvia's patterns of deceit and calculated self-disclosure, the reader is trapped as well, made cognizant of his or her own divided moral stance. Each of us is like Baudelaire's *hypocrite lecteur.* Unlike the woman taken in adultery, or Mary Magdalen, or Amanda, Silvia uses reading and writing in her own way, for self-definition and self-empowerment, not self-abnegation. Reading and writing do not convert her, turn her away from herself and from sin; they instead focus her upon herself. In Silvia, Behn depicts a female author and female sexuality, bringing the obscene onstage, making public what would normally be *ob scena.* While Behn hides her own identity from the public, she challenges her readers to move beyond the titillating characters and situation, the pornography of the text, to recognize in Silvia's conquests the potential power of author over reader. Behn is not idolizing Silvia the passionate lover. As Rose Zimbardo has suggested about the supposedly immoral comedies of the 1670s, though Silvia's writing may be pornographic, *Love-Letters* itself is not, for it "demonstrate[s] to understanding," rather than urging its audience to emulation.[60] Behn is celebrating the power of the text and is at the same time cautioning the reader about the creators of that power, even when (and perhaps especially when) they are women. It is no accident that Silvia's "masculine pen" is a central metaphor of the novel, for Silvia stands in for both male and female authors. Behn is depicting no androgyne, however. Silvia's femininity and the long tradition of relegating women to the private (and of denigrating the private) is essential to Behn's moral lessons and to her description of authors and readers in the marketplace. Silvia demonstrates that power may reside in private places and that power may be exercised by the judicious (or calculated) release of information. Silvia, the author, is the paradigm for all authors, who have the ability to determine the reader's response to their work through their purposeful craftiness with words. Like Silvia, who could wield authority under the guise of femininity, authors (and other individuals) may choose to reveal, or misrepresent, or hide their real identities. Behn's novel about a fallen woman who is not converted, who does not die, who is not imprisoned in Bridewell seems to destroy an old morality and old ways of reading and writing, in which everything was as it seemed. Behn is suggesting, perhaps, that only the wary reader will detect the private self hidden beneath the costume of the individual's public self-presentation.

Conclusion

Study our manuscripts, those Myriades
Of letters, which have past twixt thee and mee,
Thence write our Annals, and in them will bee
To all whom loves subliming fire invades,
Rule and example found.
—John Donne

IT IS PERHAPS FITTING to conclude this study with the valediction that served as its genesis. John Donne's address to his "Love," the coauthor of the letters that form the book in which "Schooles might learne Sciences, Spheares Musick, Angels Verse," is a poem that privileges private experience over public, personal correspondence over great works of literature, the mystic understanding of lovers over the learning of scholastics, lawyers, and statesmen. Donne's poem, written early in the seventeenth century, already illustrates the era's concerns with the validity of private experience and situates that experience in the reading of a book. That Donne figured his book of poems as a manuscript, and yet an obviously public document, intrigued me and set me thinking on the iconography of the book in the sixteenth and seventeenth centuries. My initial intent was to approach the relationship between privacy and print as a purely literary matter, but the seventeenth-century authors and readers in the texts I examined forced me to become at the same time more abstract and more down-to-earth in my approach: I found I had to deal with the abstractions of the "private self" but also with the implications privacy had for people's real lives in the early modern period.

In my introduction I proposed that the practice of reading led to the development of a sense of the private self. I suggested that this self was characterized by a sense of personal autonomy, a recognition of the possible differences between one's public and private roles and the right to conceal or keep secret the workings of the inner self. At the outset, however, I neglected aspects of privacy which turned out to be crucial: the overarching influence of physical space in construing the notion of privacy, the effects of gender roles on the construction of privacy, and the hints, even in the seventeenth century, that a privileging of privacy might have negative consequences.

Though I considered the changes in domestic space and architecture as an impetus for a similar psychological change, I failed to appreciate the physicality of the reading and writing experience. As though from biological necessity, readers and authors emphasized physical space, the territory surrounding the reading and writing self. Enclosed spaces—Ann Ketelbey's and Silvia's bedroom, Margaret Cavendish's and Aphra Behn's convents, the walled gardens of Silvia's lovers, and prison cells galore—all contained solitary individuals. Nearly a dozen of the characters I encountered made a point of their actual or imagined imprisonment: Thomas Worthington, Robert Southwell, John Bunyan, Charles I, Cranley and his Amanda, and John Donne, trapped with his noisome children at Micham, were just a few of these imprisoned readers. Confinement to these smaller spaces signifies both isolation and freedom—isolation from the larger community and the freedom to create a new interiority, a retreat from the usual constraints of time and place.

The consciousness of one's physical surroundings created also a new awareness of the boundaries of the human body and the experience of owning or having custody of the self and one's personal possessions. I have preferred to concentrate on the psychic, rather than the economic, lives of my readers, but in a newly developing country such as seventeenth-century England, with a rising middle class that had both more education and more leisure time, owning books—owning any personal property—must have been a new experience. Possessions can become an extension and reflection of the self; the totemic book, formerly symbolizing church and state, could now symbolize one's deepest concerns and interests, become an extension of one's personality. And the experience of reading seems to have become a highly personalized and physical activity. Recent arguments about reading books on computer screens would not be taking place if reading were solely a mental act; these seventeenth-century readers remind us that the feel and look of the book, the place and method for reading, are not incidental to the reading experience. Books and bodies and sexual activity are intermingled repeatedly: while Charles I insists on his physical and moral integrity and Donne looks forward to the reintegration of the self on the last day, Cranley and Behn present us with characters for whom the secret self is closely intertwined with the sexual self: sex and reading seem to be cognate activities.

What also seems to be emerging in the period I have studied is a new "selfishness," the creation of a self-identity, a self not defined by its relationship to God and society but a self forced to stand on its own. The oppressive and uncertain religious climate of the seventeenth century encouraged, not only private reading, but also independence from church authority. Political and religious repression must have impressed on individuals the necessity of choice and the possibility of civil disobedience; the doctrine of equivocation and outward conformity to law and custom opened up new possibilities for thinking about the self, not as the *imago dei,* a reflection of God's image, but as an autonomous human being. This spiritual autonomy evolved into a kind of secular humanism, in which the language of the psyche begins to supplant the language of the soul. James Sharpe's "Protestant private spirit" becomes Osborne's "human" spirit; Robert Southwell's chapel of the imagination turns into Cavendish's teeming brain. The apparent relationship between robust individuality, secularity, and independence from an all-seeing God has often been thought of as the invention of the Enlightenment or the romantic era, but perhaps its roots lie earlier, in the seventeenth-century reader and her book.

The great divide between public and private roles, between the inner and outer self, seems to slip in the back door for early modern readers. The social situation of Catholics during the Tudor period and of Anglicans during the Commonwealth made secrecy and concealment a necessity; surveillance generated, not only the tools for preserving secrecy, such as shorthand and ciphering, but the need for personal privacy. The Puritans alone insisted that purity of being was reflected in a consistency between the inner and outer person. One does not know what to make of Dissenter John Bunyan and revolutionary John Milton's insistence on total revelation; we are more inclined to sympathize with Charles's demand that his two bodies be respected, more inclined to believe that Jack and John Donne both had a right to exist. Even when presented with the outrageous charmer Silvia, we accept, in both real life and in literature, that people have hidden selves.

My work presents some mixed results about the gendering of privacy in the seventeenth century. The traditional assumption that men engaged in the private contemplation of virtue while women were engaged in bodily concerns in private persists into the early modern period. This assumption, however, is complicated by the ways in which private spaces (Charles's cabinet, prison cells, Ann Ketelbey's bedroom) become, not places of privation, but places in which power might be exercised. The ambiguities of privacy seem directly related to the sex of the reader; common readers (and common reading material) seem to be gendered female, while elite readers and serious reading matter are associated with the male reader and author. Female authors and readers proved to be glaring examples of a suspicion cast, not only on private reading and reading for pleasure, but on privacy itself. Women, historically deprived of public status, were the emblems of private life and thus stood in the way of any new recognition of the values of privacy and individuality. The reading of the female converts in chapter 2, the private sins of Mary Magdalen and Cranley's Amanda, the tenuous place of Behn's Silvia in her social circle (and among the novel's readers) seem inextricably tied with their status as women. Only Cavendish, with her female characters who either act like men or become consecrated virgins and renounce them altogether, is able to assume the role of public citizen that male authors could take for granted.

One of the surprising results of this retreat into readers' imaginations and secret lives was the creation of fictional forms. In nearly every genre—conversion narrative, drama, personal letter—there occurred a slippage between actual events and their reporting; every personal story turned into a kind of negotiation between author and reader about the truth of the events reported in the text. And, more often than not, the central figure of these possible fictions was a woman or an imagined woman reader. The stories of Sarah Wight, Ann Ketelbey, Cranley's Amanda, Mary Magdalen, and Silvia teetered not only between public and private territory but between fact and fiction. This perhaps explains the constant historical questioning of fictionality: fiction, like women, is "unreliable," relates to private lives, not verifiable public events. This suspicion of dangerous reading women, of fiction, of private life has wider implications as well. The gendering of privacy can help explain the modern American disdain for private reading and the scholarly life and may shed light on our schizophrenic attitudes toward honesty and self-revelation, celebrity-seeking and curiosity.

My final observations on reading and the rise of private life center on the potentially negative aspects of privacy and reading that seem to be emerging during the seventeenth century. These facets of privacy are not, of course, fully realized, but there are foreshadowings of the essential loneliness that some say characterize the modern condition. The first of these I have already alluded to: the centering on self that personal spirituality encouraged and the distancing of religious sensibilities from church doctrine and ceremony created the possibility that one could be truly private, that even God could not look in on one's private life. The despair common to readers of conversion narratives and other spiritual books confirmed one's distance from a deity, perhaps even opened up the prospect of an existence without a God.

Women readers seem to be especially affected by their reading, in peculiar ways cut off, not only from the divine, but from society and the community of other women. Sarah Wight, the female convert, remains unmarried and imprisoned by celebrity in her home, apparently to the end of her life. Other marriageable young women, such as Eva Verboon, Ann Ketelbey, and Silvia, are cut off from their families as they strive for personal independence. Margaret Cavendish attempts to incorporate women into public life but must do so by having them resist marriage, at least for a time. The most independent and successful of her female characters, Sanspareille, dies; it is significant that Cavendish's critics attribute Sanspareille's death to her virginity and her education, both of which cut her off from the experiences of other women. The successes and fame of Cavendish's Victoria reincorporate her into her society, but these stand in glaring contrast to Silvia, who also chooses to challenge custom and achieves her independence at the cost of her reputation. The striving toward privacy and autonomy seems, even at the end of the seventeenth century, not without its dangers for individuals and society.

Notes

Introduction

1. See, for example, Burckhardt, *Civilization of the Renaissance in Italy,* 1:143–50; Greenblatt, *Renaissance Self-Fashioning;* Davis, "Boundaries and the Sense of Self in Sixteenth-Century France," 53–63; Fineman, *Shakespeare's Perjured Eye;* and Maus, *Inwardness and Theater in the English Renaissance,* 1–34.

2. Ariès, introduction to *Passions of the Renaissance,* vol. 3 of *History of Private Life,* ed. Chartier, 5.

3. See Modell, *Private Self;* Morse, *England's Time of Crisis;* and Stone, *Family, Sex and Marriage in England, 1500–1800.*

4. Huebert, "Privacy." For similar observations on the history of the word, see Williams, *Keywords,* 203–4.

5. The Uniformity Act (1662) reestablished the Book of Common Prayer as the proper form for worship, required teachers in private houses to obtain licenses to teach from the archbishop, and prevented persons not ordained from holding an ecclesiastical benefice or administering the sacrament of the Lord's Supper. The Five Mile Act (1665) forbade persons "to preach in any unlawful assembly, conventicle, or meeting, under colour or pretence of any exercise of religion . . . within five miles of any parish, town, or place" (621) where they had held a religious post before the Act of Oblivion unless they took an oath swearing not "to take arms against the king." See *Documents Illustrative of English Church History,* ed. Gee and Hardy, 600–23.

6. *Public and Private Life in the Seventeenth Century,* ed. Vickers, 208. All further references will be cited parenthetically.

7. Richards, *Mental Machinery,* 53.

8. Warren and Brandeis, "The Right to Privacy," is the seminal article that brought the issue of privacy to the attention of the legal community. For more recent discussions, see Alderman and Kennedy, *Right to Privacy* (a popular account); Boling, *Privacy and the Politics of Intimate Life;* Cate, *Privacy in the Information Age;* Flaherty, *Protecting Privacy in Surveillance Societies;* and Schoeman, *Philosophical Dimensions of Privacy.* It seems relevant that much of the impetus for recent discussions of privacy revolves about the invasive and potentially destructive new technology of the computer; it is Gutenberg's invention repackaged.

9. Westin, *Privacy and Freedom,* 32. For further developments of Westin's ideas, see Ingham, "Privacy and Psychology," in *Privacy,* ed. Young, 35–58; Flaherty, *Privacy in Colonial New England;* and McLean, *Privacy and Its Invasion.*

10. Derlega and Chaikin, "Privacy and Self-Disclosure in Social Relationships."

11. Derlega et al., *Self-Disclosure,* 9.

12. Altman, "Privacy Regulation."

13. Mascuch, *Origins of the Individualist Self,* 100, argues that "reading biographical narrative allows a person to enter into an autonomous expression of the subjectivity of another person while retaining his own sense of self." My argument goes further in that I will try to show that *all* reading provides a vehicle for self-realization.

14. See Eisenstein, *Printing Press as an Agent of Change,* who has argued that the revolution was not simply technological, but made a fundamental change in the way we think and learn.

15. Kernan, *Printing Technology, Letters and Samuel Johnson,* 40–41, 220–21.

16. Duguid, "Material Matters," in *Future of the Book,* ed. Nunberg, 84.

17. Chartier, "Practical Impact of Writing," in *Passions of the Renaissance,* vol. 3 of *History of Private Life,* ed. Chartier, 116.

18. Steinberg, *Five Hundred Years of Printing,* 102.

19. Plant, *English Book Trade,* 26–29.

20. Bennett, *English Books and Readers, 1475 to 1557,* 29. Bennett bases his figures on a count of *Short-Title Catalogue* titles.

21. Bennett, *English Books and Readers, 1603 to 1640,* 230.

22. Plant, *English Book Trade,* 93.

23. Ibid., 91.

24. Cressy, "Books as Totems in Seventeenth-Century England and New England."

25. See Sheavyn, *Literary Profession in the Elizabethan Age,* 72; and Whiting, *Blind Devotion of the People,* 197.

26. See Kelly, *Early Public Libraries in Great Britain,* 70–85.

27. Steinberg, *Five Hundred Years of Printing,* 202.

28. Plant, *English Book Trade,* 244.

29. Clark, "Ownership of Books in England, 1560–1640," 98, 103. Jardine also traces the history of book ownership within the context of the new capitalism in *Worldly Goods,* 133–228, though her focus tends to be on bookish "treasures," not books for everyday use.

30. See, for example, Spufford, *Small Books and Pleasant Histories;* Watt, *Cheap Print and Popular Piety;* and Wright, *Middle-Class Culture in Elizabethan England.*

31. Clanchy, *From Memory to Written Record,* 198. See also Andrew Taylor, "Into His Secret Chamber: Reading and Privacy in Late Medieval England, in *Practice and Representation of Reading in England,* ed. Raven, Small, and Tadmor, 41–61, who notes that "private" reading could take place in solitude or in a small circle of family and friends.

32. Mascuch, *Origins of the Individualist Self,* 46.

33. For works on literacy and the measurement of literacy in the early modern period, see Adamson, "Extent of Literacy in England in the Fifteenth and Sixteenth Centuries"; Cressy, *Literacy and the Social Order;* Graff, *Legacies of Literacy;* Schofield, "Measurement of Literacy in Pre-Industrial England"; Spufford, "First Steps in Literacy"; and Stone, "Educational Revolution in England, 1560–1640."

34. Aston, *Fifteenth Century,* 83.

35. Graff, *Legacies of Literacy,* 153–54.

36. Spufford, "First Steps in Literacy," 417, 434.

37. Cressy, *Literacy and the Social Order,* 124–29.

38. Spufford, *Small Books,* 22.

39. Thus, I wish to address issues that affect the person of the author, the vulnerabilities of the private self, and not the author's traditional vulnerabilities to power, patronage, and the shades of the writers of antiquity, all of which Tylus alludes to in her introduction to *Writing and Vulnerability in the Late Renaissance.*

40. See Marotti, "Patronage, Poetry, and Print." Smith, "Woodcut Presentation Scenes in Books Printed by Caxton, de Worde, Pynson," argues that the illustrated presentation scenes in early printed books come to depict, not printer and patron, but author and reader. This transition was a gradual one, as Saunders points out in "The Social Situation of Seventeenth-Century Poetry"; authors received no royalties on profits from their work, only a fee for their manuscripts.

41. Consider, for example, the numerous prefaces that deplore the unauthorized publication of authors' works. The remedy for this act cannot be suppression of the original text but a republication, further explanation, and correction. Morse, 304, *England's Time of Crisis,* notes that Robert Burton turns the problem of his privacy, or noncelebrity, into a virtue and thereby establishes his authority and ensures his fame.

42. Bauschatz, "Montaigne's Conception of Reading in the Context of Renaissance Poetics and Modern Criticism," in *Reader in the Text,* ed. Suleiman and Crosman, 278.

43. Carlo Ginzburg's *Cheese and the Worms,* which tells the story of the sixteenth-century miller charged with heresy, illustrates the propensity of readers to make what they will of the meaning of texts, even if this happens to contradict the author's own meaning or flies in the face of religious authority.

44. Dagenais, *Ethics of Reading in Manuscript Culture,* xvii.

45. Nock, *Costs of Privacy,* 9.

46. Patterson, *Reading between the Lines.*

47. Laura E. Berk, "Children's Private Speech," in *Private Speech,* ed. Diaz and Berk, 18.

48. Paul P. Goudena, "The Problem of Abbreviation and Internalization of Private Speech," in *Private Speech,* ed. Diaz and Berk, 215–24; and Vera-John Steiner, "Private Speech among Adults," in *Private Speech,* ed. Diaz and Berk, 285–96.

49. See Love, *Scribal Publication in Seventeenth-Century England;* and Woodhuysen, *Sir Philip Sidney and the Circulation of Manuscripts, 1558–1640,* 1–203, for descriptions of manuscript transmission in this transitional era.

50. For a description of the workings of literary coteries, see Marotti, *John Donne, Coterie Poet;* and Saunders, "From Manuscript to Print."

51. Ong, "Writer's Audience Is Always a Fiction."

52. Ong, "Reading, Technology, and the Nature of Man," 133–34.

53. Denis McQuail, "Mass Media and Privacy," in *Privacy,* ed. Young, 177–92.

54. Habermas, *Structural Transformation of the Public Sphere,* 30.

55. Ong, "Reading, Technology and the Nature of Man," 140. Coleman, *Public Reading and the Reading Public,* offers a challenge to Ong's teleological notion of a move from orality to literacy, arguing that the transition was not abrupt but that oral, aural, and literate cultures coexisted throughout the late fifteenth century.

However, while she offers an extremely useful taxonomy on the variations of oral reading, she does not devise a new term for the peculiarly modern concept of a group of silent readers.

56. Clark, "Ownership of Books," 103.

57. Margolis, "Conceptions of Privacy."

58. Contamine, "Peasant Hearth to Papal Palace," in *Revelations of the Medieval World,* vol. 2 of *History of Private Life,* ed. Duby, 425–505.

59. Goffman, *Asylums.*

60. Bacon, "Of Building," in *Essayes or Counsels, Civill and Morall,* 138.

61. Barley has studied the evolution of housing standards in England, especially among the working classes. See his "Farmhouses and Cottages, 1550–1725"; and *House and Home.* For the earlier (and more elaborate) architecture of upper class homes, see Girouard, *Life in the English Country House.* For the psychological factors relating to architectural space, see Archaea, "Place of Architectural Factors in Behavioral Theories of Privacy."

62. Bold, "Privacy and the Plan," 115.

63. Alberti, *On the Art of Building in Ten Books,* 149.

64. Quoted by Hard in introduction to Wotton, *Elements of Architecture,* lxxvii.

65. Stewart, "Early Modern Closet Discovered."

66. Morse, *England's Time of Crisis,* 258, quotes Montaigne on his library and notes that "it is only there in the private sanctum that Montaigne can be truly monarch of all he surveys; it is only there that his sense of himself as lord and master returns to him."

67. Laufer and Wolfe in "Privacy as a Concept and Social Issue" discuss the importance of privacy as the proper environment for the development of the "self-ego"; such development requires separation and differentiation from the group.

68. Ferry, *"Inward" Language,* 45. Ferry's introductory chapters survey sixteenth- and seventeenth-century notions of the self in literature. She emphasizes the differences between earlier concepts of privacy and ours; I hope to elucidate the connections.

69. Fumerton, "'Secret Arts,'" has related architecture, personal revelation, and Elizabeth I's penchant for miniatures to that smallest of rooms, the sonnet, while Ziegler connects human and architectural space in "My Lady's Chamber." Ferry reviews the place of the closet, or cabinet, as a place of secrecy (*"Inward" Language,* 46–49), as does Patterson in "Re-opening the Green Cabinet." Ranum describes "the archaeology of the intimate" in "Refuges of Intimacy," in *Passions of the Renaissance,* vol. 3 of *History of Private Life,* ed. Chartier, 207–64.

70. Smith, in *Homosexual Desire in Shakespeare's England,* chap. 7, discusses the significance of the publication of Shakespeare's sonnets, with its "little rooms" enclosing intimacy and homosexual desire.

71. *OED,* s.v. "cabinet" (II.8.a), notes that the term *cabinet council* was apparently introduced at the accession of Charles I in 1625, though there are scattered references, as early as 1549 (I.6) to cabinets as "secret receptacles."

72. Basset, *Curiosities: or The Cabinet of Nature,* frontispiece.

73. Chartier, "Laborers and Voyagers"; Darnton, "What Is the History of

Books" and "First Steps toward a History of Reading," in *Kiss of Lamourette,* 107–35 and 154–87, respectively; and Hall, *Cultures of Print,* 30–34.

74. Carlo Ginzburg, "Titian, Ovid, and Sixteenth-Century Codes for Erotic Illustration," 77–95, has suggested that, in the case of erotic illustration, two "iconic circuits," one public, widespread, and socially undifferentiated, the other private, circumscribed, and socially elevated, began to merge with the advent of print. A similar opening up of all kinds of texts to new readers confounded the old rules about which readers were "fit" enough to read previously restricted texts.

75. See Pearson, "Women Reading, Reading Women," in *Women and Literature in Britain, 1500–1700,* ed. Wilcox, 80–99, for a discussion of the controversies and anxieties over women's reading in the sixteenth and seventeenth centuries.

76. Fowler, *Kinds of Literature,* 256.

77. Colie, *Resources of Kind,* 30.

78. Graham, "Women's Writing and the Self," in *Woman and Literature in Britain, 1500–1700,* ed. Wilcox, 212.

79. Gerhart, *Genre Choices, Gender Questions,* 35.

80. Dubrow, *Genre,* 31.

81. See Sharpe, *Triall of the Protestant Private Spirit.*

1: Reading and the Creation of the (Protestant) Private Spirit

1. *OED,* 2nd ed., s.v. "private" (2a).

2. Southern, in *Elizabethan Recusant Prose, 1559–1582,* 184–85, reports on the conversion of Protestant Richard Baxter upon reading Edmund Bunny's adaptation of Jesuit Robert Parsons' *Christian Exercise.* Purged of its Catholic references, it became a popular Protestant devotional work. White has documented the adaptation of traditionally Catholic materials to reform use in *Tudor Books of Private Devotion.* Alison Shell, in "Catholic Texts and Anti-Catholic Prejudice in the 17th-Century Book Trade," 33–57, shows that there was a continuum, not necessarily an opposition, between Catholic and Protestant texts; Protestant polemicists even assisted in the distribution of Catholic texts by reprinting whole documents in the course of argument.

3. Duffy, *Stripping of the Altars,* 537–43.

4. The Jesuits, it seems, made a point of casting their nets widely in their English missionary work; their proselytizing manuals give instructions on dealing with Catholics, "heretics," "schismatics," and "lukewarm Catholics." See Questier, "'Like Locusts over All the World': Conversion, Indoctrination, and the Society of Jesus in Late Elizabethan and Jacobean England," in *Reckoned Expense,* ed. McCoog, 272.

5. Wright, *Disposition or Garnishmente of the Sovle,* sig. A3v.

6. Saenger, "Books of Hours and the Reading Habits of the Later Middle Ages," 141–73; Saenger, *Space between Words,* 256–76; and Chartier, "Practical Impact of Writing," in *Passions of the Renaissance,* vol. 3 of *History of Private Life,* ed. Chartier, 124–27.

7. LeClerq, *Love of Learning and the Desire for God.*

8. Hyma, *Christian Renaissance;* Grundler, "Devotio Moderna," 176–93.

9. Zerbolt of Zutphen, "Spiritual Ascents," 286–87.

10. Retha M. Warnicke, "Lady Mildmay's Journal," 55–68, notes that Lady Mildmay, disregarding theological disputations, read the Catholic *Imitatio,* along with the Geneva Bible and Foxe's *Book of Martyrs.*

11. Thomas, "Cases of Conscience in Seventeenth-Century England," in *Public Duty and Private Conscience in Seventeenth-Century England,* ed. Morrill. Thomas also notes that this early concern with the movements of personal conscience (the "private spirit" of my title), developed into our late twentieth-century notion of the primacy of "sincerity of intention" (52).

12. Pritchard, *Catholic Loyalism in Elizabethan England,* 3–7.

13. Bossy, *English Catholic Community, 1570–1850,* 12.

14. Perez Zagorin, *Ways of Lying,* discusses religious dissidence in terms of such external observance of religious ceremony, with an accompanying clandestinity and dissimulation among recusant Catholics, the Spanish illuminists, and others.

15. Rose, *Cases of Conscience,* 222–33.

16. See Walsham, *Church Papists,* and Rose, *Cases of Conscience,* esp. 58–113 for Catholic responses to the legal repression.

17. Corthell, "'The Secrecy of Man,'" 272–90.

18. The standard bibliographies are Allison and Rogers, *Catalogue of Catholic Books in English Printed Abroad or Secretly in England, 1558–1640;* and Clancy, *English Catholic Books, 1641–1700.* See also the bibliography in Southern's *Elizabethan Recusant Prose, 1559–1582,* 367–514.

19. Roberts, introduction to *Critical Anthology of English Recusant Devotional Prose, 1558–1603,* ed. Roberts, 3–7. For more on clandestine printing in the period, see Rostenberg, *Minority Press and the English Crown.* For the relationship of printing to the Jesuit mission, see Nancy Pollard Brown, "Robert Southwell: The Mission of the Written Word," in *Reckoned Expense,* ed. McCoog, 193–213.

20. Knox, *Enthusiasm,* chap. 12.

21. Ceri Sullivan, in *Dismembered Rhetoric,* compares recusant books, and recusant catechisms in particular, to sixteenth-century courtesy manuals: "The authors write as though each reader fashions himself, building up a spiritual body by devotional exercises. Such dealing is within the reach of every member of the laity. The reader is not elected, his desire to pray is sufficient; he does not need special ability, the manuals give him all the technical knowledge needed" (123).

22. Luis de Granada, *Memoriall of a Christian Life,* sig. A1v.

23. Brown, "Robert Southwell," 208–9, notes that a reading of six recently identified manuscript versions of the *Rules* shows that the first printed edition removed all references to its woman reader, as well as making other substantive changes.

24. Southwell, *Two Letters and Short Rules of a Good Life,* 42. All further page numbers will be cited parenthetically.

25. Chartier, *Cultural Uses of Print in Early Modern France,* 223.

26. Martz, *Poetry of Meditation.*

27. Barbara Lewalski in *Protestant Poetics and the Seventeenth-Century Religious Lyric* and others, such as Chana Bloch in *Spelling the Word,* have emphasized the essentially scriptural basis for the work of these poets. But why divorce these imaginative exercises based on the Bible from the earlier Catholic tradition? Again, I

would like to suggest that though doctrinal differences existed, both Catholic and Protestant poets shared an imaginative tradition.

28. A missionary priest, accustomed to discretion in the conduct of his work, Southwell's life is almost emblematic of silent and suppressed English Catholicism. Sent to France to study as a fifteen-year-old boy, he lost fluency in English and had to relearn it before returning to England. See *Poems of Robert Southwell, S.J.*, xix–xx. Under torture by the priest-hunter Topcliffe, Southwell refused to disclose his name, only allowing that he was "a gentleman," even though, clearly, his identity was known (Pollard, introduction to *Two Letters*, xv).

29. Elsky, *Authorizing Words*, chap. 4, discusses the ways in which the era of print, with its new approaches to space, typography, and graphical elements, ushers in "the visualization of language" (128).

30. Garnet, *Societie of the Rosary*, sig. D5r.

31. See Fea, *Secret Chambers and Hiding-Places;* and Squiers, *Secret Hiding-Places.*

32. Secker, "Consolatory Literature of the English Recusants."

33. Worthington, *Rosarie of Our Ladie*, sig. *4r.

34. Hanson, "Torture and Truth in Renaissance England," 55.

35. The importance of ceremony and public prayer for the Anglican church and its diminishing of the relative significance of preaching the word are discussed in Peter Lake, "Laudian Style," 161–85.

36. See New, *Anglican and Puritan*, 72; and Davies, *Worship and Theology in England from Cranmer to Hooker, 1534–1603*, 127–293.

New looks at the sacramentalism (and concomitant sacerdotalism and dependence on priestly mediation) of the Anglicans. Davies explores the liturgical alternatives and shows that the Puritan view was not monolithic; the possibilities for the form of prayer differed as much with the individual as with the sect.

37. Robinson, *Of Religious Commvnion Private, & Publique*, sig. C3r–C3v.

38. *Dictionary of National Biography*, s.v. "Hill, Robert." Hill received his B.A. from Christ College, Cambridge, and served as chaplain to Lord Chief-Justice Popham.

39. Hill, *Pathway to Prayer and Pietie*, sig. K4v.

40. *Dictionary of National Biography*, s.v. "Parr, Elnathan." Elnathan Parr (d. 1632?) was educated at Eton and King's College, Cambridge, served as minister at Palgrave, Suffolk, a benefice that belonged to the Cornwallis family, and was the author of theological treatises and a collection of hexameter verses in Latin.

41. Parr, *Abba Father*, sig. A6r–A6v.

42. "Root and Branch Petition, A.D. 1640," in *Documents Illustrative of English Church History*, ed. Gee and Hardy, 538–41.

43. "Solemn League and Covenant," in *Documents*, ed. Gee and Hardy, 571–72.

44. Andrewes, *Manual of Private Devotions and Meditations*, sig. A4r–A5v.

45. See Guibbory, *Ceremony and Community*, esp. 11–43 and 131–38, for a discussion of ceremony and its place in religious worship after the abolition of the Book of Common Prayer.

46. Though Protestantism is frequently associated with univeral access to the Scriptures, the Bible was at first restricted to certain classes of readers. Gawthrop

and Strauss, for instance, in "Protestantism and Literacy in Early Modern Germany," discuss Luther's belief that reading was a tool for separating the able few from the many. He came to view catechisms, and not the Bible, as the best tool for teaching the masses.

Even in England, the reading of Scripture was at first highly restricted. English Law (34 & 35 Henry VIII) limited Bible-reading by sex and class: noblemen could read the Scriptures both for themselves and others; the bourgeois and female nobility could read for themselves alone; all other women and workingmen were entirely forbidden. See Gilmont, "En guise de conclusion," 482.

47. Kort, *"Take, Read,"* 35.

48. *Dictionary of National Biography,* s.v. "Ambrose, Isaac." Ambrose (1604–1663 or 1664), was one of the king's four preachers in Lancashire during the 1630s, but he eventually "associated himself with the establishment of presbyterianism in the county" and in 1662 he was ejected from his living at Garstang for nonconformity.

49. Ambrose, *Prima, the First Things,* sig. Hhh1v.

50. *Dictionary of National Biography,* s.v. "Byfield, Nicholas." Byfield (1579–1622), a Puritan minister, was a strict sabbatarian whose writings have been described as "Calvinistic."

51. The directives given in these spiritual books for the creation of commonplace books show the gradual popularization of this form among new readers and those without a classical education. Moss, *Printed Commonplace Books,* describes their use in the classical curriculum and the rigor with which teachers guided their students' marking of texts (88–89), their selection of appropriate commonplaces, and their use as rhetorical and educational (but not spiritual) tools (222–24). None of the spiritual guides I have come across exact stringent standards of their readers; the person of faith is apparently expected to rely on the spirit to guide him in this act of authorship. (This evidently was the case until the late seventeenth century, when printed commonplace books helped commercialize the genre and guide public tastes.) See Benedict, *Making the Modern Reader,* 43–44.

52. See Tickell, *Crums of Bread for the Dove in the Clefts of the Rock,* which also suggests the construction of a notebook and recommends other titles that could guide the layperson in the reading of Scripture: paraphrases, keys, commentaries, etc.

John Marbeck's (or Marbecke) *Concordance, That Is to Saie, a Work Wherein by the Ordre of the Letters of the A.B.C. Ye Maie Redely Finde Any Worde Conteigned in the Whole Bible, So Often As It Is There Expressed or Mencioned* was the first such scriptural aid in English. Marbeck is careful to explain the concept of alphabetization and apologizes for the problem of variant "Englishing" of Latin words.

53. Sharpe, *Triall of the Protestant Private Spirit,* sig. *2v–*3r.

54. Contrast this with recusant rhetoric: Sullivan argues that "the subject which a Catholic text discusses is fixed; the material of the faith is, in terms of rhetoric, a series of commonplaces. Nor can the speaker's approach be altered, since an interpretation provided by the Church is regarded as immutable. . . . Vernacular meditations, hagiographies, and catechisms were produced in order to persuade the reader to true devotion, to change himself rather than the texts" (14). In the

Protestant approach to devotional reading, the text itself can be subject to multiple meanings.

55. Rahner, *Ignatius the Theologian,* 136–80, discusses the discernment of spirits in Ignatian spirituality.

56. See how Stallybrass, in "Shakespeare, the Individual, and the Text," 594, places the term *individual* in a theological context and traces its connotations in the *OED* from indivisibility and oneness to separation and dividedness from others.

57. In chap. 19 of *The English Bible and the Seventeenth-Century Revolution,* Christopher Hill attributes the gradual dethronement of the Bible in the late seventeenth century to this sort of individual interpretation, toleration of differing religious opinions, and the discovery that any political party could cite Scripture to its benefit: "The Bible lost its universal power once it had been demonstrated that you could prove anything from it, and that there was no means of deciding once the authority of the church could not be enforced. (How right Rome had been!)" (428). It proved, Hill believes, "a sword to divide." See his *Intellectual Origins of the English Revolution Revisited,* 380.

58. Osborne, *Private Christians Non Vltra,* sig. C2r [i.e., D2r].

59. Gavison, "Privacy and the Limits of the Law," 443.

2: Authoring the Private Self

1. Curtius, *European Literature and the Latin Middle Ages,* 302–47; Gellrich, *Idea of the Book in the Middle Ages.*

2. Dante Alighieri, *Divine Comedy,* 377.

3. Thomas, *Religion and the Decline of Magic,* 45–46, 230 ff. Consider the talismanic power of the book in Christopher Marlowe's *Doctor Faustus* (c. 1588/89, published 1604) or in Thomas Middleton and William Rowley's *The Changeling* (1623), and the awe with which parish Bibles and finely decorated liturgical manuals must have been regarded. Even the modern fascination with and appreciation of books of the manuscript era (which are chiefly religious works) has less to do with their content than with their age and an appreciation of the bookmaker's craft.

4. For a description of the activity leading to the spread of the Bible in England, see Dickens, *Thomas Cromwell and the English Reformation,* esp. 116–17. In 1538 a royal proclamation had the effect of requiring that every parish in England purchase an English Bible from church funds. A circular letter from Thomas Cromwell in spring 1538 brought pressure on the bishops to conform.

5. Ong, *Orality and Literacy,* 112–13.

6. Ragussis, *Figures of Conversion,* 33.

7. Wilson, *Zachevs Converted,* sig. A6v–A7r.

8. Smith, *Admirable Convert,* sig. A3r–A4r.

9. Alleine, *True Way to Happiness,* sig. B6r–B6v.

10. This is what Joan Webber, *Eloquent "I",* 22, calls "the double intention" of John Bunyan's *Grace Abounding.* It is, however, not specific to *Grace Abounding;* all first-person narratives in some way exhibit this double purpose.

11. Delany, *British Autobiography in the Seventeenth Century,* 167.

12. Webber makes this distinction (*Eloquent "I",* 28) between the progressive,

purposeful action of the Puritan conversion narrative and the contemplative mode of the Anglican, exemplified by John Donne's *Devotions Upon Emergent Occasions.*

13. Virginia Lieson Brereton says that all conversion narratives are ipso facto success stories; we do not read the stories of those who fail in their battle against Satan. See her *From Sin to Salvation,* xiii.

14. McKeon, *Origins of the English Novel 1600–1740,* and Hunter, *Before Novels,* discuss, respectively, "histories of the individual" (90–128) and "private histories" (303–23), including religious narratives, as precursors to the novel. They might have included all four of my examples in their studies as "pre-novels." But I hope my examination of the subjects of the stories (specifically, their female protagonists and their relation to authority) may help explain, in part, the suspicion with which the novel, and female reading of the novel, has always been viewed.

15. *Dictionary of National Biography,* s.v. "Jessey, Henry."

16. Jessey, *Exceeding Riches of Grace,* sig. A2r.

17. *OED,* s.v. "Wight" (1.b), "orig. and chiefly with (good or bad) epithet, applied to supernatural, preternatural, or unearthly beings." (2.) "A human being, man or woman, person. Now *arch.* or *dial.* (often implying some contempt or commiseration)." The *OED* also traces a root from the Gothic with the meaning of "naught."

18. Women's stories of course had long been penned by men, who often assumed the first-person voice. See Hobby's *Virtue of Necessity,* 31–36, on Anna Trapnel; and Boffey's "Women Authors and Women's Literacy in Fourteenth- and Fifteenth-Century England," 159–82, in which Boffey discusses Margery Kempe's inability to read and write and the fact that she continued to use an amanuensis over a period of twenty years.

19. Bynum, in *Holy Feast and Holy Fast,* remarks on the phenomenon of "fasting girls" (74–75) and reports that not eating was viewed as supernaturally caused, but the cause could be miraculous or demonic (195). See 125, 138, and 196 for particular women whose fasts were considered to be possible cases of demonic possession.

20. Jessey, *Exceeding Riches of Grace,* 7th ed., sig. A7r–A7v.

21. Sharrock, introduction to Bunyan, *Grace Abounding to the Chief of Sinners;* Hawkins, "Double-Conversion in Bunyan's *Grace Abounding,*" 260; Bruss, *Autobiographical Acts,* 47; Hill, *Turbulent, Seditious, and Factious People,* 63–64.

22. Pooley, "*Grace Abounding* and the New Sense of Self," 110.

23. Bruss, *Autobiographical Acts,* 34.

24. Nussbaum, "By These Words I Was Sustained."

25. Gunn, *Autobiography,* 8–9.

26. Bunyan, *Grace Abounding to the Chief of Sinners,* 7. All further quotations from this edition will be cited parenthetically.

27. Louis B. Wright, in *Middle-Class Culture in Elizabethan England,* quotes William Perkins, a preacher whose *A Direction for The Government of the Tongue according to God's Word* was printed eight times between 1593 and 1634: "All this which is set down concerning speech, must as well be practiced in writing, as in speaking. Wherby are condemned ballads, books of love, all idle discourses and histories, being nothing else but enticements and baites unto manifolde sinnes." Wright mentions many other authors who inveigh against books that had no good

or useful purpose (231–35). These included romances such as *The Most Pleasant Historie of Ornatus and Artesia* (1595), *The Famous Historie of Montelyon* (1633), or the picaresque *The Pleasaunt Historie of Lazarillo de Tormes* (1586). Tales such as these had a long shelf life, and were reprinted many times after their first publication. See Wright, chap. 11, and also Davis, *Factual Fictions,* 67–69.

28. Compare the 1669 memoirs of Elizabeth White, a seventeenth-century Puritan: "I was a great lover of Histories, and other foolish Books, . . . so bewitched by them, that I could not forbear." Quoted in Caldwell, *Puritan Conversion Narrative,* 8.

29. Beal, "*Grace Abounding to the Chief of Sinners:* John Bunyan's Pauline Epistle," 147–60; Thickstun, "Preface to Bunyan's *Grace Abounding* as Pauline Epistle," 180–82.

30. Webber, *Eloquent "I,"* 21.

31. See Mullett, *John Bunyan in Context,* 30–32, where he attributes Bunyan's depression and guilt, in part, to reading the Bible as "a string of brief slogans."

32. Hill, *Turbulent, Seditious, and Factious People,* 68.

33. Murphey, "Psychodynamics of Puritan Conversion," 147.

34. Hill, *Turbulent, Seditious, and Factious People,* 73.

35. Luxon, *Literal Figures,* 143.

36. Sharrock, *Grace Abounding,* xxv–xxvi, points out that the imprisonment was a period of great productivity for Bunyan the writer, during which he published *Profitable Meditations* (1661), *Christian Behaviour* (1663), *I Will Pray with the Spirit* (1663), *One Thing is Needful* (1664?), *Prison Meditations* (1665), and *The Holy City* (1665).

37. Caldwell, *Puritan Conversion Narrative,* 50–51.

38. Greaves, *John Bunyan and English Nonconformity,* 194, sees *Grace Abounding* as "a demonstration of [Bunyan's] credentials as a religious leader."

39. Lukács, *Theory of the Novel,* 89.

40. Burnet, *Conversion & Persecutions of Eve Cohan,* pref.

41. In a study of twentieth-century converts, *Understanding Religious Conversion,* Lewis R. Rambo points out that marginal people (such as the girls of these conversion narratives) "are, in some way, disconnected from the sources of power and support of the traditional culture. The more marginal, the more likely they are to convert" (41). Through the act of conversion, the convert feels "filled with power, has access to power, or is somehow connected with either an external source of power (God) or an internal sense of power that may be perceived as spiritual or divine" (85). Perhaps their appearance as heroines of a conversion fiction bestowed on these women the sort of power that was absent from their everyday lives.

42. Shapiro, *Shakespeare and the Jews,* 120, 132.

43. Brereton notes that nineteenth-century women authors often gave up novel reading in the process of their conversions while retaining the language and style of sentimental fiction in their own work. The "feeling heart" (26) of woman linked the genres, though the chronological ordering and influences of the two were reversed during the seventeenth century.

44. Augustine regarded tears as a necessary preliminary to his own conversion: "A mighty rain of tears" preceded the command to take up the Gospel and read. See his *Confessions,* 223–25. But the salutary effects of tears begins to degenerate

into bathos during the seventeenth century. After the decidedly unsentimental treatment of weeping by Robert Southwell in *Marie Magdalens Funeral Tears* (1591) came George Herbert's "Marie Magdelene"; Richard Crashaw's "Saint Mary Magdalen, or, The Weeper," "The Teare," "A Hymne to Sainte Teresa," "The Flaming Heart," and "Hymn in the Nativity"; and Andrew Marvell's "Eyes and Tears." All of these invoke a baroque excess of sentiment in their portrayal of the female saint (Magdalen and Teresa) or the weak (the infant Christ).

45. See Damrosch, *God's Plot and Man's Stories,* 13–15, for a discussion of the displacement of God by other forces in the novel.

46. Armstrong and Tennenhouse, *Imaginary Puritan,* 204–12.

47. *Account of the Seducing of Ann,* sig. A1r. All further references will be cited parenthetically.

48. Boyarin, "Placing Reading," 24.

49. Fish, *Self-Consuming Artifacts,* 24.

50. Ibid., 3.

51. Such "histories" also cast women in an ambiguous light. As Katharine Eisaman Maus has said, in a discussion of Desdemona's and Othello's past lives, "For a beautiful young woman to have a history can mean only one thing," i.e., that she is unchaste. See *Inwardness and Theater in the English Renaissance,* 124.

3: "Extasies in Letters"

1. Hall, *Hidden Dimension,* 109.

2. Brooks, *Body Work,* 33.

3. On the relationship between privacy, territoriality, and the protection of personal space, see Hall, *Hidden Dimension,* 107–22; Altman, *Environment and Social Behaviour;* Klopfer and Rubenstein, "The Concept Privacy and Its Biological Basis," 52–65; and Altman, "Privacy as an Interpersonal Boundary Process," 113–18.

4. Elias, *Civilizing Process;* Jacques Revel, "The Uses of Civility," in *Passions of the Renaissance,* vol. 3 of *History of Private Life,* ed. Chartier, 167–205.

5. French critics and critics of French literature seem to have been especially interested in this notion of the letter as a closer of distances. See, for example, Arrou-Vignod, *Le discours des absents;* and "Men/Women of Letters," ed. Charles A. Porter, a special issue of *Yale French Studies* 71 (1986): 1–212.

6. Patterson, "Misinterpretable Donne."

7. Chartier, "Model Letters and Letter-Writing in Ancien Régime France," in *Correspondence,* 2.

8. Lisa Jardine, "Reading and the Technology of Textual Affect: Erasmus's Familiar Letters and Shakespeare's King Lear," in *Practice and Presentation of Reading,* ed. Raven, Small, and Tadmor, 77–101, argues that Erasmsus's letters contribute to this notion of "letter writing and reading as emotionally charged events" (78).

9. For contemporary and modern discussions of early modern rhetorical practice, see Hoskins, *Directions for Speech and Style,* 4–8; and Baldwin, *Medieval Rhetoric and Poetic (to 1400),* 206–27. Hoskins (1566–1638) was an acquaintance of both Donne and Ben Jonson, and his instructions "for penning of letters" was certainly known by the latter and most likely by the former writer.

10. Faulhaber, "The Letter-Writer's Rhetoric," 95.

11. From Jean Puget de La Serre's *The Secretary in Fashion,* quoted in Goldberg, *Writing Matter,* 253. Physical distancing continues to be "a symbolic definition of status," as Foddy notes in "A Critical Evaluation of Altman's Definition of Privacy as a Dialectical Process," 303, and has implications for identity within the community as well.

12. For a discussion of Erasmus's guide, see Rummel, "Erasmus's Manual of Letter-writing."

13. Day, *English Secretorie.* For an interesting discussion of Day's work and its relation to career secretaries, political secrets, and authorship, see Rambuss, *Spenser's Secret Career,* 30–48.

14. For a fuller discussion and bibliography, see Robertson, *Art of Letter Writing.*

15. The extremely popular genre included works such as Nicholas Breton's *Conceyted Letters, Newly Layde Open* (1618); *A Poste with a Madde Packet of Letters* (1602); William Fulwood's *The Enimie of Idlenesse* (1568); Thomas Gainsford's *The Secretaries Studie* (1616); I. W.'s *A Speedie Poste, with Certaine New Letters* (1625); and M. R.'s *A President for Young Pen-men: or, The Letter Writer* (1615).

16. Goldsmith, "Authority, Authenticity, and the Publication of Letters by Women," 47.

17. The first set of statistics below was compiled by examining the entries beginning with the word *letter* or *letters* in Jackson, Ferguson, and Pantzer, *Short-Title Catalogue;* Wing, *Short-Title Catalogue;* and an index to these two works, Allison and Goldsmith's *Titles of English Books.* The second set derives from a search in May 1998 of *WorldCat,* an online database, which, unfortunately, does not afford the searcher the opportunity of removing microform duplicates from the search results. Neither sample, then, is completely accurate, but one may observe, nonetheless, the increase in the publication of letters between 1475 and 1700.

PUBLISHED LETTERS, 1475–1700

	STC	*WorldCat*		*STC*	*WorldCat*
1475–1500	0	22	1601–1610	17	72
1501–1510	0	10	1611–1620	19	103
1511–1520	0	13	1621–1630	21	108
1521–1530	0	10	1631–1640	15	78
1531–1540	3	16	1641–1650	320	2001
1541–1550	2	20	1651–1660	128	686
1551–1560	5	21	1661–1670	32	496
1561–1570	2	27	1671–1680	98	1064
1571–1580	7	50	1681–1690	281	1967
1581–1590	15	69	1691–1700	257	1633
1591–1600	9	77			

18. See, for instance, the political and military letters of William Brereton (1643–45) (Wing B4368–4370); John Hotham, *Certaine Letters Sent from Sir Iohn Hotham, Young Hotham, the Major of Hull, and Others* (1643) Wing H2903; and *Letters by which it is certified, that Sir Samuell Luke Tooke at Islip. Fiftie Horse* (1644) Wing L1775.

19. The letters of Thomas Wentworth, earl of Strafford, before his execution provide a poignant (and no doubt politically inflammatory) mixture of the personal and political. See *The Earle of Strafford's Letter to his Lady. Sent by a Trvsty Messenger, with his Prayer on the Scaffold at Tower Hill, 12. of May 1641* (1641?), Wing S5788; and *A Letter Sent from the Earle of Strafford to His Lady in Ireland a Little before His Death: May 11, 1641* (1641), Wing S5786.

20. Maddison, "'King's Cabinet Opened,'" 2–9.

21. Patterson, *Censorship and Interpretation,* 209.

22. Sharpe, "Image of Virtue," 244–45, remarks that Charles had a "near obsession with privacy," replacing double locks with treble ones, and restricting access to keys and to his private apartments.

23. The staying power of Charles's "sanctity" is apparent from an article in the Jan. 25, 1994, issue of the *Chicago Tribune* (sect. 5, p. 1–2). In "Redress for a King," Glen Elsasser reported on the continued veneration of Charles by the Anglican Society of King Charles the Martyr and the annual commemoration of his death on Jan. 30.

24. Charles I, *Kings Cabinet Opened,* sig. A3r.

25. Goldberg, *Writing Matter,* 57–107.

26. James I, "Basilikon Doron," in *Political Works of James I,* ed. McIlwain, 12.

27. Schoenfeldt, "'Subject to Ev'ry Mounters Bended Knee,'" 247.

28. Quoted in Schoenfeldt, 247.

29. Goldberg, *James I and the Politics of Literature,* 149.

30. Kantorowicz, *King's Two Bodies,* 16.

31. For discussions of the *Eikon Basilike,* see Corns, *Uncloistered Virtue;* Madan, *New Bibliography of the Eikon Basilike;* Potter, *Secret Rites and Secret Writing;* and Zwicker, *Lines of Authority.*

32. Potter, *Secret Rites and Secret Writing,* 175.

33. Grossman, "Dissemination of the King," 261–63.

34. Potter, *Secret Rites and Secret Writing,* 138–39.

35. *Eikon Basilike,* ed. Knachel, 133.

36. *Rump: or an exact collection of the choycest poems and songs relating to the late times,* 1:170. Quoted in Patterson, *Censorship and Interpretation,* 209.

37. For the view of the hermaphrodite or androgyne as monster, or at least a person of mixed nature, rather than as symbol of love-union or concordia discors, see Cheney, "Spenser's Hermaphrodite and the 1590 *Faerie Queene*"; Silberman, "The Hermaphrodite and the Metamorphosis of Spenserian Allegory"; and Silberman, "Mythographic Transformations of Ovid's Hermaphrodite."

38. Milton, *Eikonoklastes,* ed. Hughes, vol. 3 of *Complete Prose Works of John Milton,* ed. Wolfe, 537–39.

39. Grossman, "Dissemination of the King," 268–72.

40. Maguire, "Theatrical Masque/Masque of Politics," 22.

41. Cable, "Milton's Iconoclastic Truth," 136.

42. Milton himself, in his *History of Britain,* insisted that "Laws are Masculin Births"—there was no room for the feminine in the rule of law. See Stevie Davies, *Feminine Reclaimed,* 180.

43. Discussions on Elizabeth's political uses of gender abound. For a sampling, see Axton, *Queen's Two Bodies;* Forster, *Icy Fire,* 122–47; Jankowski, "'As I Am Egypt's Queen'"; Levin, *"The Heart and Stomach of a King";* Marotti, "'Love Is Not Love'"; and Marcus, "Shakespeare's Comic Heroines, Elizabeth I, and the Political Uses of Androgyny."

44. Thompson and Padover, *Secret Diplomacy,* 259.

45. Trithemius was suspected of practicing black magic; his book was burned by at least one (unofficial) censor. See Galland, *Historical and Analytical Bibliography of the Literature of Cryptology;* and Shulman, *Annotated Bibliography of Cryptography.* Trithemius's fascination with secret writing was shared by Francis Bacon, who proposed a ciphered alphabet in the *Advancement of Learning* (1605). See *De Dignitate et Augmentis Scientarum,* in *Philosophical Works of Francis Bacon,* ed. Robertson, 527–29; and Robert Leslie Ellis's notes on writing in cipher, in the same volume, 636–38.

46. Smith, *Life and Letters of Sir Henry Wotton,* 1:253–69 and 2:265.

47. Henrietta Maria, *Qveen's Maiesties Gracious Answer,* sig. A2v.

48. Maddison, "'King's Cabinet Opened,'" 4.

49. Anderson, *Words That Matter,* 189, 229.

50. Altman, "Letter Book as a Literary Institution 1539–1789," 19.

51. Constable, *Letters and Letter-Collections,* 13.

52. Bennett, "Donne's *Letters to Severall Persons of Honour,*" 126.

53. Sullivan, *Influence of John Donne,* 43–46.

54. The letters have been dated in discussions by Shapiro, "The Text of Donne's *Letters to Severall Persons*"; Bennett, "Donne's Letters from the Continent in 1611–1612"; Bennett, "Donne's *Letters to Severall Persons of Honour*"; Simpson, *Study of the Prose Works of John Donne,* 291–336; and Bald, *Donne: A Life.* Gosse, in *Life and Letters of John Donne, Dean of St. Paul's,* 1:233, remarks that "John Donne the younger edited, or rather flung to the world in complete disorder" his father's letters. Keynes, in *A Bibliography of Dr. John Donne, Dean of Saint Paul's,* 247, has a similarly negative view of the younger Donne, and finds it "difficult not to suspect Donne of sharp practice." These aspersions on Donne's character are not, of course, necessarily connected with his editing practices, but they do give rise to questions about his motives and intentions in publishing his father's works.

55. Although postal carriers in the 1580s were warned against opening mail, Donne was quite right to be concerned about the privacy of his mail. By the 1650s, suspected letters were opened as a matter of course by an expert letter-opener in the employ of the Secretary of State. The Great Fire of 1666 destroyed a device that could open and reseal letters without detection. For more information, see Robinson, *British Post Office,* esp. 16, 44–45, and 54–55.

56. See especially Marotti, *John Donne, Coterie Poet.* For a more recent discussion of Donne's coterie writings within a residually oral culture, see Wollman, "The 'Press and the Fire.'"

57. Donne, *Letters to Severall Persons of Honour (1651),* 140, 226, 262. All further page numbers will be cited parenthetically.

58. Smith, *Life and Letters of Sir Henry Wotton,* 1:351.

59. Ibid., 1:345.

60. Ibid., 1:359.

61. Carey, *John Donne: Life, Mind, and Art.* See Flynn, *Donne and the Ancient Catholic Nobility,* on Donne's Catholic heritage and his early years of exile on the Continent.

62. Sackton, "Donne and the Privacy of Verse," 69.

63. Consider, for example, the bookish metaphors in "To Mr. R. W.," "The Extasie," "To the Countesse of Bedford" (II), "To the Countesse of Bedford. On New-yeares Day," "Valediction to his Booke," and "To His Mistris Going to Bed." The book serves, not only as a mark of commemoration, but as an entrée into the psyche of his (primarily) female addressees.

64. Donne, *Complete English Poems of John Donne.* For commentary on this poem as well as Donne's other verse epistles, see Pebworth and Summers, "'Thus Friends Absent Speake.'"

65. See Gilman, *Iconoclasm and Poetry in the English Reformation,* 120–24, on portraits of Donne and on his personal collection of religious art; and Phillips, *Reformation of Images,* 149–51, on Donne's support of ceremony in Church of England ritual.

66. Bynum, *Resurrection of the Body in Western Christianity, 200–1336,* 340.

67. See, for example, Donne's sermons "Preached at Lincolns Inne" (1620?), *Sermons* 3:92–93; "Preached at White-Hall, the first Friday in Lent" (1622/3), *Sermons* 4:326–27; "Deaths Duell," (1630), *Sermons* 10:238). All citations are from *The Sermons of John Donne,* ed. Potter and Simpson.

68. See Shullenberger, "Love as a Spectator Sport in John Donne's Poetry," in *Renaissance Discourses of Desire,* ed. Summers and Pebworth, 46–62.

69. Carey, "John Donne's Newsless Letters."

70. Kundera, "You're Not in Your Own House Here, My Dear Fellow," 24.

4: Margaret Cavendish and the Virtues of Publication

1. For biographical information as well as critical analyses of Cavendish and her work, see Ferguson, "A 'Wise, Wittie and Learned Lady,'" 305–40; Grant, *Margaret the First;* Jones, *Glorious Fame;* Mendelson, *Mental World of Stuart Women;* and Smith, *Reason's Disciples,* 75–95. An older, and slightly patronizing, treatment is Henry Ten Eyck Perry's joint biography, *The First Duchess of Newcastle and Her Husband as Figures in Literary History.*

2. See, for example, Newton's discussion of the publication of Jonson's *Workes* in "Jonson and the (Re-)Invention of the Book," 31–55.

3. Earlier examples of women who published their works tend to illustrate the dangers of publication for women: Mary Wroth was castigated as a "hermaphrodite in show" for her roman-à-clef, *The Countess of Montgomery's Urania;* see *The Poems of Lady Mary Wroth,* 33–34, and Lamb, *Gender and Authorship in the Sidney Circle,* 142–93. Lady Eleanor Davies was regarded as mad and confined to Bedlam (Cope,

Handmaid of the Holy Spirit, 70, 86). Elizabeth Cary's *Tragedie of Mariam* was "stolen out of [her] sister-in-law's . . . chamber and printed, but by her own pronouncement was called in"; see *The Lady Falkland: Her Life* in *The Tragedie of Mariam, The Fair Queen of Jewry, with The Lady Falkland: Her Life,* ed. Weller and Ferguson, 190. Women tended to resort to manuscript transcription rather than print in this hostile environment, as Marotti notes in *Manuscript, Print, and the English Renaissance Lyric,* 61.

4. Jones, *Glorious Fame,* 161.

5. Potter, *Secret Rites and Secret Writing,* 138–39.

6. Fitzmaurice, in "Fancy and the Family," 198–209, notes that Cavendish frequently pictured herself as a "solitary genius"—when it suited her to do so.

7. Gagen, in "Honor and Fame in the Works of the Duchess of Newcastle," 522, places Margaret Cavendish's pursuit of fame within the context of the Renaissance concept of honor, which was comprised of both an inner quality of virtue and "the reward or public recognition given to outstanding virtue or merit." Cavendish was unusual in that she was a woman who sought this twofold distinction.

8. Brown, "Margaret Cavendish: Strategies Rhetorical and Philosophical," 29, speaks of Cavendish's "evasion of moral pronouncement" in order to circumvent restrictions on women's speech. I would argue, rather, that the author is not avoiding "fixed authority" but is simply pointing out the inconsistencies between public and private acts and between the moral expectations for men and women.

9. Jones, *Glorious Fame,* 130.

10. Shortly after his return to England in 1660, Charles II gave William Davenant and Thomas Killigrew monopolies on theater performances in London and charged them also to reform the theater. There had been sporadic theatrical productions throughout the 1650s, but Charles's act made them once again legal. See Potter, "Plays and the Playwrights: 1642–60," in *Revels History of Drama in English,* ed. Leach and Craik, 4:300–301.

11. No system of citation to the volume is satisfactory: there are errors in the signature marks, in pagination, and in scene numbering; the signature marks become unwieldy in such a long folio; and there is no standardized form for the act and scene divisions of Cavendish's multipart plays. For the sake of simplicity, therefore, I use page numbers for all citations to the plays themselves and signatures for the prefatory matter, which is unpaginated.

For biographical and bibliographical information on Allestry, Martin, and Dicas, see Plomer, *Dictionary of the Booksellers and Printers,* 2–3, 64, 123; and Rostenberg, "New Science," 237–80.

12. Not all copies of the 1662 *Playes* contain this engraving. It was inserted inconsistently in several of Cavendish's works. The University of Illinois's copy of the 1668 plays, for instance, contains the portrait, while its copy of the 1662 edition does not. The University Microfilms edition, which records the copy at the Huntington Library does, however, include this illustration. See Grant, *Margaret the First,* 142–43, and Fitzmaurice's "Fancy and the Family" for further discussion on the engravings prefacing Cavendish's writings.

13. The engraving was done by Abraham van Diepenbeke (1596–1675), an Antwerp painter and student and friend of Peter Paul Rubens. He worked in England

at the behest of Charles I and painted several portraits and landscapes for William Cavendish. See the brief biography in Bénézit, *Dictionnaire critique et documentaire,* 3:573.

The illustration he created for Margaret Cavendish's books bears striking similarities to a Rubens title page for Franciscus Aguilonius's *Opticorum Libri Sex* (1613). In the Rubens, the architectural structure is formed by caryatid herms representing Mercury and Minerva, each supporting a basket of fruit on the head. Minerva reappears in the Diepenbeke illustration, along with her spear and Medusa-bearing shield. The personification of Optica, however, is seated upon a platform bearing the title, rather than standing, as does Cavendish. See *Rubens and the Book,* ed. Held, 51–52, 243.

14. Corbett and Lightbown, *Comely Frontispiece,* 6–8.

15. Strong, *Cult of Elizabeth,* 147–49.

16. *New Catholic Encyclopedia,* s.v. "Ursula, St." and "Ursulines."

17. For the iconographical significance of the mythical figures and symbols used in this frontispiece, I have relied on Hall's *Dictionary of Subjects and Symbols in Art.*

18. Panofsky, *Tomb Sculpture,* 73.

19. Carl H. Pforzheimer, in his catalog, *Carl H. Pforzheimer Library,* 1:137 collates an ideal copy as follows: 2°: A²; A3–A7²; B–8I²; [-]²; 352 leaves. My thanks to Margaret Kulis, reference librarian at the Newberry Library, for locating this information for me.

20. Masten, *Textual Intercourse,* 157, notes that, unlike the commendatory verses prefacing the collected works of Shakespeare, Jonson, and Beaumont and Fletcher, Cavendish writes her own.

21. For the history and development of the theater and the related phenomenon of closet drama during the Commonwealth period, see Harbage, *Cavalier Drama,* 215–36; Hotson, *Commonwealth and Restoration Stage,* 3–58; Potter, "Plays and the Playwrights: 1642–60," in *Revels History of Drama in English,* ed. Leach and Craik, 4:261–304; Randall, *Winter Fruit;* and Wright, "Reading of Plays during the Puritan Revolution," 73–108.

22. See, for instance, her poem "Of Many Worlds in This World," in *Penguin Book of Renaissance Verse 1509–1659,* ed. Norbrook, 479.

23. For details on William Cavendish's own dramatic efforts (including those improved upon by James Shirley and Thomas Shadwell), consult Bentley, *Jacobean and Caroline Stage,* 3:142–51; Harbage, *Cavalier Drama;* and Randall, *Winter Fruit.* The Duke's literary interests also rubbed off on his daughters, Jane Cavendish and Elizabeth Brackley, who wrote their own closet piece, "The Concealed Fansyes."

24. Newcastle was one of Jonson's last patrons, commissioning him to write three masques: *The Entertainment at Blackfriars* (1624), *The King's Entertainment at Welbeck* (1633), and *Love's Welcome at Bolsover* (1634). See Kay, *Ben Jonson: A Literary Life,* 179–80. The influence of Jonson's "humorous" drama is evident in the plays of both Cavendishes.

25. See Rosenthal, *Playwrights,* 58–104.

26. In the prefatory letter to her husband in *Life of the Thrice Noble, High and*

Puissant Prince, William Cavendishe (1667), Margaret complains of these inconsistencies in her critics. See *Lives of William Cavendishe, Duke of Newcastle, and of His Wife, Margaret Duchess of Newcastle,* xx.

27. On the attacks on the stage and the suppression of stage-plays after 1642, see Butler, *Theatre and Crisis 1632–1642;* Gildersleeve, *Government Regulation of the Elizabethan Drama; English Drama and Stage under the Tudor and Stuart Princes 1543–1664,* esp. 63–70 and 231–52; Heinemann, *Puritanism and Theatre,* 18–47; and Thompson, *Controversy between the Puritans and the Stage.*

28. In addition to Henrietta Maria's controversial participation in a masque in 1633, the English royal family in exile acted along with members of the French nobility around 1654. See Harbage, *Cavalier Drama,* 11–18, 207; and *Revels History of Drama in English,* ed. Leach and Craik, 4:lii–liii.

29. For definitions of closet drama and their suitability for reading rather than the stage, see Barish, "Problem of Closet Drama in the Italian Renaissance," 4–30; and Hogendoorn, "Reading on a Booke," 50–66.

30. It appears Cavendish's own work habits mirrored her instructions for reading plays. Grant (*Margaret the First,* 113) repeats the possibly apocryphal story of Cavendish dictating her thoughts to her secretary and quotes Cavendish's own statements from *Nature's Pictures* about her habit of speaking her compositions aloud before she set pen to paper.

31. Newcastle's laudatory verse in the 1662 *Playes* is just one such example. He provided others for *The World's Olio* (1655), *The Philosophical and Physical Opinions* (1655), *Nature's Pictures* (1656) and *Sociable Letters* (1664).

32. Randall, *Winter Fruit,* 331, speaks of Cavendish being "refracted into more than one character" in her plays.

33. See Slights, *Ben Jonson and the Art of Secrecy,* 29, on disguise as an allusion to the secret self; it is a mode for both self-display and self-disguise.

34. Michael Shapiro examines the trope of the female page (and the inevitable sexual attraction between lord and squire) in *Gender in Play on the Shakespearean Stage,* 17, 209–11. Margaret Cavendish often combines Shapiro's roles of woman warrior and cross-dressed page in her "Heroickesses."

35. Dolores Paloma remarks that the fighting women in Cavendish's plays are able to defend themselves in battle precisely because of their moral power. See "Margaret Cavendish: Defining the Female Self," 56–57.

36. In her autobiography, Cavendish comments on her bashfulness among strangers and her social difficulties at court. See *True Relation* in her *Lives,* 278–80.

37. Quoted in Brett, *Charles II and His Court,* 5.

38. For a similarly perplexing attitude toward the marriage contract, see Cavendish's play *The Religious* (*Playes,* 1662) in which two young people, Lord Melancholy and Lady Perfection, are betrothed at a young age and later separated by their parents. The young man's forced marriage to another prevents their reunion, so Perfection leaves the world and becomes a hermit. The death of the man's wife does not even free them to marry because of her vow. Only some jesuitical quibbling by a pair of friars enables them to marry and to found a new religious order of chastity in marriage. It is unclear at the end of the play whether the "Religious Generation"

they will beget is a spiritual community of descendants or actual flesh-and-blood children. The important point I wish to make is that Cavendish reforms the marriage bond into a relationship that is primarily spiritual.

39. Jonson, *Ben Jonson: The Complete Poems,* ed. Parfitt, 211–15. For an explication of the poem, see Peterson, *Imitation and Praise in the Poems of Ben Jonson,* 195–232.

40. Jonson, "An Epigram. To William, Earl of Newcastle," in *Complete Poems,* 200.

41. Cavendish, *Lives,* 309.

42. Mendelson, *Mental World of Stuart Women,* 25–26.

43. Cavendish, *Lives,* 280.

44. See Trease, *Portrait of a Cavalier,* 95; and Margaret Cavendish's defense of his actions (and his orthodoxy) in *Lives,* 232–33.

45. Grant, *Margaret the First,* 28–29, 39.

46. Murray, *Antwerp in the Age of Plantin and Brueghel,* 73.

47. William Cavendish, *Ideology and Politics on the Eve of the Restoration,* 12, 20.

48. Elliott, *Spiritual Marriage,* 5.

49. *Female Academy,* the last play in the volume, offers a compromise: a life of solitude and a cloistered education for young girls, marriage thereafter.

50. See Marotti, *John Donne, Coterie Poet;* and Saunders, "Stigma of Print," 139–64.

51. Findley and Hobby in "Seventeenth Century Women's Autobiography," 30–31, see this conflict as the genesis for Cavendish's autobiography.

52. Plato, *Plato's Phaedrus,* ed. Hackworth, 156–57.

53. Neptune, after raping the beautiful Caenis, offers to fulfil any wish of hers. "Grant me / To cease to be a woman." Her wish granted, she spends the rest of her days in men's pursuits, renamed Caeneus. See Ovid, *Metamorphoses,* ed. Kenney, 279–80.

54. Seznec, in *Survival of the Pagan Gods,* 99–103, describes the Renaissance belief that hieroglyphs could prevent sacred mysteries from being comprehended by the uninitiated.

55. Pearson, *Prostituted Muse,* 9–10.

56. "Ben Jonson's Conversations with William Drummond of Hawthornden," in *Complete Poems,* 462.

57. Two critics pinpoint the cause of Sanspareille's death: her separation from the female community. Jacqueline Pearson, in "'Women May Discourse,'" 40, states that "a woman who is educated breaks her links with other women, and cannot function as a woman within society." Linda R. Payne, "Dramatic Dreamscape: Women's Dreams and Utopian Vision in the Works of Margaret Cavendish, Duchess of Newcastle," in *Curtain Calls,* ed. Schofield and Macheski, 29, asks whether it might have been "inconceivable that this remarkable woman could continue to bloom in a public role, particularly when further estranged from her sex by the vow of celibacy."

58. Grant, *Glorious Fame,* 218–22.

59. Kramer, in "'Thus by the Musick of a Ladyes Tongue,'" 57–79, empha-

sizes Sanspareille's educational successes but glosses over the character's death. She also offers a much more negative view of Innocence and Mother Love, making Sanspareille the only heroine of the play.

60. Pearson, "'Women May Discourse,'" 36–39, rightly notes that the fates of characters such as Innocence and Sanspareille reveal Cavendish's own ambivalences about the role of speaking and publishing women in a male-dominated society.

61. The Lady Victoria's politics appear to be those of Margaret Cavendish herself. In "Embracing the Absolute," 24–39, Gallagher argues that Cavendish's Toryism and feminism converge to create a connection between "the *roi absolu* and the *moi absolu.*"

5: Discovery, Pornography, and the Novel

1. The *OED* offers three definitions which are pertinent to our discussion of self-disclosure and the private self: 3.a. "To disclose or expose to view (anything covered up, hidden, or previously unseen), to reveal, show. (earliest usage, c. 1450)"; 4. "To divulge, reveal, disclose to knowledge (anything secret or unknown), to make known. *arch.* (earliest usage, 1300)"; 6. "To reveal the identity of (a person); hence, to betray. *arch.* (earliest usage, 1320)."

2. For a review of the social and critical reckoning of Aphra Behn and her writing, see Gallagher, *Nobody's Story,* 1–48; and Heidi Hutner, "Rereading Aphra Behn: An Introduction," in *Rereading Aphra Behn,* ed. Hutner, 2–3.

3. See entry under "Pornographer," *OED,* (f. Gr. harlot + writing, writer).

4. See Richetti, "Love Letters," 17, for comments on the novel's "double voicing" and the fact that, within the world of the novel, "no one's discourse can be trusted and . . . no one actually speaks to anyone else except for expressive or self-serving rhetorical purposes."

5. For the history of pornographic writing during the Renaissance, see Foxon, *Libertine Literature in England 1660–1745;* Fryer, *Private Case—Public Scandal,* 70–82; Thompson, *Unfit for Modest Ears;* Frantz, *Festum Voluptatis;* and *Invention of Pornography,* ed. Lynn Hunt.

For the simultaneous development of the novel in the seventeenth and eighteenth centuries, see McKeon, *Origins of the English Novel, 1600–1740* and Hunter, *Before Novels.*

6. There is a voluminous literature on the actual and supposed dangers of novel-reading and its relation to intimacy, privacy, sexuality, and the imagination. See, for example, Watt, *Rise of the Novel,* 198–200; Hunter, "Loneliness of the Long-Distance Reader," 455–85; Beaujour, "Exemplary Pornography," 325–49; Davis, *Factual Fictions,* 116–17; and Hunter, "World as Stage and Closet," 271–87.

7. For discussions of the ways in which women's writing and erotic writing may be regarded as equally transgressive, see Suleiman, "Pornography, Transgression, and the Avant-Garde," 117–36, esp. 119–21; Frappier-Mazur, "Marginal Canons," 112–28; and Pearson, *Prostituted Muse,* 6–14.

8. Jacob, "Materialist World of Pornography," in *Invention of Pornography,* ed. Hunt, 165.

9. The French tradition, with its links to "philosophy" and political subver-

sion, has been dealt with extensively in Goulemot, *Forbidden Texts;* and Darnton, *Forbidden Best-Sellers of Pre-Revolutionary France.* Though these two studies deal with a later period than that of which I treat, they are important for their consideration of the relationship between the spread of print culture and the accessibility of literary pornography.

10. Goulemot, *Forbidden Texts,* 62.

11. As I suggested in a previous chapter, certain seventeenth-century conversion narratives appeared to evolve into fictional narratives, precursors of the eighteenth- and nineteenth-century female-centered novel. The "downward" fate of the women in erotic fiction may further explain, as Judith Kegan Gardiner suggests, why women's erotic fiction has been effaced from the canon. See her "First English Novel," 202. Unlike sentimental fiction or the novel of manners in which the heroine is satisfactorily married in the end, the heroine's break from conventional social expectations made her an unacceptable model for impressionable female readers.

12. Norberg, "Libertine Whore," in *Invention of Pornography,* ed. Hunt, 227.

13. Shuger, *Renaissance Bible,* 190.

14. John Calvin, for instance, sees no significance in Christ's writing on the ground; he says it simply shows that he "despised them." However, he does emphasize their hypocrisy and notes that a "single word" from Christ "breaks the pride of hypocrites." See his commentary on John 8 in *John,* ed. McGrath and Packer, 204–5.

15. The role of men in the story of Lucrece provides a useful backdrop to the Gospel story. See Dubrow's "A Mirror for Complaints," 406–7 and Wall, *Imprint of Gender,* 216–17.

16. Susan Haskins traces and sorts out the various legends and representations of Mary Magdalen in *Mary Magdalen,* esp. 16–29, 93–97. For literary treatments of Mary Magdalen from the Middle Ages onward, see Karras, "Holy Harlots"; and Jacobs, "Image of Mary Magdalene in Seventeenth-Century Poetry," 62–78.

17. As Karras, *Common Women,* 141, points out, women were defined by their sexuality, and lust was the archetypal female sin; the redeemed whore therefore became a powerful (and peculiarly gender-informed) symbol of repentance.

18. My analysis follows closely that of Shuger, *Renaissance Bible,* 170–86, who discusses this sermon, along with other Magdalen texts, in conjunction with the theme of the abandoned woman and its roots in Ovid's *Heroides.*

19. Andrewes, "Sermon 14 of the Resurrection, Easter 1620," in *Sermons,* ed. Story, 194.

20. Wall, *Imprint of Gender,* 270.

21. See, for example, Lucas van Leyden's (ca. 1494–1533) engraving "Christ Appearing to the Magdalen" (1519), his ca. 1506 etching of the same title, and his engraving "Mary Magdalen in the Clouds" (1518) (in which she bears the vase of oils), or his naked and "Repentant Magdalen" (1505–6), all of which are reproduced in Harbison, "Lucas van Leyden," 117–29. Donatello played with baroque sentiments in his sculpture of the emaciated ascetic (15th cent.), in which the Magdalen's hair forms her only dress.

22. Reproductions of these artworks may be found in Harbison, "Lucas van

Leyden," Haskins, *Mary Magdalen,* 264, 301, 304, 305; and Shuger, *Renaissance Bible,* figs. 1–3.

23. Cranley, *Amanda: or, The Reformed Whore,* sig. A2r. Another edition was issued as *The Converted courtezan, or, the reformed whore* in 1639. The only extended discussion of Cranley's work is in Schmitz's *Fall of Women in Early English Narrative Verse,* 217–22.

24. See, for example, the epigrams of Martial and Ben Jonson, and Coiro's *Robert Herrick's Hesperides and the Epigram Book Tradition.*

25. Momus was the sleepy god of the Greeks who was "always railing and carping." Asked to judge the merits of Poseidon, Hephaestus, and Athena, Momus rebuked them all. Zoilus (4th cent. B.C.) was a Greek rhetorician nicknamed *Homeromastix* (Homer's Scourge) for his attacks on Homer's epics. See *Benet's Reader's Encyclopedia.*

26. Donne, "Elegie XVI. On his Mistris," in *Complete English Poems of John Donne,* ed. Patrides, 173–75.

27. According to Pendry, *Elizabethan Prisons and Prison Scenes,* 208–10, the Fleet housed prisoners of some social status, who, for a fee to the warden, were granted the freedom of the house.

28. The power of the refiner's fire to purge the dross out of base metal is a frequent biblical trope. See for example Daniel 11:35, Zechariah 13:9, and Malachi 3:3.

29. Johann Gutenberg was a goldsmith, and the skills of goldsmiths were often indispensable to early engravers and typefounders. See Steinberg, *Five Hundred Years of Printing,* 17, 23–24, and McMurtrie, *The Book,* 133.

30. Chaucer's *Troilus and Criseyde,* the pseudo-Chaucerian *The Complaint of the Lover of Christ Saint Mary Magdaleyn* (ca. 1520), Samuel Daniel's *The Complaint of Rosamund* (1592), John Sweetnam's *St. Mary Magdalen's Pilgrimage to Paradise* (1617), and Lope de Vega's *Las lágrimas de la Madalena* (1614) were all written in rime royal. See Schmitz, *Fall of Women in Early English Narrative Verse,* 175, 180, 219; and Davis, "Woman, Why Weepest Thou?" 42.

31. For a discussion of the Renaissance discomfort with the openness of women's bodies, see Stallybrass, "Patriarchal Territories," 123–42 and Paster, "Leaky Vessels."

32. Kendrick, in *Secret Museum,* 13, points out that the term *pornographer*—"whore-painter" or "whore-writer"—is ambiguous, and the maker of pornography has become tainted by the object he represents. Cranley is barely able to mask his interest in Amanda with religious zeal, while Behn strips her characters of this cover.

33. For Behn's complaints about this literary double standard, see Jessica Munns, "'Good, Sweet, Honey, Sugar-Candied Reader,'" in *Rereading Aphra Behn,* ed. Hutner, 51–53.

34. Paz, *Double Flame,* 16.

35. Sontag, "Pornographic Imagination," 47–48.

36. McLuhan, *Gutenberg Galaxy,* 191, 196.

37. Frantz, *Festum Voluptatis,* 144–45.

38. Weil, "Sometimes a Scepter Is Only a Scepter," in *Invention of Pornography,* ed. Hunt, 145–47.

39. In contrast, Ruth Perry writes of "the impotent suffering of the embattled heroine" of the epistolary novel in *Women, Letters, and the Novel,* 22.

40. Behn's anonymity was probably a matter of self-protection, given the abuse she had already suffered for her playwrighting by this time. Randal Taylor, publisher of *Love-Letters,* was known as a "trade" publisher (i.e., one who could shield the author against prosecution). See Todd, *Secret Life of Aphra Behn,* 310–11). But note that Susan Suleiman regards anonymity as one indication of the pornographic status of texts ("Pornography," 117).

41. Foucault, *History of Sexuality,* 1:21, 58–59.

42. Behn, *Love-Letters Between a Nobleman and His Sister (1684–7),* ed. Todd, ix. All further references to the novel and to the transcript of the trial (Appendix I) will be cited parenthetically. For other background information on the writing and publication of the novel, see Duffy, *Passionate Shepherdess,* 221–25.

43. Link, *Aphra Behn,* 131.

44. Kauffman, *Discourses of Desire,* 25.

45. Both Perry, *Women, Letters, and the Novel,* 26, and Day, *Told in Letters,* 160, emphasize Philander's "seduction" of Silvia and her attempts at resistance.

46. See Gardiner, "Aphra Behn: Sexuality and Self-Respect," 67–78, who says that Behn "consistently sees sexual passion—which involves a generous giving of oneself to others—as the root of all social impulse. Its emotional opposite is egotistical concentration on one's 'interests'" (77). Zimbardo, in "Aphra Behn: A Dramatist in Search of the Novel," in *Curtain Calls,* ed. Schofield and Macheski, 380–81, comments that the author "saw love itself as the boundary-breaking, elevating passion—not an idea of love that exists in the service of an idea of honor, as in the traditional love-and-honor formula, but rather as an idea of love that by itself *subsumes* honor and is in itself heroic." I agree that passion is almost always boundary-breaking, but in *Love-Letters,* it is hardly elevating or honorable.

47. A character named Silvia also appears in Behn's poetry (Behn, *Poetry,* ed. Todd). The Silvia/Sylvia of "A Dialogue for an Entertainment at Court, between Damon and Sylvia" (87–88) is the cruel fair, the beloved of a shepherd. "Song" (6), with its slightly bawdy innuendo, is reminiscent of the novel in depicting a Silvia who yields easily. The Silvia of "A Song in Dialogue" (354), like her counterpart in the novel, resists the shepherd's advances for fear of his inconstancy (see *Love-Letters,* 25–26,on Silvia's initial support of her sister). And Silvia is the addressee of a number of carpe diem poems ("The Golden Age, 30–35; "The Counsel," 79; "A Paraphrase on the Eleventh Ode Out of the first Book of Horace," 99). For the novelistic Silvia, the brevity of youth makes her resolved to make the most of her beauty before it is spoken of in the past tense.

48. See Vickers, "Diana Described," 265–79; and "'Blazon of Sweet Beauty's Best.'"

49. For discussions of the political subplot and the implications of Behn's Tory views in the novel, see Backschneider, *Spectacular Politics,* 107–24; Jacobs, "The Seduction of Aphra Behn," 395–403; Pollak, "Beyond Incest: Gender and the Politics of Transgression in Aphra Behn's Love-Letters between a Nobleman and His Sister," in *Rereading Aphra Behn,* ed. Hutner, 151–86; and Wehrs, "Eros, Ethics, Identity," 461–78.

50. See Pearson, "Gender and Narrative in the Fiction of Aphra Behn," 182. Silvia seems to experience none of the anxiety about "coition and composition" that seems to be the fate of male pornographic writers; see Boehrer, "Behn's 'Disapppointment' and Nashe's 'Choice of Valentines,'" 172–87.

51. Todd, "Who Is Silvia?" 202.

52. Pearson, "Gender and Narrative," 49, notes that, "in a world where the sexual double standard operates," dissimulation can be a woman's only resource. Pearson wishes to mitigate Silvia's "sins" in the name of some sort of female right to be equally as immoral as men.

53. Gallagher, *Nobody's Story,* 21.

54. Turner, "*Whores Rhetorick.*"

55. Warren Chernaik, *Sexual Freedom in Restoration Literature,* 176, 183, says that Behn's use of androgynous figures "calls into question the traditional boundaries of gender"; beauty is difficult to pin down as male or female, and "creativity, rational persuasion, and the spirit which is capable of giving life to inanimate matter are, paradoxically, both male in their nature and equally distributed among men and women."

56. Pearson, *Prostituted Muse,* 101–3, suggests that cross-dressing may be erotically stimulating and not especially subversive in Restoration drama. The female transvestite is a sympathetic figure because her disguise is not hypocritical but "a demonstration of a deeper truth." Silvia's cross-dressing is more complex: it does indeed reveal her inner truth—that she is like a man, but it at the same time also reveals her hypocrisy, her capacity for disguising her real self.

57. Ballaster, in "'Pretences of State': Aphra Behn and the Female Plot," in *Rereading Aphra Behn,* ed. Hutner, 205–6, makes a similar claim for the female narrator of *Oroonoko,* in which feminine clothing not only enhances female difference and arouses curiosity but bestows power: "The clothing that conceals her body, the writing that obscures the woman, only heightens the reader's pleasure, keeping possession out of reach and sustaining the libidinous drive of the text."

58. Pearson, "Gender and Narrative," 181.

59. Miller, *Novel and the Police,* 206.

60. Zimbardo, *Mirror to Nature,* 11.

Bibliography

Primary Sources

An Account of the Seducing of Ann, the Daughter of Edward Ketelbey, of Ludlow, Gent. to the Popish Religion, with Some Very Extraordinary Passages Relating Thereto, Particularly, of the Gross Prevarications, and Insolent Boldness of the Two Popish Bishops Leyborn and Gifforn in the Management of It. Humbly Presented to the Lords Spiritual and Temporal, and Commons, Now Assembled in Parliament. London: Printed and sold by J. Nutt, 1700. Wing A382.

Alberti, Leon Battista. *On the Art of Building in Ten Books.* Trans. Joseph Rykwert, Neil Leach, and Robert Tavernor. Cambridge: MIT Press, 1988.

Alleine, Joseph. *The True Way to Happiness, in a Serious Treatise, Shewing I. What Conversion Is Not. . . .* London: Printed, to be sold by Nevil Simmons, 1675. Wing A981.

Ambrose, Isaac. *Prima, the First Things, in Reference to, the Middle and Last Things: or, The Doctrine of Regeneration, the New Birth, the Very Beginning of a Godly Life.* London: By T. R. and E. M. for I. A. to be sold by Nathanael Webb and William Grantham, 1654. Wing A2965.

Andrewes, Lancelot. *A Manual of Private Devotions and Meditations of the Right Reverend Father in God, Lancelot Andrews, Late L. Bishop of Winchester. Translated out of a fair Greek MS of his Amanuensis.* London: Printed by T. N. for Anne Moseley, 1670. Wing A3136.

———. "Sermon 14 of the Resurrection, Easter 1620." In *Sermons,* ed. G. M. Story. Oxford: Clarendon Press, 1967.

Augustine. *Confessions.* Washington DC: Catholic Univ. of America Press, 1953.

Bacon, Francis. *Advancement of Learning (1605). De Dignitate et Augmentis Scientarum.* In *The Philosophical Works of Francis Bacon.* Ed. John M. Robertson from the texts . . . of Robert Leslie Ellis and James Spedding. Freeport NY: Books for Libraries Press, 1970.

———. "Of Building." *The Essayes or Counsels, Civill and Morall.* Ed. Michael Kiernan. Oxford: Clarendon Press, 1985.

Basset, R. *Curiosities: or The Cabinet of Nature. Containing Phylosophical, Naturall, and Morall Questions Fully Answered and Resolved.* London: Printed by N. and I. Okes, 1637. STC 1557.

Behn, Aphra. *Love-Letters Between a Nobleman and His Sister (1684–7).* Ed. Janet Todd. Columbus: Ohio State Univ. Press, 1993.

———. *Poetry.* Ed. Janet Todd. Columbus: Ohio State Univ. Press, 1992.

Bunyan, John. *Grace Abounding to the Chief of Sinners.* Ed. Roger Sharrock. Oxford: Clarendon Press, 1962.

Burnet, Gilbert. *The Conversion & Persecutions of Eve Cohan, Now Called Elizabeth Verboon, a Person of Quality of the Jewish Religion. Who Was Baptized the 10th of October, 1680. At*

St. Martins in the Fields, by the Right Reverend Father in God, William, Lord Bishop of St. Asaph. London: Printed by J. D. for Richard Chiswell, 1680. Wing B5772.

Byfield, Nicholas. *Directions for the Private Reading of the Scriptures . . . The fourth Edition. Wherein the Analyticall Tables Are Much and Profitably Inlarged, and Helps Prescribed to Those that Cannot Write or Read: By Jo. Geree M.A. and Pastour of Saint Faiths London. Whereunto Is Annexed a Pithy Direction to Reconcile Places of Scripture Which Seem Repugnant.* London: By M. F. for P. Stephens, 1648. Wing B6383.

Calvin, John. *John.* Ed. Alister McGrath and J. I. Packer. Wheaton: Crossway Books, 1994.

Cary, Elizabeth Cary. "The Lady Falkland: Her Life." In *The Tragedie of Mariam, The Fair Queen of Jewry, with The Lady Falkland: Her Life.* Ed. Barry Weller and Margaret W. Ferguson. Berkeley: Univ. of California Press, 1994.

Cavendish, Jane, and Elizabeth Brackley. "The Concealed Fansyes: A Play by Lady Jane Cavendish and Lady Elizabeth Brackley." Transcribed by Nathan Comfort Starr. *PMLA* 46 (1931): 802–28.

Cavendish, Margaret. *The Lives of William Cavendishe, Duke of Newcastle, and of His Wife, Margaret Duchess of Newcastle.* Ed. Mark Antony Lower. London: John Russell Smith, 1872.

———. *Playes.* London: Printed by A. Warren for John Martyn, James Allestry, and Tho. Dicas, 1662. Wing N868.

Cavendish, William. *Ideology and Politics on the Eve of the Restoration: Newcastle's Advice to Charles II.* Ed. Thomas P. Slaughter. Philadelphia: American Philosophical Society, 1984.

Charles I. *The Kings Cabinet Opened: or, Certain Packets of Secret Letters & Papers, Written with the Kings Own Hand, and Taken in His Cabinet at Nasby-Field, June 14. 1645.* London: Printed for Robert Bostock, 1645. Wing C2358.

Cranley, Thomas. *Amanda: Or, The Reformed Whore.* London: J. Norton, 1635. STC 5988.

———. *The Converted Courtezan, or, The Reformed Whore.* London: For B. Langford, 1639. STC 5989.

Dante Alighieri. *The Divine Comedy.* Paradiso. Trans. Charles S. Singleton. Princeton: Princeton Univ. Press, 1975.

Day, Angel. *The English Secretorie.* London: Printed by Robert Waldegrave, 1586. STC 6401.

Donne, John. *The Complete English Poems of John Donne.* Ed. C. A. Patrides. London: Dent, 1985.

———. *Letters to Severall Persons of Honour (1651).* Ed. M. Thomas Hester. Delmar NY: Scholars' Facsimiles & Reprints, 1977.

———. *The Sermons of John Donne.* Ed. George R. Potter and Evelyn M. Simpson. Berkeley: Univ. of California Press, 1953–62.

Eikon Basilike: The Portraiture of His Sacred Majesty in His Solitudes and Sufferings. Ed. Philip A. Knachel. Ithaca: Published for the Folger Shakespeare Library by Cornell Univ. Press, 1966.

Garnet, Henry. *The Societie of the Rosary.* [London?: S.n., 1596–97]. STC 11617.5 (formerly 19939a).

Gouge, William. *Of Domesticall Duties.* London: Printed by John Haviland for William Bladen, 1622. STC 12119.

Grundler, Otto. "Devotio Moderna." In *Christian Spirituality: High Middle Ages and Reformation,* ed. Jill Raitt, 176–93. New York: Crossroad, 1988.

Henrietta Maria. *The Queen's Maiesties Gracious Answer to the Lord Digbies Letter, and the*

Parliaments Censure to the 18. Rebels. With the Examination and Confession of Captain Butler, before the Committee. Likewise the True Relation of 36 Other Rebels, Apprehended and Taken in Milford-Lane, by Many Constables, and a Strong Watch, Who Intended to Fire the City of London, Had They Not Bin Prevented. Printed at London: for Tho. Powell, and averred by I. B. Clev., [1642]. Wing H1458.

Herbert, George. *The English Poems of George Herbert.* Ed. C. A. Patrides. London: Dent, 1974.

Hill, Robert. *The Pathway to Prayer and Pietie.* London: Printed by W. S. for Edward Blunt and William Barret, 1613. STC 13474.

Hoskins, John. *Directions for Speech and Style.* Ed. Hoyt H. Hudson. Princeton: Princeton Univ. Press, 1935.

James I. "Basilikon Doron." In *The Political Works of James I,* ed. Charles Howard McIlwain, 3–52. New York: Russell & Russell, 1965.

Jessey, Henry. *The Exceeding Riches of Grace Advanced by the Spirit of Grace, in an Empty Nothing Creature, viz. M[ris] Sarah Wight, Lately Hopeles and Restles, Her Soule Dwelling as far from Peace of Hopes of Mercy, As Ever Was Any . . . Published for the Refreshing of Poor Souls, by an Eye and Ear-witness of a Good Part Thereof, Henry Jesse, a Servant of Jesus Christ.* London: Printed by Matthew Simmons for Henry Overton, and Hannah Allen, 1647. Wing J687.

———. *The Exceeding Riches of Grace Advanced by the Spirit of Grace, in an Empty Nothing Creature, (viz) Mrs. Sarah Wight. . . .* The Seventh Edition, Corrected. London: Printed by J. C. for Henry Mortlock, 1658. Wing J692.

Jonson, Ben. *Ben Jonson: The Complete Poems.* Ed. George Parfitt. London: Penguin, 1988.

Luis de Granada. *A Memoriall of a Christian Life.* Rouen: Imprinted by George L'oyselet, 1586. STC 16903.

Marbeck, John. *A Concordance, That Is to Saie, a Work Wherein by the Ordre of the Letters of the A.B.C. Ye Maie Redely Finde Any Worde Conteigned in the Whole Bible, So Often As It Is There Expressed or Mencioned.* London: Richard Grafton, 1550. STC 17300.

Milton, John. *Complete Prose Works of John Milton.* Ed. Don M. Wolfe. New Haven: Yale Univ. Press, 1953–82.

Osborne, Francis. *The Private Christians Non Vltra, or, A Plea for the Lay-Man's Interpreting the Scriptvres. Written by Philolaoclerus.* Oxford: Printed by H. Hall, Printer to the Univ., for Tho. Robinson, 1656. Wing O521.

Ovid. *Metamorphoses.* Trans. A. D. Melville. Ed. E. J. Kenney. Oxford: Oxford Univ. Press, 1987.

Parr, Elnathan. *Abba Father: or, A Plaine and Short Direction Concerning Priuate Prayer.* London: Imprinted by F. K. for Samuel Man, 1618. STC 19312.

Plato. *Plato's Phaedrus.* Trans. and introd. R. Hackworth. Cambridge: Cambridge Univ. Press, 1952.

Public and Private Life in the Seventeenth Century: The Mackenzie-Evelyn Debate: Being a Facsimile Edition of George Mackenzie, A Moral Essay, Preferring Solitude to Publick Entertainment, and All It's Appanages; Such as Fame, Command, Riches, Pleasures, Conversation, &c. (1665) and John Evelyn, Publick Employment and an Active Life Prefer'd to Solitude, and All Its Appanages, Such as Fame, Command, Riches, Conversation, &c. In Reply to a Late Ingenious Essay of a Contrary Title (1667). Ed. Brian Vickers. Delmar NY: Scholars' Facsimiles & Reprints, 1986.

Robinson, John. *Of Religious Commvnion Private, & Publique: with the Silenceing of the Clamours Raysed by Mr Thomas Helvvisse agaynst Our Reteyning the Baptism Receaved in Engl: & Administering of Bapt. vnto Infants. As Also a Survey of the Confession of Fayth Published in Certayne Conclusions by the Remaynders of Mr Smithes Company.* [S.l.: S.n.], 1614. STC 21115.

Sharpe, James. *The Triall of the Protestant Private Spirit.* [S. Omer: English College Press], 1630. STC 22370.

Southwell, Robert. *Marie Magdalens Funeral Tears (1591).* Delmar NY: Scholar's Facsimiles & Reprints, 1975.

———. *The Poems of Robert Southwell, S. J.* Ed. James H. McDonald and Nancy Pollard Brown. Oxford: Clarendon Press, 1967.

———. *Two Letters and Short Rules of a Good Life.* Ed. Nancy Pollard Brown. Charlottesville: Univ. Press of Virginia, 1973.

Wilkins, John. *Mercury, or the Secret and Swift Messenger: Shewing, How a Man May with Privacy and Speed Communicate His Thoughts to a Friend at Any Distance.* London: Printed by I. Norton, for Iohn Maynard, and Timothy Wilkins. . . , 1641. Wing W2202.

Wilson, John. *Zachevs Converted: or, The Rich Publicans Repentance. Restitution. In Which, the Mysteries of the Doctrine of Conversion, Are Sweetly Laid Open and Applyed for the Establishing of the Weakest. . . .* London: Printed by T. Cotes, for Fulke Clifton, 1631. STC 25770.

Worthington, Thomas. *The Rosarie of our Ladie, Otherwise Called Our Ladies Psalter.* Antverpiae: Apud Ioannem Keerbergium, 1600. STC 17546.

Wotton, Henry. *The Elements of Architecture.* Charlottesville: Published for the Folger Shakespeare Library, Univ. Press of Virginia, 1968.

Wright, Thomas. *The Disposition or Garnishmente of the Sovle To Receiue Worthily the Blessed Sacrament. . . .* At Antwerpe [i.e., England]: Ioachim Trognesius, 1596.

Wroth, Mary. *The Poems of Lady Mary Wroth.* Ed. Josephine A. Roberts. Baton Rouge: Louisiana State Univ. Press, 1983.

Zerbolt, of Zutphen, Gerard. "The Spiritual Ascents." In *Devotio Moderna: Basic Writings,* trans. and introd. John H. Van Engen, 245–315. New York: Paulist Press, 1988.

Secondary Sources

Adamson, J. W. "The Extent of Literacy in England in the Fifteenth and Sixteenth Centuries: Notes and Conjectures." *The Library,* 4th ser. 10 (1929): 163–93.

Alderman, Ellen, and Caroline Kennedy. *The Right to Privacy.* New York: Knopf, 1995.

Allison, A. F., and D. M. Rogers. *A Catalogue of Catholic Books in English Printed Abroad or Secretly in England, 1558–1640.* London: Wm. Dawson & Sons, 1968.

Allison, A. F., and V. F. Goldsmith. *Titles of English Books (and of Foreign Books Printed in England): An Alphabetical Finding-List by Title of Books Published under the Author's Name, Pseudonym or Initials.* Hamden CT: Archon Books, 1977.

Altman, Irving. "Privacy Regulation: Culturally Universal or Culturally Specific?" *Journal of Social Issues* 33 (1977): 66–84.

Altman, Janet Gurkin. "The Letter Book as a Literary Institution, 1539–1789: Toward a Cultural History of Published Correspondences in France." *Yale French Studies* 71 (1986): 17–62.

Anderson, Judith H. *Words That Matter: Linguistic Perception in Renaissance English.* Stanford: Stanford Univ. Press, 1996.

Archaea, John. "The Place of Architectural Factors in Behavioral Theories of Privacy." *Journal of Social Issues* 33 (1977): 116–37.

Armstrong, Nancy, and Leonard Tennenhouse. *The Imaginary Puritan: Literature, Intellectual Labor, and the Origins of Personal Life.* Berkeley: Univ. of California Press, 1992.

Arrou-Vignod, Jean-Philippe. *Le discours des absents.* [Paris]: Gallimard, 1993.

Aston, Margaret. *The Fifteenth Century: The Prospect of Europe.* [New York]: Harcourt, Brace & World, 1968.

Axton, Marie. *The Queen's Two Bodies: Drama and the Elizabethan Succession.* London: Royal Historical Society, 1977.

Backschneider, Paula R. *Spectacular Politics: Theatrical Power and Mass Culture in Early Modern England.* Baltimore: Johns Hopkins Univ. Press, 1993.

Bald, R. C. *Donne: A Life.* Oxford: Oxford Univ. Press, 1970.

Baldwin, Charles Sears. *Medieval Rhetoric and Poetic (to 1400): Interpreted from Representative Works.* New York: Macmillan, 1928.

Barish, Jonas. "The Problem of Closet Drama in the Italian Renaissance." *Italica* 71 (1994): 4–30.

Barley, M. W. "Farmhouses and Cottages, 1550–1725." *Economic History Review,* 2d ser. (1954): 291–306.

———. *The House and Home.* London: Vista Books, 1963.

Beal, Rebecca S. "*Grace Abounding to the Chief of Sinners:* John Bunyan's Pauline Epistle." *Studies in English Literature, 1500–1900* 21 (1981): 147–60.

Bell, Maureen, George Parfitt, and Simon Shepherd. *A Biographical Dictionary of English Women Writers, 1580–1720.* Boston: G. K. Hall, 1990.

Benedict, Barbara M. *Making the Modern Reader: Cultural Mediation in Early Modern Literary Anthologies.* Princeton: Princeton Univ. Press, 1996.

Benet's Reader's Encyclopedia. 3d ed. Ed. Katherine Baker Siepmann. New York: Harper & Row, 1987.

Bénézit, Emmanuel. *Dictionnaire critique et documentaire des peintres, sculpteurs, dessinateurs et graveurs de tous les temps et de tous les pays.* New ed. Paris: Grund, 1976.

Bennett, H. S. *English Books and Readers, 1475 to 1557.* Cambridge: University Press, 1952.

———. *English Books and Readers, 1603 to 1640.* Cambridge: University Press, 1970.

Bennett, Roger E. "Donne's Letters from the Continent in 1611–1612." *Philological Quarterly* 19 (1940): 66–78.

———. "Donne's *Letters to Severall Persons of Honour.*" *PMLA* 56 (1941): 120–40.

Bentley, Gerald Eades. *The Jacobean and Caroline Stage.* 7 vols. Oxford: Clarendon Press, 1956.

Bloch, Chana. *Spelling the Word: George Herbert and the Bible.* Berkeley: Univ. of California Press, 1985.

Boehrer, Bruce Thomas. "Behn's 'Disapppointment' and Nashe's 'Choice of Valentines': Pornographic Poetry and the Influence of Anxiety." *Essays in Literature* 16 (1989): 172–87.

Boffey, Julia. "Women Authors and Women's Literacy in Fourteenth- and Fifteenth-Century England." In *Women and Literature in Britain, 1150–1500,* ed. Carol M. Meale, 159–82. Cambridge: Cambridge Univ. Press, 1993.

Bold, John. "Privacy and the Plan." In *English Architecture Public and Private: Essays for Kerry Downes,* ed. John Bold and Edward Chaney, 107–19. London: Hambledon Press, 1993.

Bone, Quentin. *Henrietta Maria: Queen of the Cavaliers.* Urbana: Univ. of Illinois Press, 1972.

Bossy, John. *The English Catholic Community, 1570–1850.* London: Darton, Longman & Todd, 1979.

Boyarin, Daniel. "Placing Reading: Ancient Israel and Medieval Europe." In *The Ethnography of Reading,* ed. Jonathan Boyarin, 10–37. Berkeley: Univ. of California Press, 1993.

Brett, A. C. A. *Charles II and His Court.* London: Methuen, 1910.

Brooks, Peter. *Body Work: Objects of Desire in Modern Narrative.* Cambridge: Harvard Univ. Press, 1993.

Brown, Sylvia. "Margaret Cavendish: Strategies Rhetorical and Philosophical against the Charge of Wantonness, or Her Excuses for Writing So Much." *Critical Matrix* 6 (1991): 20–45.

Bruss, Elizabeth W. *Autobiographical Acts: The Changing Situation of a Literary Genre.* Baltimore: Johns Hopkins Univ. Press, 1976.

Burckhardt, Jacob. *The Civilization of the Renaissance in Italy.* Trans. S. G. C. Middlemore. 3 vols. New York: Harper, 1958.

Butler, Martin. *Theatre and Crisis, 1632–1642.* Cambridge: Cambridge Univ. Press, 1984.

Bynum, Carolyn. *Holy Feast and Holy Fast: The Religious Significance of Food to Medieval Women.* Berkeley: Univ. of California Press, 1987.

———. *The Resurrection of the Body in Western Christianity, 200-1336.* New York: Columbia Univ. Press, 1995.

Cable, Lana. "Milton's Iconoclastic Truth." In *Politics, Poetics, and Hermeneutics in Milton's Prose,* ed. David Loewenstein and James Grantham Turner, 135–52. Cambridge: Cambridge Univ. Press, 1990.

Caldwell, Patricia. *The Puritan Conversion Narrative: The Beginnings of American Expression.* Cambridge: Cambridge Univ. Press, 1983.

Carey, John. *John Donne: Life, Mind, and Art.* New ed. London: Faber & Faber, 1990.

———. "John Donne's Newsless Letters." *Essays and Studies* 34 (1981): 45–65.

Cate, Fred H. *Privacy in the Information Age.* Washington DC: Brookings Institution Press, 1997.

Chartier, Roger. *The Cultural Uses of Print in Early Modern France.* Princeton: Princeton Univ. Press, 1987.

———. Introduction: "An Ordinary Kind of Writing: Model Letters and Letter-Writing in Ancien Régime France." In Roger Chartier, Alain Boureau, and Cécile Dauphin, *Correspondence: Models of Letter-Writing from the Middle Ages to the Nineteenth Century,* 1–23. Princeton: Princeton Univ. Press, 1997.

———. "Laborers and Voyagers: From the Text to the Reader." *Diacritics* 22 (1992): 49–61.

———, ed. *Passions of the Renaissance.* Vol. 3 of *A History of Private Life,* ed. Philippe Ariès and Georges Duby. Cambridge: Belknap Press of Harvard Univ. Press, 1989.

Cheney, Donald. "Spenser's Hermaphrodite and the 1590 *Faerie Queene.*" *PMLA* 87 (1972): 192–200.

Chernaik, Warren. *Sexual Freedom in Restoration Literature.* Cambridge: Cambridge Univ. Press, 1995.

Clanchy, M. T. *From Memory to Written Record: England, 1066–1307.* London: Edward Arnold, 1979.

Clancy, Thomas H. *English Catholic Books, 1641–1700: A Bibliography.* Chicago: Loyola Univ. Press, 1974.

———. *English Catholic Books, 1641–1700: A Bibliography.* Rev. ed. Brookfield VT: Scolar Press, 1996.

Clark, Peter. "The Ownership of Books in England, 1560–1640: The Example of Some Kentish Townfolk." In *Schooling and Society: Studies in the History of Education,* ed. Lawrence Stone, 95–111. Baltimore: Johns Hopkins Univ. Press, 1976.

Coiro, Ann Baynes. *Robert Herrick's Hesperides and the Epigram Book Tradition.* Baltimore: Johns Hopkins Univ. Press, 1988.

Coleman, Joyce. *Public Reading and the Reading Public in Late Medieval England and France.* Cambridge: Cambridge Univ. Press, 1996.

Colie, Rosalie. *The Resources of Kind: Genre Theory in the Renaissance.* Berkeley: Univ. of California Press, 1973.

Constable, Giles. *Letters and Letter-Collections.* Turnhout: Editions Brepols, 1976.

Cope, Esther S. *Handmaid of the Holy Spirit: Dame Eleanor Davies, Never Soe Mad a Ladie.* Ann Arbor: Univ. of Michigan Press, 1992.

Corbett, Margery, and Ronald Lightbown. *The Comely Frontispiece: The Emblematic Title-Page in England, 1550–1660.* London: Routledge & Kegan Paul, 1979.

Corns, Thomas N. *Uncloistered Virtue: English Political Literature, 1640–1660.* New York: Clarendon Press, 1992.

Corthell, Ronald J. "'The Secrecy of Man': Recusant Discourse and the Elizabethan Subject." *English Literary Renaissance* 19 (1989): 272–90.

Cressy, David. "Books as Totems in Seventeenth-Century England and New England." *Journal of Library History, Philosophy and Comparative Librarianship* 21 (1986): 92–106.

———. *Literacy and the Social Order: Reading and Writing in Tudor and Stuart England.* Cambridge: Cambridge Univ. Press, 1980.

Curtius, Ernst Robert. *European Literature and the Latin Middle Ages.* Trans. Willard Trask. New York: Pantheon Books, 1953.

Dagenais, John. *The Ethics of Reading in Manuscript Culture: Glossing the Libro De Buen Amor.* Princeton: Princeton Univ. Press, 1994.

Damrosch, Leopold. *God's Plot and Man's Stories: Studies in Fictional Imagination from Milton to Fielding.* Chicago: Univ. of Chicago Press, 1985.

Darnton, Robert. *The Forbidden Best-Sellers of Pre-Revolutionary France.* New York: Norton, 1995.

———. *The Kiss of Lamourette: Reflections in Cultural History.* New York: Norton, 1990.

Davies, Horton. *Worship and Theology in England from Cranmer to Hooker, 1534–1603.* Princeton: Princeton Univ. Press, 1970.

Davies, Stevie. *The Feminine Reclaimed: The Idea of Woman in Spenser, Shakespeare, and Milton.* Lexington: Univ. of Kentucky Press, 1986.

Davis, Elizabeth B. "'Woman, Why Weepest Thou?' Re-visioning the Golden Age Magdalen." *Hispania* 76 (1993): 38–48.

Davis, Lennard J. *Factual Fictions: The Origins of the English Novel.* New York: Columbia Univ. Press, 1983.

Davis, Natalie Zemon. "Boundaries and the Sense of Self in Sixteenth-Century France." In *Reconstructing Individualism: Autonomy, Individuality, and the Self in Western Thought,* ed. Thomas C. Heller et al., 53–63. Stanford: Stanford Univ. Press, 1986.

Day, Robert Adams. *Told in Letters: Epistolary Fiction before Richardson.* Ann Arbor: Univ. of Michigan Press, 1966.

Delany, Paul. *British Autobiography in the Seventeenth Century.* London: Routledge & Kegan Paul, 1969.

Derlega, Valerian J., and Alan L. Chaikin. "Privacy and Self-Disclosure in Social Relationships." *Journal of Social Issues* 33 (1977): 102–15.

Derlega, Valerian J. et al. *Self-Disclosure.* Newbury Park: Sage Publications, 1993.

Diaz, Rafael M., and Laura E. Berk, eds. *Private Speech: From Social Interaction to Self-Regulation.* Hillsdale NJ: L. Erlbaum, 1992.

Dickens, A. G. *Thomas Cromwell and the English Reformation.* New York: Macmillan, 1959.

Documents Illustrative of English Church History. Ed. Henry Gee and William John Hardy. New York: Kraus Reprint, 1966.

Dubrow, Heather. *Genre.* London: Methuen, 1982.

———. "A Mirror for Complaints: Shakespeare's Lucrece and Generic Tradition." In *Renaissance Genres: Essays in Theory, History, and Interpretation,* ed. Barbara Kiefer Lewalski, 399–417. Cambridge: Harvard Univ. Press, 1986.

Duby, Georges, ed. *Revelations of the Medieval World.* Vol. 2 of *A History of Private Life,* ed. Philippe Ariès and Georges Duby. Cambridge: Belknap Press of Harvard Univ. Press, 1988.

Duffy, Eamon. *The Stripping of the Altars: Traditional Religion in England, c. 1400–c. 1580.* New Haven: Yale Univ. Press, 1992.

Duffy, Maureen. *The Passionate Shepherdess: Aphra Behn 1640–89.* London: Jonathan Cape, 1977.

Duguid, Paul. "Material Matters: The Past and Futurology of the Book." In *The Future of the Book,* ed. Geoffrey Nunberg, 63–101. Berkeley: Univ. of California Press, 1996.

Eisenstein, Elizabeth. *The Printing Press as an Agent of Change: Communications and Cultural Transformations in Early-Modern Europe.* 2 vols. Cambridge: Cambridge Univ. Press, 1979.

Elias, Norbert. *The Civilizing Process: The History of Manners.* New York: Urizen Books, 1978.

Elliott, Dyan. *Spiritual Marriage: Sexual Abstinence in Medieval Wedlock.* Princeton: Princeton Univ. Press, 1993.

Elsasser, Glen. "Redress for a King." *Chicago Tribune,* 25 Jan. 1994, sec. 5, pp. 1–2.

Elsky, Martin. *Authorizing Words: Speech, Writing, and Print in the English Renaissance.* Ithaca: Cornell Univ. Press, 1989.

Faulhaber, Charles B. "The Letter-Writer's Rhetoric: The Summa Dictaminis of Guido Faba." In *Medieval Eloquence: Studies in the Theory and Practice of Medieval Rhetoric,* ed. James J. Murphy, 85–111. Berkeley: Univ. of California Press, 1978.

Fea, Allan. *Secret Chambers and Hiding-Places: Historic, Romantic, and Legendary Stories and Traditions about Hiding-Holes, Secret Chambers, etc.* 1901. Reprint, Detroit: Singing Tree Press, 1971.

Ferguson, Moira. "A 'Wise, Wittie and Learned Lady.'" In *Women Writers of the Seventeenth Century,* ed. Katharina M. Wilson and Frank J. Warnke, 305–40. Athens: Univ. of Georgia Press, 1989.

Ferry, Anne. *The "Inward" Language: Sonnets of Wyatt, Sidney, Shakespeare, Donne.* Chicago: Univ. of Chicago Press, 1983.

Findley, Sandra, and Elaine Hobby. "Seventeenth Century Women's Autobiography." In *1642: Literature and Power in the Seventeenth Century: Proceedings of the Essex Conference on the Sociology of Literature,* ed. Francis Barker, 11–54. Essex: University of Essex, 1981.

Fineman, Joel. *Shakespeare's Perjured Eye: The Invention of Poetic Subjectivity in the Sonnets.* Berkeley: Univ. of California Press, 1986.

Fish, Stanley E. *Self-Consuming Artifacts: The Experience of Seventeenth-Century Literature.* Berkeley: Univ. of California Press, 1972.

Fitzmaurice, James. "Fancy and the Family: Self-Characterizations of Margaret Cavendish." *Huntington Library Quarterly* 53 (1990): 198–209.

Flaherty, David H. *Privacy in Colonial New England.* Charlottesville: Univ. Press of Virginia, 1972.

———. *Protecting Privacy in Surveillance Societies: The Federal Republic of Germany, Sweden, France, Canada, and the United States.* Chapel Hill: Univ. of North Carolina Press, 1989.

Flynn, Dennis. *John Donne and the Ancient Catholic Nobility.* Bloomington: Indiana Univ. Press, 1995.

Forster, Leonard. *The Icy Fire: Five Studies in European Petrarchism.* London: Cambridge Univ. Press, 1969.

Fowler, Alastair. *Kinds of Literature: An Introduction to the Theory of Genres and Modes.* Cambridge: Harvard Univ. Press, 1982.

Foxon, David. *Libertine Literature in England, 1660–1745.* New Hyde Park NY: University Books, 1965.

Frantz, David O. *Festum Voluptatis: A Study of Renaissance Erotica.* Columbus: Ohio State Univ. Press, 1989.

Frappier-Mazur, Lucienne. "Marginal Canons: Rewriting the Erotic." *Yale French Studies* 75 (1988): 112–28.

Fryer, Peter. *Private Case—Public Scandal.* London: Secker & Warburg, 1966.

Fumerton, Patricia. "'Secret' Arts: Elizabethan Miniatures and Sonnets." *Representations* 15 (summer 1986): 57–97.

Gagen, Jean. "Honor and Fame in the Works of the Duchess of Newcastle." *Studies in Philology* 56 (1959): 519–38.

Gallagher, Catherine. "Embracing the Absolute: The Politics of the Female Subject in Seventeenth-Century England." *Genders* 1 (1988): 24–39.

———. *Nobody's Story: The Vanishing Acts of Women Writers in the Marketplace, 1670–1820.* Berkeley: Univ. of California Press, 1994.

Galland, Joseph S. *An Historical and Analytical Bibliography of the Literature of Cryptology.* Evanston: Northwestern University, 1945.

Gardiner, Judith Kegan. "Aphra Behn: Sexuality and Self-Respect." *Women's Studies* 7 (1980): 67–78.

———. "The First English Novel: Aphra Behn's Love Letters, the Canon, and Women's Tastes." *Tulsa Studies in Women's Literature* 8 (1989): 201–22.

Gavison, Ruth. "Privacy and the Limits of the Law." *Yale Law Journal* 89 (1980): 421–71.

Gawthrop, Richard, and Gerald Strauss. "Protestantism and Literacy in Early Modern Germany." *Past and Present* 104 (1984): 31–55.

Gellrich, Jesse. *The Idea of the Book in the Middle Ages: Language Theory, Mythology, and Fiction.* Ithaca: Cornell Univ. Press, 1985.

Gerhart, Mary. *Genre Choices, Gender Questions.* Norman: Univ. of Oklahoma Press, 1992.

Gildersleeve, Virginia Crocheron. *Government Regulation of the Elizabethan Drama.* 1908. Reprint, New York: Burt Franklin, 1961.

Gilman, Ernest B. *Iconoclasm and Poetry in the English Reformation: Down Went Dagon.* Chicago: Univ. of Chicago Press, 1986.

Gilmont, Jean François. "En guise de conclusion . . ." In *La réforme et le livre: l'Europe de l'imprime (1517-v. 1570),* ed. Jean François Gilmont, 479–504. Paris: Éditions du Cerf, 1990.

Ginzburg, Carlo. *The Cheese and the Worms: The Cosmos of a Sixteenth-Century Miller.* Baltimore: Johns Hopkins Univ. Press, 1980.

———. "Titian, Ovid, and Sixteenth-Century Codes for Erotic Illustration." In *Clues, Myths, and the Historical Method,* 77–95. Baltimore: Johns Hopkins Univ. Press, 1989.

Girouard, Mark. *Life in the English Country House: A Social and Architectural History.* New Haven: Yale Univ. Press, 1978.

Goffman, Erving. *Asylums: Essays on the Social Situation of Mental Patients and Other Inmates.* Garden City NY: Anchor Books, 1961.

Goldberg, Jonathan. *James I and the Politics of Literature: Jonson, Shakespeare, Donne, and Their Contemporaries.* Baltimore: Johns Hopkins Univ. Press, 1983.

———. *Writing Matter: From the Hands of the English Renaissance.* Stanford: Stanford Univ. Press, 1990.

Goldsmith, Elizabeth C. "Authority, Authenticity, and the Publication of Letters by Women." In *Writing the Female Voice: Essays on Epistolary Literature,* ed. Elizabeth C. Goldsmith, 46–59. Boston: Northeastern Univ. Press, 1989.

Gosse, Edmund. *The Life and Letters of John Donne, Dean of St. Paul's.* 2 vols. 1899. Reprint, Gloucester MA: Peter Smith, 1959.

Goulemot, Jean Marie. *Forbidden Texts: Erotic Literature and Its Readers in Eighteenth-Century France.* Trans. James Simpson. Philadelphia: Univ. of Pennsylvania Press, 1994.

Graff, Harvey J. *The Legacies of Literacy: Continuities and Contradictions in Western Culture and Society.* Bloomington: Indiana Univ. Press, 1987.

Grant, Douglas. *Margaret the First: A Biography of Margaret Cavendish Duchess of Newcastle, 1623–1673.* Toronto: Univ. of Toronto Press, 1957.

Greenblatt, Stephen. *Renaissance Self-Fashioning: More to Shakespeare.* Chicago: Univ. of Chicago Press, 1980.

Grossman, Marshall. "The Dissemination of the King." In *The Theatrical City: Culture, Theatre and Politics in London, 1576–1649,* ed. David L. Smith, Richard Strier, and David Bevington, 260–81. Cambridge: Cambridge Univ. Press, 1995.

Guibbory, Achsah. *Ceremony and Community from Milton to Herbert: Literature, Religion, and Cultural Conflict in Seventeenth-Century England.* Cambridge: Cambridge Univ. Press, 1998.

Gunn, Janet Varner. *Autobiography: Towards a Poetics of Experience.* Philadelphia: Univ. of Pennsylvania Press, 1982.

Habermas, Jürgen. *The Structural Transformation of the Public Sphere: An Inquiry into a Category of Bourgeois Society.* Trans. Thomas Burger. Cambridge: MIT Press, 1991.

Hall, David D. *Cultures of Print: Essays in the History of the Book.* Amherst: Univ. of Massachusetts Press, 1996.

Hall, Edward T. *The Hidden Dimension.* Garden City NY: Doubleday, 1966.

Hall, James. *Dictionary of Subjects and Symbols in Art.* Rev. ed. London: John Murray, 1979.

Hanson, Elizabeth. "Torture and Truth in Renaissance England." *Representations* 34 (1991): 53–84.

Harbage, Alfred. *Cavalier Drama: An Historical and Critical Supplement to the Study of the Elizabethan and Restoration Stage.* New York: Modern Language Association, 1936.

Harbison, Craig. "Lucas van Leyden, the Magdalen and the Problem of Secularization in Early Sixteenth Century Northern Art." *Oud Holland* 98 (1984): 117–29.

Haskins, Susan. *Mary Magdalen: Myth and Metaphor.* New York: Harcourt Brace & Co., 1993.

Hawkins, Anne. "The Double-Conversion in Bunyan's *Grace Abounding.*" *Philological Quarterly* 61 (1982): 259–76.

Hazlitt, W. C. *The English Drama and Stage Under the Tudor and Stuart Princes 1543–1664: Illustrated by a Series of Documents, Treatises and Poems.* 1869. Reprint, New York: Burt Franklin, [1964].

Heinemann, Margot. *Puritanism and Theatre: Thomas Middleton and Opposition Drama under the Early Stuarts.* Cambridge: Cambridge Univ. Press, 1980.

Held, Julius S., ed. *Rubens and the Book: Title Pages by Peter Paul Rubens.* Williamstown MA: Williams College, 1977.

Helgerson, Richard. *Self-Crowned Laureates: Spenser, Jonson, Milton, and the Literary System.* Berkeley: Univ. of California Press, 1983.

Hill, Christopher. *The Bible and the English Revolution.* London: Penguin, 1994.

———. *Intellectual Origins of the English Revolution Revisited.* Oxford: Clarendon Press, 1997.

———. *A Turbulent, Seditious, and Factious People: John Bunyan and His Church, 1628–1688.* Oxford: Clarendon Press, 1988.

———. *The World Turned Upside Down: Radical Ideas during the English Revolution.* New York: Viking, 1972.

Hobby, Elaine. *Virtue of Necessity: English Women's Writing, 1649–88.* Ann Arbor: Univ. of Michigan Press, 1989.

Hogendoorn, Wiebe. "Reading on a Booke: Closet Drama and the Study of Theatre Arts." In *Essays on Drama and Theatre: Liber Amicorum Benjamin Hunningher,* 50–66. Amsterdam: Moussault, 1973.

Hotson, Leslie. *The Commonwealth and Restoration Stage.* Cambridge: Harvard Univ. Press, 1928.

Huebert, Ronald. "Privacy: The Early Social History of a Word." *Sewanee Review* 105 (1997): 21–38.

Hunt, Lynn, ed. *The Invention of Pornography: Obscenity and the Origins of Modernity, 1500–1800.* New York: Zone Books, 1993.

Hunter, J. Paul. *Before Novels: The Cultural Contexts of Eighteenth-Century English Fiction.* New York: Norton, 1990.

———. "The Loneliness of the Long-Distance Reader." *Genre* 10 (1977): 455–85.

———. "The World as Stage and Closet." In *British Theatre and the Other Arts, 1660–1800,* ed. Shirley Strum Kenny, 271–87. Washington DC: Folger Shakespeare Library, 1984.

Hutner, Heidi, ed. *Rereading Aphra Behn: History, Theory, and Criticism.* Charlottesville: Univ. Press of Virginia, 1993.

Hyma, Albert. *The Christian Renaissance: A History of the "Devotio Moderna."* 2d ed. Hamden CT: Archon Books, 1965.

Jackson, W. A., F. S. Ferguson, and Katharine F. Pantzer, eds. *A Short-Title Catalogue of Books Printed in England, Scotland & Ireland and of English Books Printed Abroad, 1475–1640.* London: Bibliographical Society, 1976–91.

Jacobs, Linda L. "The Image of Mary Magdalene in Seventeenth-Century Poetry." *Publications of the Mississippi Philological Association,* 1987, 62–78.

Jacobs, Naomi. "The Seduction of Aphra Behn." *Women's Studies* 18 (1991): 395–403.

Jankowski, Theodora A. "'As I Am Egypt's Queen': Cleopatra, Elizabeth I, and the Female Body Politic." *Assays: Critical Approaches to Medieval and Renaissance Texts* 5 (1989): 91–110.

Jardine, Lisa. *Worldly Goods: A New History of the Renaissance.* New York: Doubleday, 1996.

Jones, Kathleen. *A Glorious Fame: The Life of Margaret Cavendish, Duchess of Newcastle, 1623–1673.* London: Bloomsbury, 1988.

Kantorowicz, Ernst H. *The King's Two Bodies: A Study in Mediaeval Political Theology.* Princeton: Princeton Univ. Press, 1957.

Karras, Ruth Mazo. *Common Women: Prostitution and Sexuality in Medieval England.* New York: Oxford Univ. Press, 1996.

———. "Holy Harlots: Prostitute Saints in Medieval Legend." *Journal of the History of Sexuality* 1 (1990): 3–32.

Kauffman, Linda S. *Discourses of Desire: Gender, Genre, and Epistolary Fictions.* Ithaca: Cornell Univ. Press, 1986.

Kay, W. David. *Ben Jonson: A Literary Life.* New York: St. Martin's Press, 1995.

Kelly, Thomas. *Early Public Libraries: A History of Public Libraries in Great Britain before 1850.* London: Library Association, 1966.

Kendrick, Walter. *The Secret Museum: Pornography in Modern Culture.* New York: Viking, 1987.

Kernan, Alvin. *Printing Technology, Letters and Samuel Johnson.* Princeton: Princeton Univ. Press, 1987.

Keynes, Geoffrey. *A Bibliography of Dr. John Donne, Dean of Saint Paul's.* 4th ed. Oxford: Clarendon Press, 1973.

Knox, Ronald A. *Enthusiasm: A Chapter in the History of Religion with Special Reference to the XVII and XVIII Centuries.* Oxford: Clarendon Press, 1950.

Kort, Wesley A. *"Take, Read": Scripture, Textuality, and Cultural Practice.* University Park: Pennsylvania State Univ. Press, 1996.

Kramer, Annette. "'Thus by the Musick of a Ladyes Tongue': Margaret Cavendish's Dramatic Innovations in Women's Education." *Women's History Review* 2 (1993): 57–79.

Kundera, Milan. "You're Not in Your Own House Here, My Dear Fellow." *New York Review of Books,* 21 Sept. 1995, 21–24.

Lake, Peter. "The Laudian Style: Order, Uniformity and the Pursuit of Holiness in the 1630s." In *The Early Stuart Church, 1603–1642,* ed. Kenneth Fincham, 161–85. Stanford: Stanford Univ. Press, 1993.

Lamb, Mary Ellen. *Gender and Authorship in the Sidney Circle.* Madison: Univ. of Wisconsin Press, 1990.

Laufer, Robert S., and Maxine Wolfe. "Privacy as a Concept and Social Issue: A Multidimensional Developmental Theory." *Journal of Social Issues* 33 (1977): 22–42.

Leach, Clifford, and T. W. Craik, eds. *The Revels History of Drama in English.* 8 vols. London: Methuen, 1981.

Leclerq, Jean. *The Love of Learning and the Desire for God: A Study of Monastic Culture.* New York: Fordham Univ. Press, 1982.

Levin, Carole. *"The Heart and Stomach of a King": Elizabeth I and the Politics of Sex and Power.* Philadelphia: Univ. of Pennsylvania Press, 1994.

Lewalski, Barbara. *Protestant Poetics and the Seventeenth-Century Religious Lyric.* Princeton: Princeton Univ. Press, 1979.

Lieson, Virginia. *From Sin to Salvation: Stories of Women's Conversion, 1800 to the Present.* Bloomington: Indiana Univ. Press, 1991.

Link, Frederick M. *Aphra Behn.* New York: Twayne, 1968.

Love, Harold. *Scribal Publication in Seventeenth-Century England.* Oxford: Clarendon Press, 1993.

Lukács, Georg. *The Theory of the Novel: A Historico-Philosophical Essay on the Forms of Great Epic Literature.* Cambridge: MIT Press, 1971.

Luxon, Thomas H. *Literal Figures: Puritan Allegory and the Reformation Crisis in Representation.* Chicago: Univ. of Chicago Press, 1995.

Madan, F. F. *A New Bibliography of the Eikon Basilike of King Charles the First, with a Note on the Authorship.* Oxford: Oxford Univ. Press, 1949.

Maddison, R. E. "'The King's Cabinet Opened': A Case Study in Pamphlet History." *Notes and Queries,* n.s. 13 (1966): 2–9.

Maguire, Nancy Klein. "The Theatrical Mask/Masque of Politics: The Case of Charles I." *Journal of British Studies* 29 (1989): 1–22.

Marcus, Leah S. "Shakespeare's Comic Heroines, Elizabeth I, and the Political Uses of Androgyny." In *Women in the Middle Ages and the Renaissance: Literary and Historical Perspectives,* ed. Mary Beth Rose, 135–53. Syracuse: Syracuse Univ. Press, 1986.

Margolis, Stephen T. "Conceptions of Privacy: Current Status and Next Steps." *Journal of Social Issues* 33 (1977): 5–21.

Marotti, Arthur F. *John Donne, Coterie Poet.* Madison: Univ. of Wisconsin Press, 1986.

———. "'Love Is Not Love': Elizabethan Sonnet Sequences and the Social Order." *ELH* 49 (1982): 396–428.

———. *Manuscript, Print, and the English Renaissance Lyric.* Ithaca: Cornell Univ. Press, 1995.

———. "Patronage, Poetry, and Print." *Yearbook of English Studies* 21 (1991): 1–26.

Martz, Louis L. *The Poetry of Meditation: A Study in English Religious Literature of the Seventeenth Century.* New Haven: Yale Univ. Press, 1954.

Mascuch, Michael. *Origins of the Individualist Self: Autobiography and Self-Identity in England, 1591–1791.* Stanford: Stanford Univ. Press, 1996.

Masten, Jeffrey. *Textual Intercourse: Collaboration, Authorship, and Sexualities in Renaissance Drama.* Cambridge: Cambridge Univ. Press, 1997.

Maus, Katharine Eisaman. *Inwardness and Theater in the English Renaissance.* Chicago: Univ. of Chicago Press, 1995.

McCoog, Thomas M., ed. *The Reckoned Expense: Edmund Campion and the Early English Jesuits.* Woodbridge UK: Boydell Press, 1996.

McKeon, Michael. *The Origins of the English Novel, 1600–1740.* Baltimore: Johns Hopkins Univ. Press, 1987.

McLuhan, Marshall. *The Gutenberg Galaxy: The Making of Typographic Man.* Toronto: Univ. of Toronto Press, 1965.

McMurtrie, Douglas C. *The Book: The Story of Printing and Bookmaking.* London: Oxford Univ. Press, 1943.

Mendelson, Sara Heller. *The Mental World of Stuart Women: Three Studies.* Amherst: Univ. of Massachusetts Press, 1987.

Miller, D. A. *The Novel and the Police.* Berkeley: Univ. of California Press, 1988.

Modell, Arthur H. *The Private Self.* Cambridge: Harvard Univ. Press, 1993.

Morse, David. *England's Time of Crisis: From Shakespeare to Milton.* New York: St. Martin's Press, 1989.

Moss, Ann. *Printed Commonplace-Books and the Structuring of Renaissance Thought.* Oxford: Clarendon Press, 1996.

Mullett, Michael. *John Bunyan in Context.* Pittsburgh: Duquesne Univ. Press, 1997.

Murphey, Murray G. "The Psychodynamics of Puritan Conversion." *American Quarterly* 31 (1970): 135–47.

Murray, John J. *Antwerp in the Age of Plantin and Brueghel.* Norman: Univ. of Oklahoma Press, 1970.

New, John F. H. *Anglican and Puritan: The Basis of Their Opposition, 1558–1640.* Stanford: Stanford Univ. Press, 1964.

Newton, Richard C. "Jonson and the (Re-)Invention of the Book." In *Classic and Cavalier: Essays on Jonson and the Sons of Ben,* ed. Claude J. Summers and Ted-Larry Pebworth, 31–55. Pittsburgh: Univ. of Pittsburgh Press, 1982.

Nock, Steven L. *The Costs of Privacy: Surveillance and Reputation in America.* New York: Aldine de Gruyter, 1993.

Norbrook, David, ed. *The Penguin Book of Renaissance Verse, 1509–1659.* London: Penguin, 1992.

Nussbaum, Felicity A. "By These Words I Was Sustained: Bunyan's *Grace Abounding.*" *ELH* 49 (1982): 18–34.

Ong, Walter J. *Orality and Literacy: The Technologizing of the Word.* London: Methuen, 1982.

———. "Reading, Technology, and the Nature of Man: An Interpretation." *Yearbook of English Studies* 10 (1980): 132–49.

———. "The Writer's Audience Is Always a Fiction." *PMLA* 90 (1975): 9–21.

Paloma, Dolores. "Margaret Cavendish: Defining the Female Self." *Women's Studies* 7 (1980): 55–66.

Panofsky, Erwin. *Tomb Sculpture: Four Lectures on Its Changing Aspects from Ancient Egypt to Bernini.* Ed. H. W. Janson. New York: Abrams, 1992.

Patterson, Annabel. *Censorship and Interpretation: The Conditions of Writing and Reading in Early Modern England.* Madison: Univ. of Wisconsin Press, 1984.

———. *Reading between the Lines.* Madison: Univ. of Wisconsin Press, 1984.

———. "Re-opening the Green Cabinet: Clement Marot and Edmund Spenser." *English Literary Renaissance* 16 (1986): 44–70.

Paz, Octavio. *The Double Flame: Love and Eroticism.* New York: Harcourt Brace & Co., 1995.

Pearson, Jacqueline. "Gender and Narrative in the Fiction of Aphra Behn." *Review of English Studies,* n.s. 42 (1991): 40–56, 179–90.

———. *The Prostituted Muse: Images of Women and Women Dramatists, 1642–1737.* New York: St. Martin's Press, 1988.

———. "'Women May Discourse . . . as Well as Men': Speaking and Silent Women in the

Plays of Margaret Cavendish, Duchess of Newcastle." *Tulsa Studies in Women's Literature* 4 (1985): 33–45.

Pebworth, Ted-Larry, and Claude J. Summers. "'Thus Friends Absent Speake': The Exchange of Verse Letters between John Donne and Henry Wotton." *Modern Philology* 81 (1984): 361–77.

Pendry, E. D. *Elizabethan Prisons and Prison Scenes.* Salzburg, Austria: Institut für Englische Sprache und Literatur, 1974.

Perry, Henry Ten Eyck. *The First Duchess of Newcastle and Her Husband as Figures in Literary History.* Boston: Ginn, 1918.

Perry, Ruth. *Women, Letters, and the Novel.* New York: AMS Press, 1980.

Peterson, Richard S. *Imitation and Praise in the Poems of Ben Jonson.* New Haven: Yale Univ Press, 1981.

Pforzheimer, Carl Howard. *The Carl H. Pforzheimer Library: English Literature, 1475–1700* 3 vols. [New York: The Author], 1940.

Phillips, John. *The Reformation of Images: Destruction of Art in England, 1535–1660.* Berkeley Univ. of California Press, 1973.

Plant, Marjorie. *The English Book Trade: An Economic History of the Making and Sale of Books.* 3d ed. London: Allen & Unwin, 1974.

Plomer, Henry R. *A Dictionary of the Booksellers and Printers Who Were at Work in England Scotland and Ireland from 1641 to 1667.* London: Bibliographical Society, 1907.

Pooley, Roger. "*Grace Abounding* and the New Sense of Self." In *John Bunyan and His England, 1628–88,* ed. Anne Laurence, W. R. Owens, and Stuart Sim, 105–14. London: Hambledon Press, 1990.

Porter, Charles A., ed. "Men/Women of Letters." *Yale French Studies* 71 (1986): 1–212.

Potter, Lois. *Secret Rites and Secret Writing: Royalist Literature, 1641–1660.* Cambridge: Cambridge Univ. Press, 1989.

Pritchard, Arnold. *Catholic Loyalism in Elizabethan England.* Chapel Hill: Univ. of North Carolina Press, 1979.

Ragussis, Michael. *Figures of Conversion: "The Jewish Question" and English National Identity.* Durham: Duke Univ. Press, 1995.

Rahner, Hugo. *Ignatius the Theologian.* New York: Herder & Herder, 1968.

Rambo, Lewis R. *Understanding Religious Conversion.* New Haven: Yale Univ. Press, 1993.

Rambuss, Richard. *Spenser's Secret Career.* Cambridge: Cambridge Univ. Press, 1993.

Randall, Dale B. J. *Winter Fruit: English Drama, 1642–1660.* Lexington: Univ. Press of Kentucky, 1995.

Raven, James, Helen Small, and Naomi Tadmor, eds. *The Practice and Representation of Reading in England.* Cambridge: Cambridge Univ. Press, 1996.

Richards, Graham. *Mental Machinery: The Origins and Consequences of Psychological Ideas, Part I: 1600–1850.* Baltimore: Johns Hopkins Univ. Press, 1992.

Richetti, John. "*Love Letters Between a Nobleman and His Sister:* Aphra Behn and Amatory Fiction." In *Augustan Subjects: Essays in Honor of Martin C. Battestin,* ed. Albert J. Rivero, 13–28. Newark: Univ. of Delaware Press, 1997.

Roberts, John, ed. *A Critical Anthology of English Recusant Devotional Prose, 1558–1603.* Pittsburgh: Duquesne Univ. Press, 1966.

Robertson, Jean. *The Art of Letter Writing: An Essay on the Handbooks Published in England during the Sixteenth and Seventeenth Centuries.* London: Univ. Press of Liverpool, 1942.

Robinson, Howard. *The British Post Office: A History.* Princeton: Princeton Univ. Press, 1948.

Rose, Elliott. *Cases of Conscience: Alternatives Open to Recusants and Puritans under Elizabeth I and James I.* London: Cambridge Univ. Press, 1975.

Rosenthal, Laura J. *Playwrights and Plagiarists in Early Modern England: Gender, Authorship, Literary Property.* Ithaca: Cornell Univ. Press, 1996.

Rostenberg, Leona. *The Minority Press and the English Crown: A Study in Repression, 1558–1625.* Nieuwkoop, the Netherlands: B. De Graaf, 1971.

———. "The New Science: John Martyn, 'Printer to the Royal Society.'" In *Literary, Political, Scientific, Religious and Legal Publishing, Printing and Bookselling in England, 1551–1700: Twelve Studies,* 237–80. New York: Burt Franklin, 1965.

Rummel, Erika. "Erasmus' Manual of Letter-Writing: Tradition and Innovation." *Renaissance and Reformation / Renaissance et réforme* 25 (1989): 299–312.

Sackton, Alexander. "Donne and the Privacy of Verse." *Studies in English Literature, 1500–1900* 7 (1967): 67–82.

Saenger, Paul. "Books of Hours and the Reading Habits of the Later Middle Ages." In *The Culture of Print: Power and the Uses of Print in Early Modern Europe,* ed. Roger Chartier, 141–73. Princeton: Princeton Univ. Press, 1987.

———. *Space between Words: The Origins of Silent Reading.* Stanford: Stanford Univ. Press, 1997.

Saunders, J. W. "From Manuscript to Print: A Note on the Circulation of Poetic MSS. in the Sixteenth Century." *Proceedings of the Leeds Philosophical and Literary Society, Literary and Historical Section* 6 (1951): 507–28.

———. "The Social Situation of Seventeenth-Century Poetry." In *Metaphysical Poetry,* ed. Malcolm Bradbury and David Palmer, 237–59. New York: St. Martin's Press, 1970.

———. "The Stigma of Print: A Note on the Social Bases of Tudor Poetry." *Essays in Criticism* 1 (1951): 139–64.

Schmitz, Götz. *The Fall of Women in Early English Narrative Verse.* Cambridge: Cambridge Univ. Press, 1990.

Schoeman, Ferdinand David, ed. *Philosophical Dimensions of Privacy: An Anthology.* Cambridge: Cambridge Univ. Press, 1984.

Schoenfeldt, Michael C. "'Subject to Ev'ry Mounters Bended Knee': Herbert and Authority." In *The Historical Renaissance: New Essays on Tudor and Stuart Literature and Culture,* ed. Heather Dubrow and Richard Strier, 242–69. Chicago: Univ. of Chicago Press, 1988.

Schofield, Mary Ann, and Cecilia Macheski, eds. *Curtain Calls: British and American Women and the Theater, 1660–1820.* Athens: Ohio Univ. Press, 1991.

Schofield, R. S. "The Measurement of Literacy in Pre-Industrial England." In *Literacy in Traditional Societies,* ed. Jack Goody, 311–25. Cambridge: Cambridge Univ. Press, 1968.

Secker, Josephine Evetts. "Consolatory Literature of the English Recusants." *Renaissance and Reformation / Renaissance et réforme* 6 (1982): 122–41.

Seznec, Jean. *The Survival of the Pagan Gods: The Mythological Tradition and Its Place in Renaissance Humanism and Art.* New York: Pantheon Books, 1953.

Shapiro, I. A. "The Text of Donne's *Letters to Severall Persons.*" *Review of English Studies* 7 (1931): 291–301.

Shapiro, James. *Shakespeare and the Jews.* New York: Columbia Univ. Press, 1996.

Shapiro, Michael. *Gender in Play on the Shakespearean Stage: Boy Heroines and Female Pages.* Ann Arbor: Univ. of Michigan Press, 1994.

Sharpe, Kevin. "The Image of Virtue: The Court and Household of Charles I, 1625–1642." In *The English Court: From the Wars of the Roses to the Civil War,* ed. David Starkey, 226–60. London: Longman, 1987.

———. *The Personal Rule of Charles I.* New Haven: Yale Univ. Press, 1992.

Sheavyn, Phoebe. *The Literary Profession in the Elizabethan Age.* 2d ed. Rev. J. W. Saunders. Manchester: Manchester Univ. Press, 1967.

Shell, Alison. "Catholic Texts and Anti-Catholic Prejudice in the 17th-Century Book Trade." In *Censorship and the Control of Print in England and France, 1600–1910,* ed. Robin Myers and Michael Harris, 33–57. Winchester UK: St. Paul's Bibliographies, 1992.

Shuger, Debora. *Habits of Thought in the English Renaissance: Religion, Politics, and the Dominant Culture.* Berkeley: Univ. of California Press, 1990.

———. *The Renaissance Bible: Scholarship, Sacrifice, and Subjectivity.* Berkeley: Univ. of California Press, 1994.

Shullenberger, William. "Love as a Spectator Sport in John Donne's Poetry." In *Renaissance Discourses of Desire,* ed. Claude J. Summers and Ted-Larry Pebworth, 46–62. Columbia: Univ. of Missouri Press, 1993.

Shulman, David. *An Annotated Bibliography of Cryptography.* New York: Garland, 1976.

Silberman, Lauren. "The Hermaphrodite and the Metamorphosis of Spenserian Allegory." *English Literary Renaissance* 17 (1987): 207–23.

———. "Mythographic Transformations of Ovid's Hermaphrodite." *Sixteenth Century Journal* 19 (1988): 643–52.

Simpson, Evelyn M. *A Study of the Prose Works of John Donne.* 2d ed. Oxford: Clarendon Press, 1948.

Slights, William W. E. *Ben Jonson and the Art of Secrecy.* Toronto: Univ. of Toronto Press, 1994.

Smith, Bruce R. *Homosexual Desire in Shakespeare's England: A Cultural Poetics.* Chicago: Univ. of Chicago Press, 1991.

Smith, Hilda L. *Reason's Disciples: Seventeenth-Century English Feminists.* Urbana: Univ. of Illinois Press, 1982.

Smith, Julie A. "Woodcut Presentation Scenes in Books Printed by Caxton, de Worde, Pynson." *Gutenberg Jahrbuch* 61 (1986): 322–43.

Smith, Logan Pearsall. *The Life and Letters of Sir Henry Wotton.* 2 vols. Oxford: Clarendon Press, 1907.

Sontag, Susan. "The Pornographic Imagination." In *Styles of Radical Will,* 35–73. New York: Farrar, Straus & Giroux, 1969.

Southern, A. C. *Elizabethan Recusant Prose, 1559–1582.* London: Sands, 1950.

Spufford, Margaret. "First Steps in Literacy: The Reading and Writing Experiences of the Humblest Seventeenth-Century Spiritual Autobiographers." *Social History* 4 (1979): 407–35.

———. *Small Books and Pleasant Histories: Popular Fiction and Its Readership in Seventeenth-Century England.* Athens: Univ. of Georgia Press, 1982.

Squiers, Granville. *Secret Hiding-Places: The Origins, Histories and Descriptions of English Secret Hiding-Places Used by Priests, Cavaliers, Jacobites and Smugglers.* Detroit: Tower Books, 1971.

Stallybrass, Peter. "Patriarchal Territories: The Body Enclosed." In *Rewriting the Renaissance: The Discourses of Sexual Difference in Early Modern Europe,* ed. Margaret W. Ferguson,

Maureen Quilligan, and Nancy J. Vickers, 123–42. Chicago: Univ. of Chicago Press, 1986.

———. "Shakespeare, the Individual, and the Text." In *Cultural Studies,* ed. Lawrence Grossberg, Cary Nelson, and Paula Treichler, 593–612. New York: Routledge, 1992.

Steinberg, S. H. *Five Hundred Years of Printing.* 3d ed. Harmondsworth, England: Penguin, 1974.

Stewart, Alan. "The Early Modern Closet Discovered." *Representations* 50 (spring 1995): 76–100.

Stone, Lawrence. "The Educational Revolution in England, 1560–1640." *Past and Present* 28 (1964): 41–80.

———. *The Family, Sex and Marriage in England, 1500–1800.* New York: Harper & Row, 1977.

Strong, Roy. *The Cult of Elizabeth: Elizabethan Portraiture and Pageantry.* London: Thames & Hudson, 1977.

Suleiman, Susan Rubin. "Pornography, Transgression, and the Avant-Garde: Bataille's Story of the Eye." In *The Poetics of Gender,* ed. Nancy K. Miller, 117–36. New York: Columbia Univ. Press, 1986.

Suleiman, Susan Rubin, and Inge Crosman, eds. *The Reader in the Text: Essays on Audience and Interpretation.* Princeton: Princeton Univ. Press, 1980.

Sullivan, Ceri. *Dismembered Rhetoric: English Recusant Writing, 1580 to 1603.* Madison NJ: Fairleigh Dickinson Univ. Press, 1995.

Sullivan, Ernest W., II. *The Influence of John Donne: His Uncollected Seventeenth-Century Printed Verse.* Columbia: Univ. of Missouri Press, 1993.

Thickstun, Margaret Olofson. "The Preface to Bunyan's *Grace Abounding* as Pauline Epistle." *Notes and Queries,* n.s. 32 (1985): 180–82.

Thomas, Keith. "Cases of Conscience in Seventeenth-Century England." In *Public Duty and Private Conscience in Seventeenth-Century England: Essays Presented to G. E. Aylmer,* ed. John Morrill, Paul Slack, and Daniel Woolf, 29–56. Oxford: Clarendon Press, 1993.

———. *Religion and the Decline of Magic: Studies in Popular Beliefs in Sixteenth and Seventeenth Century England.* London: Weidenfeld & Nicolson, 1971.

Thompson, Elbert N. S. *The Controversy between the Puritans and the Stage.* New York: Russell & Russell, 1966.

Thompson, James Westfall, and Saul K. Padover. *Secret Diplomacy: Espionage and Cryptography, 1500–1815.* New York: Frederick Ungar, 1963.

Thompson, Roger. *Unfit for Modest Ears: A Study of Pornographic, Obscene and Bawdy Works Written or Published in England in the Second Half of the Seventeenth Century.* London: Macmillan, 1979.

Todd, Janet. *The Secret Life of Aphra Behn.* New Brunswick NJ: Rutgers Univ. Press, 1996.

———. "Who Is Silvia? What Is She? Feminine Identity in Aphra Behn's *Love-Letters Between a Nobleman and His Sister.*" In *Aphra Behn Studies,* 199–218, ed. Janet Todd. Cambridge: Cambridge Univ. Press, 1996.

Trease, Geoffrey. *Portrait of a Cavalier: William Cavendish, First Duke of Newcastle.* London: Macmillan, 1979.

Turner, James Grantham. "*The Whores Rhetorick:* Narrative, Pornography, and the Origins of the Novel." *Studies in Sixteenth-Century Culture* 24 (1995): 297–306.

Tylus, Jane. *Writing and Vulnerability in the Late Renaissance.* Stanford: Stanford Univ. Press, 1993.

Vickers, Nancy. "'The Blazon of Sweet Beauty's Best': Shakespeare's *Lucrece.*" In *Shakespeare and the Question of Theory,* ed. Patricia Parker and Geoffrey Hartman, 95–115. New York: Methuen, 1985.

———. "Diana Described: Scattered Women and Scattered Rhyme." *Critical Inquiry* 8 (1981): 265–79.

Wall, Wendy. *The Imprint of Gender: Authorship and Publication in the English Renaissance.* Ithaca: Cornell Univ. Press, 1993.

Walsham, Alexandra. *Church Papists: Catholicism, Conformity and Confessional Polemic in Early Modern England.* Woodbridge UK: Boydell Press, 1993.

Warnicke, Retha M. "Lady Mildmay's Journal: A Study in Autobiography and Meditation in Reformation England." *Sixteenth Century Journal* 20 (1989): 55–68.

Warren, Samuel D., and Louis D. Brandeis. "The Right to Privacy." *Harvard Law Review* 4 (1890): 193–220.

Watt, Ian. *The Rise of the Novel: Studies in Defoe, Richardson and Fielding.* Berkeley: Univ. of California Press, 1957.

Watt, Tessa. *Cheap Print and Popular Piety.* Cambridge: Cambridge Univ. Press, 1991.

Webber, Joan. *The Eloquent "I": Style and Self in Seventeenth Century Prose.* Madison: Univ. of Wisconsin Press, 1968.

Wehrs, Donald R. "Eros, Ethics, Identity: Royalist Feminism and the Politics of Desire in Aphra Behn's Love Letters." *Studies in English Literature, 1500–1900* 32 (1992): 461–78.

Westin, Alan F. *Privacy and Freedom.* New York: Atheneum, 1967.

White, Helen C. *The Tudor Books of Private Devotion.* Madison: Univ. of Wisconsin Press, 1951.

Whiting, Robert. *The Blind Devotion of the People: Popular Religion and the English Reformation.* Cambridge: Cambridge Univ. Press, 1989.

Wilcox, Helen, ed. *Women and Literature in Britain, 1500–1700.* Cambridge: Cambridge Univ. Press, 1996.

Williams, Raymond. *Keywords: A Vocabulary of Culture and Society.* New York: Oxford Univ. Press, 1976.

Wing, Donald. *Short-Title Catalogue of Books Printed in England, Scotland, Ireland, Wales, and British America and of English Books Printed in Other Countries, 1641–1700.* New York: Modern Language Association, 1972–88 [rev. v. 1, 1994].

Wollman, Richard B. "The 'Press and the Fire': Print and Manuscript Culture in Donne's Circle." *Studies in English Literature, 1500–1900* 33 (1993): 85–97.

Woudhuysen, H. R. *Sir Philip Sidney and the Circulation of Manuscripts, 1558–1640.* Oxford: Clarendon Press, 1996.

Wright, Louis B. *Middle-Class Culture in Elizabethan England.* Chapel Hill: Univ. of North Carolina Press, 1935.

———. "The Reading of Plays during the Puritan Revolution." *Huntington Library Bulletin* 6 (1934): 73–108.

Young, John B., ed. *Privacy.* Chichester, England: John Wiley, 1978.

Zagorin, Perez. *Ways of Lying: Dissimulation, Persecution, and Conformity in Early Modern Europe.* Cambridge: Harvard Univ. Press, 1990.

Ziegler, Georgianna. "My Lady's Chamber: Female Space, Female Chastity in Shakespeare." *Textual Practice* 4 (1990): 73–90.

Zimbardo, Rose. *A Mirror to Nature: Transformations in Drama and Aesthetics, 1660–1732.* Lexington: Univ. Press of Kentucky, 1986.

Zwicker, Steven N. *Lines of Authority: Politics and English Literary Culture, 1649–1689.* Ithaca: Cornell Univ. Press, 1993.

Index

Italicized page numbers refer to illustrations.